GW00503530

'You're good at languages. That means ɥ_____
Diplomatic', pronounced the father of the teenage Michael
Burton.

And so began a diplomatic career, ranging from
Khartoum to the Khyber Pass, that encompassed a wide
variety of experiences: resolving tribal uprisings among
Gulf Arabs, helping from Paris to achieve Britain's entry
into Europe, smoothing the path to a united Germany
in Berlin after the fall of The Wall, and serving as British
Ambassador in a post from which he had been banned by
the Foreign Office twenty-eight years earlier.

Sir Michael Burton's fascinating memoir describes inter-
actions with four British Prime Ministers, an American
President, an Arab King and a master Soviet spy – not to
mention facilitating royal visits to several of his postings,
which displayed Britain's 'soft power' in action.

In the process, Burton vividly illustrates British diplomacy at work, and reveals an aspect of Britain's govern-
ance that rarely sees the light of day.

MICHAEL BURTON was educated at Bedford School
and Magdalen College, Oxford and began his diplomatic life in 1960, following National Service with
active combat duty as a young subaltern in the jungles of
Malaya, during the communist insurgency there. He was
then sent to the Foreign Office's so-called 'Spy School'
in Shemlan, Lebanon, to learn Arabic. Thereafter Sir
Michael's career spanned a number of important postings
in the Middle East and in Europe. He served in Berlin as
the Minister and Head of the British Mission in Berlin
during the crucial period covering both the collapse of
the Wall and of the German Democratic Republic. He
was then appointed British Ambassador to Prague in the
Czech Republic.

Following his retirement Sir Michael and Lady Henrietta
Burton have lived in London and in Sussex.

'A sparkling book by one of the UK's most versatile and experienced diplomats. This rich account by someone who had a ring-side seat at some of the most significant and exciting events in post-war period is a joy to read.'

Peter Frankopan, Professor of Global History at Oxford University and author of The Silk Roads

'Michael Burton's career took him to fascinating places at times of profound change. His warm and evocative memoir sparkles with incident and colour, and brings to life moments of history that have helped shape our modern world. Highly recommended.'

Lord Ricketts, former UK National Security Advisor, UK Ambassador to France and Head of HM Diplomatic Service

'Michael Burton has been in all the places that mattered at the right times. His riveting, very personal account of these game-changing events and people make this a compelling read.'

Peter Snow, historian, journalist and BBC Newsnight

'Sir Michael Burton gives a very engaging account of a diplomatic career … He was in the front line of some of the major crises and events of the day including the Six Day War in 1967, Britain's negotiations to enter the European Community in 1972, and the fall of the Berlin Wall and its consequences.

Burton combines analysis of policy and the major players with anecdotal detail and insight … He also captures the human dimension of diplomatic negotiations superbly, as well as the value added to diplomacy by his wife Henrietta …

His book is a must read for anyone interested in foreign policy.'

Charles Anson, former Press Secretary to HM The Queen, and former diplomat

ON HER MAJESTY'S DIPLOMATIC SERVICE

ON HER MAJESTY'S DIPLOMATIC SERVICE

From the Arab World to the Berlin Wall

Michael Burton

Published by iB2 Media

First edition published in 2022

Copyright © Sir Michael Burton 2022

*The right of Sir Michael Burton to be identified as the author of this work
has been asserted by him in accordance with the Copyright, Designs
and Patents Act 1988.*

*British Library Cataloguing in Publication Data
Data available*

*Typeset by
Mach 3 Solutions Ltd, Bussage, Gloucestershire*

*Printed in Great Britain by
TJ Books Ltd, Padstow, Cornwall*

ISBN 978-1-915248-00-8

To
my wife, Henrietta Jindra
my partner on this journey,
my children Nicholas and Amanda
my grand-children Lydia, Daniel, Joey and Celine
and to the memory of
Samantina

Contents

Abbreviations

ACC	Allied Control Commission (Berlin)
AK	Allied Kommandatura (Berlin)
BASC	Berlin Air Safety Centre
BEBO	British Embassy Berlin Office
BMG	British Military Government
BMH	British Military Hospital
BOAC	British Overseas Airways Corporation
COBRA	Cabinet Office Briefing Room A
CT	Communist Terrorist (in the Malayan Emergency)
EEC	European Economic Community
ESA	European Space Agency
G7	Group of Seven (industrialised countries)
GDR	German Democratic Republic
ITN	Independent Television News
JWS	Jungle Warfare School
KHF	Know How Fund
MECAS	Middle East Centre for Arab Studies
MED	Middle East Department (FCO)
MCP	Malayan Communist Party
MNLA	Malayan National Liberation Army
MOD	Ministry of Defence
MPAJA	Malayan People's Anti-Japanese Army
NAAFI	Navy, Army and Air Force Institute
NASA	National Air and Space Agency
NENAD	Near East and North Africa Department (FCO)
ODS	Civil Democratic Party
OPEC	Organization of Petroleum Exporting Countries
PIA	Pakistan International Airlines
PO	Potential Officer
QA	Quadripartite Agreement (on Berlin)
SAS	Special Air Service

SHAPE	Supreme Headquarters Allied Powers Europe
SNOPG	Senior Naval Officer Persian Gulf
TOS	Trucial Oman Scouts
UNWRA	United Nations Relief and Works Agency
WMD	Weapons of Mass Destruction
WOSBY	War Office Selection Board
UAE	United Arab Emirates

Preface

I started writing these memoirs in 2011. The reason they have taken me so long is due mainly to a certain hesitation at adding to the already substantial corpus of diplomatic memoirs. To overcome this reticence, I had to convince myself that there was a story worth telling. I was helped, in overcoming this hurdle, not only by the encouragement of friends and family, but also by a number of people attending lectures I have given, whose interest had been sparked by some aspect of my diplomatic career, such as the fall of the Berlin Wall, or background to the international and diplomatic events and circumstances which in so many instances drove the relationships between states. They were also interested in learning what a diplomat actually does.

In the events I recount, apart from my early days in the Gulf, I worked in partnership with my wife, Henrietta. It was not always an easy journey. Our getting married was problematic, due to the Foreign Office's objections, for Cold War reasons, to my marrying a Czech-born girl (as described in Chapter 3). After we were eventually able to marry, without my having to resign from the Service, our first child was born with a congenital condition, which led to her untimely death at the age of 2. We came through this together. My wife's loyalty and devotion at my side, were what, above all, enabled me to achieve whatever I have achieved. It was only fitting that my final posting should have been as ambassador in the land of her birth, after it emerged from its communist experience.

As regards my methodology, I kept no diaries, so I have relied largely on my memory, reinforced by a few key documents to which I have had access and the numerous memory-jogging photographs I have taken throughout. I have worked on the principle that only those incidents of which I have a clear recollection have been worth recording. I have tried to minimise recounting events where I felt my memory was not entirely accurate and checked whatever I can. Those errors that have survived are entirely my responsibility.

I am deeply indebted to my editors, Iradj Bagherzade and Elizabeth Stone, for guiding me through the process, and giving me confidence that the end product would be worthwhile. I am also grateful for the patience of my family.

Fulham, London
August 2021

Introduction

These sketches of my career in Britain's Diplomatic Service cover a wide canvas, from the sands of southern Arabia (in what is now the United Arab Emirates), before the advent of oil riches, to the banks of the Nile in Khartoum, the Khyber Pass and Afghanistan under Soviet control, to Paris in the sixties, and then to Berlin before and after the Fall of the Wall. They culminate with my appointment as ambassador in Prague, a post in which I had been told I could never serve for security reasons when I married my Czech-born wife, twenty-five years earlier. The wheel had come full circle.

They also range over some of the main themes of British foreign policy during the last four decades of the twentieth century: the problems of the Middle East – from the Six Day Arab-Israel War in 1967 to the optimistic moment of the Oslo Agreement in 1993; the crucial Anglo-French Summit in Paris in 1971 which paved the way for Britain to join the Common Market; to the ending of the Cold War following the fall of the Berlin Wall; and reconnecting thereafter with the post-communist countries in Central Europe.

Along the way, I was involved in three features of that period which have now almost, or completely, disappeared into the mists of time. The first of these is National Service for which I was one of the last young men to be called up. The complaint of many of my contemporaries was that it was a waste of two years, and that they were thoroughly bored. This was not my experience. After going through the ranks, and then obtaining a National Service commission, I commanded a rifle platoon on active service during communist-inspired insurgency in Malaya at the time of the Emergency (as recounted in Chapter 2). This was not boring.

Secondly, there was my first Foreign Office posting, as an Assistant Political Agent, in what were then called the Trucial States, in the southern Persian Gulf (described in Chapter 3). This was a loose group of sheikhdoms in an exclusive treaty arrangement with Britain, which provided both their protection and security. At that time a perceived threat to the old-world sheikhly system was the Arab nationalism inspired by Egypt's President Gamal Abdel Nasser, whose adversarial rhetoric and warm relations with the Soviet Union were regarded as hostile to British interests. For anyone with an appreciation of the simplicities of the desert Arabs' way of life, the Trucial States seemed like a delightful anachronism, which would not long survive those winds of Arab nationalism after Britain's departure, which took place in 1971. As it turned out, the system, and the foundations Britain laid on which modern states could be built, proved durable. On them, powered by oil wealth, arose the gleaming skyscrapers of the United Arab Emirates of today.

Thirdly, we jump forward to the British Military Government in the Berlin of the 1980s, still under the protection of the Allies who had occupied the city since the end of the Second World War. I was destined to be the last Minister (a diplomatic rank) at its head, before it lost its function, and disappeared, with the reunification of Germany and Berlin in 1990. Again, this looked like an anachronism (which, in my view, its title was), but the reality was that the continued presence of the Western Allies guaranteed the freedom and security of the West Berliners against the potential threat from the surrounding Soviet forces (Chapter 9 tells the tale).

My diplomatic career, like that of most other senior diplomats, encompassed a wide range of experiences, from the adventurous – close encounters with armed and hooded men on a mountain road in Lebanon, manning the command centre in London during a critical hostage crisis which had to involve the SAS, or a tense Berlin face-off with the Soviets over my initiative to assist escapees from the East – to more standard diplomatic fare such as negotiating with the Iranian government for the lifting of the *fatwa* on the author Salman Rushdie, working to adapt the UK position on the Arab/Israel dispute following the dramatic breakthrough in the Oslo Process, or pointing out to London certain realities in the immediate aftermath of the opening of the Berlin Wall, such as the hunger of the East Germans for the purchasing power of the D-Mark, which would drive the process of reunification – something that many in the West, including our own Prime Minister Margaret Thatcher, did not immediately welcome. And occasionally a royal visit, or twice representing Britain at the Cannes Film Festival, added a welcome touch of glamour.

My career in the Diplomatic Service lasted thirty-seven years, ending in 1997. The cast list in these memoirs is therefore quite extensive and includes, apart from foreign personalities from all the countries in which I served, four Prime Ministers with whom I had dealings: Edward Heath, Margaret Thatcher, John Major and Tony Blair.

But the outstanding figure is that of the Queen. I played an increasingly senior role in the organisation of four of her overseas state visits, accompanied by the Duke of Edinburgh, each of which had its own particular significance: France, in 1972, celebrated a re-set in Anglo-French relations following the lifting of the French veto on Britain joining the EEC; Kuwait, in 1979, was the first visit by a British monarch to the Gulf States, which had been under British protection prior to achieving independence in 1961 (in the case of Kuwait) and 1971 for the others; Berlin, in 1992, celebrated the peaceful reunification of Germany, and Berlin, with her walk through the Brandenburg Gate (and a controversial visit to Dresden); and Prague, in 1997, a few months before my retirement, marked the return of the Czechs to the Western democratic family, from which they had been torn by the infamous Munich Agreement of 1938 in which Britain and France acquiesced in Nazi Germany's occupation of the Sudetenland (which was followed by the invasion and occupation of the remainder of Czechoslovakia shortly afterwards) – all in an eventually futile attempt to preserve 'peace in our time' in Europe.

There were many lighter moments along the way. What I have tried to show above all else is what a diplomat actually does – although, of course, every diplomatic career is different – in an attempt to demystify the particular profession to which I have devoted thirty-seven years of my life. I was fortunate that, in my case, it brought me into contact with some of the significant events of the last forty years of the twentieth century, as well as having the privilege of being a member of that family which is Her Majesty's Diplomatic Service.

Chapter 1

In the Beginning: Family, Wartime Childhood and Schooldays

Why would anyone go into a life of diplomacy, as I did? In my case, no previous member of my family, on either side, had taken this exotic route. The idea came from my father, who had been a brigadier in the Indian Army, when he called me in for a career discussion. I was studying French and German in the sixth form at school at the time. The conversation, as I remember it, went something like this:

Pa: Mike, you're good at languages.
Me: Yes, Pa.
Pa: That means you go into the Diplomatic.
Me: What's that, Pa?
Pa: I don't quite know, but it's what you do if you're good at languages!

I won't pretend that this rather ridiculous conversation settled the matter for good and all. My obedience was not unquestioning, and my father and I were actually having some quite vigorous arguments at this stage (on questions like whether Picasso was a great artist, as I asserted, or a fraud). But the idea, once it entered my head, never quite left it. An ambition began to take shape.

This fateful career talk took place in the drawing room of our family house in Bedford where my two brothers and I attended Bedford School. The family had moved to Bedford when my father left India, on retirement from the British Indian Army, at Independence in 1947. There wasn't much money, and Bedford at the time offered favourable terms for the sons of overseas military and civilian families.

As for my father, he came from a family with a long tradition of service in India. He had been born in India and, after Sandhurst, had taken a commission in the 5th Royal Gurkha Rifles, the elite of the Gurkha regiments, and the only one to have 'Royal' in its title. His father,

1. My father, Brigadier Guy Burton DSO and two Bars. 'You're good at languages. That means you go into the Diplomatic' was his career advice to me. (Photo: author)

my grandfather Pop, had been in the Indian Police and had risen to become the Deputy Inspector General of Police in the United Provinces (now Uttar Pradesh), the largest state in India. More of him later.

Pop's father was a captain in the navy of the East India Company, and the family man of mystery. He is said to have turned down a title in England following a violent argument with his family. The story, true or not, is that a lawyer wearing a tall black hat who was rowed out to his ship at Madras in order to bring him the glad news was sent packing. Great-grandfather also changed his name, from Thomas St Just Bridgeman to John St Edmund Burton – that much is factual. I was given his middle name.

During the war my father fought in the 14th Army, under Lieutenant-General William (Bill) Slim (later Field Marshal Sir William, then Viscount Slim), throughout the Burma campaign against the invading Japanese Imperial Army. He was the youngest brigade commander. As the Japanese army advanced through Burma, he was one of the few battalion commanders to withdraw his troops back across the Sittang River with their arms and equipment intact. For this action he was awarded his first of three DSOs.

He went on to receive two Bars to the DSO in the course of the campaign, the first in the brutal battle for the Tiddim Road in the Battle of Imphal, the key engagement of the war, which blocked the Japanese advance into India. And the second Bar was a rare Immediate Award in the field for his role in defeating the Japanese at the Battle of Meiktila in 1945, the last major action before their surrender at Rangoon. This made him one of the most highly decorated soldiers of the war.

Of course, this all meant that the family saw little of my father at this time. He himself felt the lack of contact keenly and it was one of the reasons he decided not to remain in the Army after the Independence of India in 1947. He resigned and returned to make a new life at home.

During my father's absence my mother had held the fort in the family. I had been born in 1937, two years before the outbreak of conflict, and my brother Clive two years earlier. My younger brother Derek came along four years after me.

Throughout the war we lived in Camberley, which was then a sleepy Surrey town with a distinctly military flavour, due to the presence of the Royal Military Academy, Sandhurst, and the Army Staff College. There were also numerous retired officers, many of them from the Indian Army. Both my sets of grandparents lived there. Pop and my grandmother, Munna, lived in a large house up the hill from the centre of town on the Portsmouth road. My mother's parents, Ganna and Grandpa, lived further down the hill on Bath Road, an unmade cul-de-sac which gave access to the private road leading to the Staff College and the RMA.

My mother, Barbara, a warm and positive woman, must have had in earlier years a touch of John Betjeman's poetic fancy Miss Joan Hunter Dunn about her ('Furnish'd and burnish'd by Aldershot sun'). Indeed, we used to play tennis at the Officers Club at Aldershot. My mother wasn't a typical army wife and had not much enjoyed life with the regiment before the war in Abbottabad, the regimental depot on the North West Frontier, where my brother Clive was born. It has won notoriety in more recent times as the place where Osama bin Laden met his end.

My mother's whole life was her family. She also employed her excellent organisational and secretarial skills in support of causes dear to her heart, ranging from the election campaign of our Bedford MP, Christopher Soames (later my ambassador in Paris), to raising money for the Save the Children Fund. In her final years she turned to typing books in Braille for the blind. These commendable activities sometimes crowded out, I felt, the more mundane demands of the household chores. The fridge was occasionally best left unopened!

My parents were deeply devoted to each other. Their greatest pleasure, in later years, was driving at a leisurely pace down to the South of France in their vintage (and not wholly reliable) Bentley, to spend a few days in Monte Carlo. My mother plotted the route with great care, avoiding motorways and choosing scenic roads and villages which held out the prospect of welcoming inns with good (but not overly fancy) food. She became very good at this. In Monte Carlo they stayed, if the budget that year allowed, at the Metropole Hotel. When my father had checked in, as a regular guest, there was just time for Reception to alert Monsieur Sheikh at the bar so that he could greet my father on arrival with the words 'Bonjour, mon Général'. I accompanied my parents on one of these trips.

My mother's family had, if anything, a more military slant than my father's, although more on the naval side. Further back up the tree the emphasis was heavily on clergymen. My mother was good at her family's genealogy, and one egregious star she laid claim to (although she could not trace the exact link), was Master Betty, the child actor at

2. My mother, Barbara, née Kemmis Betty: not a typical army wife.
(Photo: author)

the turn of the nineteenth century, who created a sensation in London with his performance of Hamlet. The House of Commons adjourned early in order to enable Members to attend. A painting of him has pride of place in the Garrick Club.

My mother's family name was Kemmis Betty. This came about when, in 1867, Catherine Kemmis, the widow of the Revd William Betty (the Rector of a parish in County Meath, Ireland), together with her three children, gave notice that they henceforth intended to use the surname Kemmis together with Betty, and before it.

My grandpa, Colonel Hubert Kemmis Betty DSO OBE, had gone to Canada before the Great War to make his fortune. He did not succeed. He then returned to Europe as a senior officer in the Canadian Expeditionary Force to fight in the trenches of Flanders, and was gassed at the Battle of Ypres, which badly affected his lungs. After the war he took his family to live for a time in Switzerland for the sake of his lungs, where he developed his talent for watercolour painting and carving wooden furniture. I remember him as a sweet and kindly man. He spent much of the Second World War, apart from his service in the Home Guard, making wooden toys in his garden shed. He was assisted by a German POW called Hans, who must have been on parole. Grandpa and Hans made a happy pair.

As for grandmother Ganna (Ethel Kemmis Betty, née Watts), she was a real star. She was brought up in South Africa. On coming to England, she became a nurse at Great Ormond Street Children's Hospital before she married. A striking woman of unfailing good humour and common sense, she was a source of good advice and a rock of support to me until her death at the age of 93. She also taught me to drive.

Enough of family affairs, apart from mentioning two uncles, my mother's brothers. Both were in the army. The elder brother, Mervyn, was an Indian Mountain Gunner. His great enthusiasm in life was skiing. He took Clive and me skiing at Grindelwald in Switzerland when I was ten. It was our first foreign trip. 1947 was the depth of post-war austerity and one could not take more than £50 out of the country. We sat up all night in the train. Uncle Mervyn kept our spirits up by telling us of the amazing omelettes we would have when we reached the station restaurant at Basel.

He was right. The omelettes were frothy concoctions made with seemingly limitless eggs. For travellers coming from gloomy, rationed Britain the experience was magical. And then there was the unrationed chocolate which Clive and I put away in vast quantities. We also learned to ski, while gazing in awe at the Eiger and Jungfrau mountains.

As for my mother's much younger brother, Uncle Peter, he also became a Gurkha officer, in the 2nd King Edward VII's Own Goorkha Rifles. Peter, who was also my godfather, died only in 2016, having just passed his hundredth birthday. His (lead) obituary in *The Times*, illustrated with the picture of him as a dashing young Gurkha officer, captured him accurately under the heading 'Impeccably mannered Gurkha officer awarded the Military Cross for holding a vital bridge in Malaya'. This occurred during the Japanese advance down the Malayan Peninsula towards the capture of Singapore in 1941. After the fall of the island, Peter's unit, who had taken up a defensive position on the road north to the causeway, were ordered, to their total chagrin, to cease fighting and march into captivity at Changi.

As a POW at Changi, Peter and a fellow Gurkha officer cultivated a vegetable patch to supplement the meagre rations of the Changi prisoners, those in hospital and the Gurkha soldier captives held else-where on the island. In consequence, he was never included in a draft to work on the infamous Burma railway. Afterwards he acknowledged that the Japanese had done unspeakable things to Commonwealth prisoners, but had effectively left him alone.

In 1945 my grandmother took me up on the train up from Camberley, gazing at the barrage balloons over London as we approached Waterloo station, to visit the Madame Tussauds waxworks. When we were halfway round the exhibition an official climbed onto a chair and announced in jubilant tones that Japan had surrendered. At the thought of Peter's release from captivity Ganna became faint, and I went to find a chair for her, and a cup of tea. It was an emotional moment.

As a child growing up in Camberley during the war, I remember little of it, apart from sweet rationing. There was the occasional excitement when the air-raid sirens sounded, announcing a Luftwaffe raid targeted at the RMA down the road. Clive and I would spend the night in a cupboard under the stairs, which we much enjoyed. We also had a scare when Lord Haw-Haw, the Irish traitor William Joyce, who broadcast nightly propaganda for the Nazis from Berlin, announced – after his customary drawled introduction of 'Germany calling, Germany calling' – that the Luftwaffe intended next night to bomb Camberley High Street, aiming particularly at our grocers Tietgens. To our enormous relief, the raid did not take place.

When I was seven my schooling started in earnest. My mother drove me the few miles to Windlesham to become a boarder at Woodcote House. It was a no-nonsense family-run traditional boys' school with about seventy-five pupils. The headmaster was Mr Paterson. Successive generations of the Paterson family have run the school to this day. I have nothing but happy memories of it. The teaching must have been good because when I moved on, rather prematurely because of my father's return from India, to my public school in Bedford, I found that I was somewhat ahead of my classmates – which did not make me popular. I had also acquired a taste, and aptitude, for acting.

One memory that I do have of Woodcote House is of the whole school being assembled to hear on the radio the judges in Nuremberg passing sentence on the Nazi war criminals. I suspect, but cannot be sure, that we raised a hearty cheer each time the death sentence by hanging was imposed. We also felt cheated by the news that Hermann

Goering had escaped the hangman's noose by taking poison. I little knew that forty years later I would encounter Rudolf Hess, Hitler's deputy, who, by feigning mental instability, had been lucky to escape a death sentence that day.

It is a striking coincidence that two of my contemporaries at Woodcote House would be colleagues in Germany, also forty years later. Christopher Mallaby was the ambassador in Bonn when I was minister in Berlin and Patrick Brooking, by then a Major-General, was the British Commandant in Berlin. It is a sort of testimony to the old-boy network that this small prep school in Surrey provided the three top British officials in Germany at that time.

At school the boy who made the biggest impression on me was the one destined for the most louche and entertaining future. Willie Donaldson, a strongly built, ginger-haired boy would go on to enjoy a huge inheritance. He used it to finance the satirists of the 1960s in Beyond the Fringe. He also took to crack cocaine and lived in a brothel and then, in the persona of Henry Root, 'wet-fish merchant', wrote hilarious spoof letters to assorted members of the establishment, including Margaret Thatcher, enclosing the generous sum of £1 for their respective causes! The published replies became a source of deep embarrassment to the victims.

I was pretty miserable to leave Woodcote House, at the age of 10, when the family made the move to Bedford. It was the start of a new chapter.

*   *   *

Bedford in the late 1940s was an attractive county town. The main feature was the River Ouse which flowed through municipal gardens only about 100 yards from our family house. Rowing was a major sporting activity for the boys' schools in the town, culminating in a regatta in July which was the climax of the summer season. When I arrived at Bedford School it was basking in the glory of having won the Princess Elizabeth Cup at Henley for the past three years – which I think entitled it to keep the cup.

The school had received a Licence of Letters Patent from Edward VI in 1552, the 400th anniversary of which was commemorated while I was at the school in 1952 with a memorable visit by Princess Margaret (whose beauty quite dazzled me). It was then endowed in 1566 by Sir William Harpur, a citizen of Bedford who became Lord

3. A drawing of the Bedford School main building by John Western. My time at the
school coincided with its 400th anniversary in 1952. (Photo: author)

Mayor of London. The endowment provided also for the foundation
of a girls' school, Bedford High School. Two other schools founded
later also benefited from the Harpur Trust, so that education was a
major feature of the town.

The Headmaster when I arrived was a stern martinet named
Humphrey Grose Hodge, a short man with a fine head of silver hair
and a commanding presence. My teachers, as I progressed up the
school, were mostly 'old school' in their approach, but effective in
instilling the basics into their pupils.

The German teacher, PK Bourne, the brother of a distinguished
general, had a rather forbidding manner, always striding as if sideways
with a stiff neck. On Cadet (CCF) days he'd squeeze himself into the
uniform of an Army major, delighting in playing the role of wartime
officer once more. He drummed the essentials of German grammar
into our heads with the aid of his 'dotty ditties' to help one remember
the exceptions to the rules. But if time remained in the period after this
tedious business he would bring out a small battered suitcase which
contained his photographs and postcards from travelling in Germany
before the war. These were a revelation to me. Pictures, for example,
of the baroque glories of Dresden before the Allied air-raid of 1945
awoke an interest in me to visit these places one day.

It was evident to my parents that my particular bent was for modern languages. When I became a teenager, they furthered my progress by arranging a summer holiday exchange with a French boy. A cousin of my mother's, Fred, owned a yacht in which he regularly took part in a race to Dinard, the fashionable seaside town in Brittany across the River Rance from St Malo. At the Dinard Yacht Club he met a family of prosperous textile manufacturers from Lille, called Bigo, who were in the habit of renting a villa in Dinard for the summer. The Bigos were looking for an English family to take their son Christian, to improve his English. Cousin Fred passed the proposal on to us.

So it was, that in the summer of 1952 our family crossed the Channel and drove through Normandy to Dinard. For the first time I sampled French white wine, unchilled but delicious. The Bigos welcomed us warmly, but when the exchange had taken place and I watched the family, plus Christian, disappear down the road to head home, I felt a great feeling of desolation.

However, I quickly settled in. The younger Bigo boy, Daniel, and I had fun sailing a dinghy in the bay of La Rance and swimming in the tide-filled pool below the villa on Place du General de Gaulle. I spent two more summers at the Bigos, although Christian opted out of his side of the exchange. My confidence in French grew. In time girls became part of the picture, with impossibly glamorous names like Solange.

I used to read *Paris Match*, mainly for the pictures. The French Prime Minister, the socialist Pierre Mendès-France, who was generally considered the best hope to bring greater stability into the political scene, fell from power on the question of establishing a European defence entity. This saga sparked my interest in French and European politics.

A more poignant story in *Paris Match* was that of a party of French schoolgirls who were swept to their deaths by a flash flood in the ravine (known as the *siq*) leading to the 'lost' city of Petra in Jordan. It was an appalling tragedy. Years later, when stationed in Jordan, I saw how the Jordanians, following the accident, had built retaining walls and excavated ancient run-off channels to prevent it ever happening again.

My parents also found a way of raising the level of my German. They invited a young German woman, Gisela Stitz, to spend some time with us in Bedford. Rather reluctantly, although I was the right age for it, I found myself ploughing through Goethe's tale of a young man literally dying for love, *Die Leiden des Jungen Werther's*. At a later stage I returned Gisela's visit and stayed with her family in Düsseldorf, earning some money on the side, very agreeably, by coaching the girls in her office at tennis.

The master at Bedford who had the most impact on me was JL St G (John) Eyre, the sixth-form history teacher. He stood out from most of the others in being unashamedly an intellectual in a school that prized athletic prowess above other qualities. A tall lanky man with deeply sunken cheeks, his wayward forelock reinforced his bohemian image (although he had had a very creditable war as an officer in the Irish Guards).

I was not the only boy who looked to Eyre as a beacon of civilisation in a largely philistine landscape. Those who contributed reminiscences of him to Richard Lindley's obituary in *The Guardian* in 2006 included (Lord) Paddy Ashdown who wrote, 'Pretty well single-handed [John Eyre] converted a rough tearaway schoolboy interested in rugby and sport into somebody who discovered the benefits of music, poetry, literature and art which have stayed with me and probably improved me ever since.'

The way that Eyre changed my life was in choosing me to play the lead in his production of *Hamlet* in my final year at school. I had worked my way up the ranks of the Dramatic Society, starting with playing women's parts (as was the practice before the school teamed up later with the girls of Bedford High School). The most successful of these was my debut, aged 13, playing the brothel keeper, Mrs Trapes, in John Gray's *The Beggars' Opera*. I made my mark doing a solo song and dance number, front of stage, with the lyric:

> In the days of my youth I could sing like a dove,
> Like a sparrow I always was ready for Love,
> Fol do diddle day-de-de (reptd)
> Fol de de, day de de, fol de diddle day de de.

Eyre was rehearsing another boy, John Percival, and me in tandem for the lead part in *Hamlet* before making his final decision. The day I heard that Percival had been chosen was one of the worst in my life. Happily, it was a false rumour and I played the Prince, and Percival played Laertes. (Perhaps the ghost of Master Betty had something to do with it!) It all added to the drama of our duel in the final act.

The experience of playing the longest and most demanding part in the English language is life-changing. On a practical level it taught me

4. 'Alas poor Yorick': playing Hamlet in the school play, Christmas 1954.
(Photo: author)

to speak clearly and project my voice. Eyre would sit at the back of the Great Hall and shout out whenever he could not hear a syllable. This invaluable training has stood me in good stead in public speaking for the rest of my life.

As a reward for my efforts John Eyre took me up to London to see Paul Schofield in a play at the old St James's Theatre, followed by dinner at the Savile Club. I felt I had grown up. In the 1990s he and Richard Lindley (a star reporter of *Panorama* and ITN), together with Carole Stone, a networker of genius, who later became Richard's wife, who co-produced *Hamlet* as well as playing the Ghost, visited me in Prague, where I was ambassador. He had lost none of his restless intellectual energy.

I left Bedford in 1955 having won the William Doncaster Scholarship (an Open Scholarship in German) to Magdalen College, Oxford. But before taking it up I first had to do my National Service.

Chapter 2

The Path to Diplomacy: From the Malayan Jungles to Magdalen, Oxford

National Service was a two-year period of military service which was obligatory for all male school leavers. It was both fair and democratic in that no exceptions were granted, other than on medical grounds, although you could be deferred if you had some valid educational reason.

But it was not generally popular, and most young men considered it an unwelcome interruption in their progression from school to further education or work, and a waste of time. My year was one of the last to be called up, although I doubt whether we realised that at the time. I personally, brought up, as I was, in the military ethos, looked upon it as a challenge and an adventure.

As far as I was concerned it started on a farcical note. My call-up papers instructed me to report for basic training to the Rifle Depot at Peninsula Barracks, Winchester. There was an affecting scene as, still two months short of my eighteenth birthday, the family waved me goodbye on my way to join the army. On arrival at the depot I was surprised to find only two other recruits, both self-assured Wykehamists. It turned out that there had been a mistake over the call-up papers and we were a week early. We were issued with rail passes to go home and come back in a week's time.

But first we had to sleep the night in the barrack-room, which was deserted. Three delicately brought-up young men undressed and went to bed. Almost immediately the inhabitants of the barrack-room returned from their evening's carousals in the NAAFI. They stood round our beds in mocking ribaldry, as we feigned to be in the deepest sleep. Never had we heard such juicy profanity. We learned that our status in life was that of 'f***ing POs' (Potential Officers) and that we were certainly given to unnatural practices. We survived, and next day returned home to find, in my case, the family less than overjoyed to see me, having expended so much emotion on my original departure.

My regiment was the Rifle Brigade (The 95th), one of the elite regiments of the British Army. Raised during the Napoleonic Wars, it had seen distinguished service during the Peninsula Campaign (hence the name of the Barracks, which it shared with its sister regiment, the King's Royal Rifle Corps) when Sir Arthur Wellesley, later Duke of Wellington, defeated the French armies. It prided itself on its dark green uniform, its speed of marching, shooting skills and number of VCs won. It was also an article of faith that the officers led by example, rather than by the imposition of rigid discipline on the men. The upper reach of the army is regularly populated with former Rifle Brigade officers.

Since my two years' service, the Rifle Brigade has been through a number of amalgamations, culminating in it now being one of the regiments of the Rifles. In fiction, the regiment featured prominently in Bernard Cornwell's 'Sharpe' novels.

The regiment traditionally did its recruiting in the East End of London. So, the barrack-room, when our twelve weeks of basic training finally got under way, was a mixture of POs and cockneys. Although wary of each other, we all got along pretty well, once the strangeness had worn off. Hanging over us POs was the crucial War Office Selection Board ('Wosby') which would decide which of us went on to officer cadet training.

We were addressed on our first day by the major commanding the Training Company. He had a definite air of authority, but we felt that he was unlikely to be destined for higher things. We were wrong. He was Edwin Bramall, the future Field Marshal and Chief of the Defence Staff, whom I would come to know many years later as Lord Bramall when we were fellow non-executive directors of Vickers Defence Systems, which was building the Challenger II tank. An important part of future Field Marshal 'Dwin's' role was choosing the wine for our board dinner.

I found 'Wosby', when my turn came round, to be a well-tuned series of tests for judging leadership qualities. One of the tricks for getting through was to master the principle of the 'cantilever' for getting the platoon across a (notional) raging river with the aid of a plank which was not long enough to reach the other side. Everyone stood on one end of the plank to provide a counterweight. Each man then ran along it and jumped over in turn. I cannot remember what happened to the last man to cross – but he was presumably expendable.

To my huge relief, I passed the Board. It was painful to see the disappointment of those who did not make it.

The next stop, Eaton Hall outside Chester, in the bitter January of 1956, was the Officer Cadet School for National Service infantrymen. In normal times the home of the Duke of Westminster, it was a Victorian pile, set in a large estate – which incorporated an enjoyable golf course. Rather incongruously for a military establishment, it sported a large and no doubt priceless painting by Rubens in the Great Hall. The sixteen-week course had the reputation of being tough, particularly the two-week Battle Camp in North Wales in the final fortnight.

We officer cadets always knew what to expect, because if we went down to the popular dance hall in Chester on a Saturday night, the girls, who had known our many predecessors on the course, could tell us exactly what point we were at, and, in lurid detail, what horrors lay ahead. This was rarely comforting. My course took some pride in the fact, however, that, when we were halfway through the dreaded Battle Camp at Trawsfynydd in North Wales (later the site of a nuclear power station), it had to be cancelled due to the appalling weather conditions. This had never happened before.

One of my lasting memories is of attending the Grand National at Aintree that year, to which I had driven in my old banger of a car together with a few friends. Like most of those present, I had backed the Queen Mother's horse, Devon Loch, ridden by none other than the champion jockey Dick Francis. When Devon Loch sailed over the final fence far in the lead and commenced his run-in to the finishing line, I turned to the bookie to claim my winnings. He was about to pay out when a sudden commotion on the track distracted his attention. To the fury of much of the nation, Devon Loch had stumbled and fallen for some reason which has ever since been hotly debated. We were left to drown our sorrows.

Many years later I was able to ask the two persons most closely involved if they had an explanation. Firstly, there was Dick Francis. A bestselling and prolific writer of novels relating to the Turf, he enjoyed a, proportionately, very high readership in the Czech Republic, thanks to his Czech translator, Jara Moserova. When he visited Prague, to meet his fan base, Jara, who was a good friend of ours, suggested that we invite him to tea at my residence together with his family. In some ways the Devon Loch incident had made him, because it started him on his highly successful career as a novelist. But even he could offer no clear explanation for the horse's fall.

The other person to profess herself similarly in the dark was the Queen Mother herself. She had come to Berlin, where I was Minister, to attend the St Patrick's Day Parade of her beloved Irish Guards, as was her habit. After dinner in the Commandant's house, the Villa Lemm, I plucked up my courage to ask her about the Devon Loch mystery. She had clearly given the matter much thought over the years, but finally concluded that 'We have never been able to work it out'.

*   *   *

On passing out from Eaton Hall, I was commissioned, to my great delight, back into the Rifle Brigade as a 2nd Lieutenant. The regiment had just finished a tour of duty in Kenya (fighting the Mau Mau) and transferred to Malaya, which came to be known as Malaysia in 1963, to take part in the Emergency. I was to fly out on a trooping flight from Northolt to Singapore to join it at the Kota Tinggi Jungle Warfare School (JWS) just across the Singapore causeway in Malaya. At that time Singapore was a part of Malaya (and later Malaysia) until it declared its independence in 1965. A flight (my first) of that length on what seemed like a barely serviceable propeller-driven Hermes aircraft was quite an adventure, taking three days. We stayed overnight in such exotic locations as Mrs Milwalla's Grand Hotel in the desert outside Karachi. I was appointed o/c troops on the plane, army jargon ('officer commanding') for being in charge of the military personnel on board. The other passengers were families with young

5. A so-called CT ('Communist Terrorist'), one of the insurgents in the Malayan Emergency, who were eventually defeated by British, Malayan and Commonwealth forces. (Photo: author)

children. The only other officer was a gloomy brigadier from the Pay Corps. He suggested that we stick to whisky at Mrs Milwalla's. This proved to be wise advice, as we found when boarding the plane the next day that we were the only passengers not to be brought down by Mrs Milwalla's cuisine.

When we eventually reached Singapore I was met by my Uncle Peter's wife, Aunt Gemma. Peter was up country as second in command of his regiment, the 2nd, King Edward's Own, Sirmoor Gurkha Rifles. The family had a married quarter in Johore Bahru across the causeway from Singapore and Gemma had obtained permission for me to spend the weekend with them before joining my regiment on Monday. We drove along the jungle-fringed trunk road which, Gemma explained, had only recently been declared 'white', or free from the risk of attack by Communist Terrorists (CTs).

The Malayan Emergency was the only confrontation with communist forces which the West actually won (apart from the Cold War itself). The background to it was that Malaya (as it was still called in 1956) was a multiracial British colony, due to achieve independence (called Merdeka) in the year following my arrival. About half the population of some 6 million were Malay, a Muslim people who were overwhelmingly monarchist, revering their rulers, the Sultans who ruled the nine sultanates that made up the country.

The largest minority was Chinese, who had originally been imported as labourers. In contrast to the Malays, they were largely secular, and conscious of their good fortune in having settled in Malaya and left their tormented motherland.

The surrender of the British garrison in Singapore to the Japanese Imperial Army in 1942 had done huge damage to Britain's standing throughout South East Asia. During the following years of Occupation, resistance to the Japanese had been kept alive by the Malayan People's Anti-Japanese Army (MPAJA), a largely Chinese force made up of the Malayan Communist Party (MCP), led by the forceful and charismatic Chin Peng, a dedicated communist who was intent on driving the British out of Malaya, as Ho Chi Minh, another communist, was determined to do to the French in Indo-China.

Fighting alongside the MPAJA in the jungle was the British Force 136, among whose officers was the legendary Colonel Freddie Spencer Chapman, who left a vivid account of the privations and dangers of jungle fighting in his powerful book *The Jungle is Neutral*. This showed that, for guerrilla operations such as those of Force 136, the jungle provided an excellent base for those who understood it and were acclimatised to it. In 1948, at the start of the Emergency, the communist insurgents were both jungle-trained and acclimatised.

The insurrection that broke out in that year – later given the name of the 'Emergency' – developed into an intense jungle war fought by British, Commonwealth and Malay forces against the Malayan National Liberation Army (MNLA), led by Chin Peng. The MNLA fed on the fact that, at the end of the war, the Chinese community harboured a sense of grievance, feeling that they had lost out in the post-war arrangements.

A new constitution, which the British introduced, designed to centralise political power in Malaya and also to improve the position of immigrants such as the Chinese, ran into strong resistance from the Malay majority. As a result, the Chinese were left as what they regarded as second-class citizens, which played into the hands of the communists, who claimed that without them the Japanese would not have surrendered.

The communists' dream was to make Malaya into a People's Republic. This dream was founded on two errors of judgement: firstly, that tolerant, relatively prosperous Malaya was ripe for revolution, and secondly, that the British would be a push-over – neither proved to be the case.

By the time of my arrival in Malaya, the MNLA was on the back foot, due to the authorities using a judicious mixture of carrot and stick policies. The carrot grew out of an imaginative counter-insurgency strategy known as the Briggs Plan. The main thrust of this was that the best way to defeat the insurgency was to cut off the insurgents from their supporters in the population at large. This led to the forced relocation of some 500,000 rural Malayans, including 400,000 Chinese, from squatter communities on the fringes of the forests into guarded camps known as New Villages.

These villages were newly constructed in most cases and were surrounded by barbed wire, police posts and floodlit areas, the purpose of which was to keep the inhabitants in and the guerrillas out. People understandably resented this at first, but then became relatively content with the better living standards in the villages. Also, they were given money and, importantly, ownership of the land they lived on.

The stick element in the policy mix came with the appointment as High Commissioner (after the assassination in October 1951 of Sir Henry Gurney) of Lieutenant General (later Field Marshall) Sir Gerald Templar. A tough, no-nonsense, soldier, he pressed ahead with the Briggs Plan and sped up the formation of a Malayan army. He also increased the financial rewards any civilian could win for detecting insurgents, and expanded the intelligence network (Special Branch). Both these moves played a major part in the eventual defeat of the MNLA under Templar's creative leadership.

On joining the regiment, I was given command of 13 Platoon in I company, taking over from Simon Horne, who had distinguished himself in the regiment's previous tour of duty in Kenya. The next year would be spent with my platoon patrolling the jungle, particularly the fringe where 'secondary' jungle adjoined the rubber plantations, in order to secure any New Village in an area and thus to prevent the inhabitants from taking out food and medical supplies to the insurgents hiding near the jungle edge and mounting the occasional jungle ambush.

But first I had to survive the Jungle Warfare School! The course was an in-at-the-deep-end introduction to the charms of jungle warfare. There was plenty of live firing at pop-up targets and wading through leech-infested streams.

Less uncomfortable, but scarcely less daunting, was my introduction into the regimental Officers Mess. A National Service subaltern was a low form of life and, although one's fellow subalterns were friendly enough, one could not, at least at the start, expect to be noticed by any more senior officer. The Commanding Officer was a martinet of short stature who rejoiced in the nickname, behind his back, of Bootface. But, fortunately, I Company was a happy ship, under the command of Major Peter Hudson.

When I Company was stationed in a location apart from the main regiment we set up a monthly dining club, called the Monday Club. This had two rules designed to bamboozle the Colonel; firstly, each officer was responsible in turn for arranging a good dinner in our company mess on Thursdays; and secondly the menu on Mondays

6. With my platoon at the company base in Malaya (as it was) between jungle operations. For a raw, young ex-schoolboy, the experience of responsibility and command was an eye-opener. (Photo: author)

– since the colonel, once he had heard of the Club, was bound to descend on us for a good dinner on that day – was bully beef, nobody's favourite military meal!

In contrast to the battles that marked the later Vietnam War, the Malayan Emergency was largely a platoon commander's war. My platoon consisted of about twenty men. Our patrolling took place mainly within a mile or so of the jungle's edge, rather than in the deep jungle. Usually the platoon's task was based on the intelligence of likely insurgents' movements provided by Special Branch. The platoon moved through the jungle with great care, trying to make as little noise as possible so as not to alert any insurgents in the area. Smoking, even during rest breaks, was strictly forbidden, since the smell of cigarette smoke carried a considerable distance.

The main problem for the platoon commander was not to get lost. This was not straightforward as the maps were rudimentary. Any stream one came across should usually not be there, according to the map, or should be flowing in the opposite direction, and there was hardly ever a point of reference visible through the thick wall of foliage. Many were the times when a feeling of panic gripped me that we were lost again!

A night in the jungle was an uncomfortable experience. I would choose a clearing where there was a stream for water and silently indicate that this was to be the camp site. The platoon would then sling their individual hammocks, called *bashas*, between two trees with a waterproof covering on a rope over them. The evening meal would be a Spartan affair. The platoon would be issued with a tot of rum, which most of them did not like, and passed on to me. After that it was a matter of trying to get some sleep and not thinking too much about the millipedes and other biting insects that might be inching hungrily towards one!

If the intelligence was firmer and more specific, the platoon would be sent out to mount an ambush in the jungle. This was normally both arduous and frustrating. Once the location of the ambush had been reconnoitred, the essential point was that, when getting into position, the platoon should, as far as possible, leave no sign of its presence. A crushed nettle, a single footprint or a wilting leaf could give away the ambush position.

The ambush might be in the secondary jungle adjoining a rubber plantation. From dawn until the rubber tappers left the plantation at about two in the afternoon, everyone had to keep absolutely still and

7. My platoon in at the deep end, undergoing jungle warfare training in Malaya, and getting acquainted with the leeches. (Photo: author)

silent, often with tappers working only a few yards away. After that, the troops could leave their positions but there still had to be no cooking, no smoking and no noise for fear of detection. All this might go on for three days, which was as long as the average man could stand. By this time everyone was wet, cramped, tired, covered in insect bites and, if there had been no contact, a bit flat (although aching for the taste of a cold beer!). With my platoon I never actually had a contact in an ambush, at which I was frustrated, but also, I must confess, somewhat relieved.

All of this sounds very arduous and uncomfortable. And so it was, when the platoon was on patrol or lying in ambush for extended periods. But the discomforts were usually short-lived, and nothing compared with what my father must have endured during the Burma campaign, as I would frequently reflect lying in a muddy hole. Furthermore, my more abiding memory of the Malayan jungle is the heavy burden of responsibility I felt for the men in my platoon, and fulfilling the mission we had been set without making a mess of it.

This was made more complicated, in my first few months in command of I Platoon, by having as my number two an insubordinate platoon sergeant – a few years older than me – who resented me as a 'green' new

8. A National Service subaltern in The Rifle Brigade, back from active service in the Malayan Emergency, and quite proud of his uniform. (Photo: author)

officer and showed it with displays of insolence which undermined my authority with the men. Eventually I managed to get rid of him when he questioned my command for no-smoking when the platoon was setting up an ambush position in the jungle, and the smell of smoke, which carries in the pure jungle air, could have given away our position.

The experience of commanding men on active service left me, at the end, with increased confidence and maturity. It also developed my leadership skills – not least through absorbing the (Rifle) regiment's ethos of leading by example, and having to earn the men's respect and obedience, rather than having it drilled into them in the manner of Guards regiments.

My service in Malaya also left me with memories of camaraderie in the mess, the beauty of the country (other than having to hack one's way through its jungles) and the laid-back lifestyle of this soon to be ex-British colony in south-east Asia, as experienced, for example, in the Tanglin Club in Singapore.

More broadly, there was the satisfaction that in fighting the Emergency we were convinced that we were doing something worthwhile; helping to bring stability to Malaya to achieve its goal of independence from Britain the following year as a democratic country, free from the threat of an insurgency inspired by the West's Cold War communist adversaries. British recognition of a legitimate aspiration by a colonial Malaya for independence from its imperial overlords stands in sharp contrast with Britain's actions in Egypt at about the same time; colluding with Israel and France to take back the Suez Canal, which had been (perfectly legally) nationalised by Gamal Abdel Nasser's revolutionary government and thus seeking to retain control over Egypt's future. This dubious imperialist exploit cast a long shadow over my later diplomatic career.

For the last few months of my National Service I was posted back in the summer of 1957 to the regimental depot in Winchester as a training officer. But now I lived in the elegant Officers' Mess on the far side of the parade ground from the barrack room I had inhabited during my basic training – with my Malayan campaign medal as a reminder of the contrast with the primitive nature of my recent accommodation!

I remember this as a sun-kissed time. I began to think ahead to Oxford and even studied some economics with a lecturer who visited from Southampton University. There was golf in the hills above Winchester, and dinghy racing in an Enterprise at Bosham on the Solent on Wednesday afternoons, acting as crew for the adjutant, Robin Somerset. And there were many parties.

When I was duty officer, as I marched smartly across the parade ground at ten in the evening, in my rifle green uniform with cross-belt and sword, to inspect the guard, I felt the attraction of a glorious regimental tradition. I was almost tempted to extend my time in the army. But it was time to move on to the next phase and to take up my place at Magdalen College. Oxford awaited me.

*   *   *

Magdalen is one of the most beautiful colleges in Oxford, with its soaring tower dominating the bridge across the Cherwell River at the bottom of the High Street. The bridge becomes dangerously congested at dawn on May Morning, when the college choir, in a traditional ceremony, heralds the arrival of spring, and the start of the punting season, from its top.

Arriving as a freshman, it was impossible not to be aware of one's good fortune to have gained a place there. But, although there was a fair sprinkling of wealthy undergraduates, the college was far from being a haven for the rich and idle. The Prelims exams at the end of the second term were a demanding test, after which the ranks thinned out.

I had chosen not to read Modern Languages but to switch to Politics, Philosophy and Economics, universally recognised as PPE. To begin with it was all rather strange. In particular, the Oxford school of linguistic philosophy seemed almost pointless in its neglect of what are thought of as the grand philosophical themes, in favour of a minute dissection of language. The ultimate dead-end seemed to be having to write an essay on the meaning of meaning. But there was an undoubted cachet in studying the gnomic sayings of Ludwig Wittgenstein, the cult philosopher of the hour. More than that, the intellectual rigour in the use of language, and reasoning generally – instilled by the philosophy course – stood me in good stead in my future profession where clarity of thinking and expression were an essential qualification.

In time the mental rigour engendered in the philosophy course became a powerful intellectual weapon when studying the other subjects, politics and economics, which, more obviously, reinforced and illuminated each other. I was doubly fortunate that all my tutors were of the highest calibre: Ken Tite, Peter Pulzer, Jeremy Wolfenden and Anthony King in politics; Harry Weldon and Geoffrey Warnock in philosophy; and David Worswick in economics.

As far as I was concerned the outstanding lecturers of the day were firstly the philosopher Isaiah Berlin, who was capable of making a single sentence last for five minutes; secondly the rich and controversial art historian Douglas Cooper who was a friend and promoter of Picasso's (apart from his later work) and collector of the works of Braque; and thirdly the historian AJP Taylor – a Fellow of Magdalen – who took pride in being the only lecturer in the University able to fill the lecture hall at 9am, and made a satisfying amount of money with his ground-breaking history lectures on TV, delivered straight to camera, not to mention his lucrative journalism with the Beaverbrook press.

The college President, TSR Boase, was the acme of urbanity, who entertained the undergraduates to elegant dinners in his Lodging – with the exception, it was said, of the future super-star Dudley Moore, whom he apparently did not think it worth troubling over. A historian and chronicler of the Crusades, Boase had his great moment, in our eyes, when the then US Vice-President Richard Nixon visited Oxford. Boase was Vice-Chancellor of the university at the time. When Nixon called on him at the college and greeted him with the words 'How d'you do, Mr President?', Boase took delight in replying, with a beatific smile 'How d'you do, Mr Vice-President?'

My long vacations were mostly spent abroad, travelling through Europe and trying to soak up different aspects of the continent's cultural offerings, or discovering Africa where my father had become the director of the British civil engineering consultants building the harbour for the coastal town of Tema in Ghana, the largest artificial harbour on the continent. Ghana was in the first flush of independence under the charismatic leadership of Kwame Nkrumah, who had turned his country into an exciting place to visit.

Several of the country's ministers came to our house in Tema for dinner. Sadly, most of them would later become mired in scandal. But at the time exuberant optimism over the country's future was the order of the day.

Back at Oxford I continued to aim to take the Foreign Office examination in my final year. Whether influenced by my single-mindedness or not, several of my friends decided to take the same route, including John Coles who would become Permanent Under-Secretary in the FCO, and Brian Fall whose final post was ambassador in Moscow. I hedged against failure in the exam by applying for, and winning, a scholarship to study for a year at the prestigious Science Po at the Sorbonne in Paris.

Magdalen had so much to offer that, for many of us, it was a world unto itself, and friendships made there tended to last throughout life. For example, both Coles and Fall are members of the Trogiron Club (trog = prole), a club of (mostly) former Magdalen members which still meets for lunch once or twice a year to this day. It was set up to take advantage of the college's excellent kitchen, with a self-deprecating title intended to distinguish it from the somewhat pretentious (as we saw it) Gridiron Club. The original hard-core members included Lewis Rudd, the distinguished producer of children's TV; Stephen Cretney, academic lawyer and Fellow of All Souls; Gerald Bowden, MP for Dulwich; Frederic Reynold QC; Jonathan Cecil, the actor; Adrian Berry (Lord Camrose); John Stopford Birch; Jonathan Alexander; Antony Birley; and Anthony Freemantle, the college aesthete.

And so it was that, with the French scholarship secured, and the Foreign Office exam passed with a result near the top of the order, I indulged myself with a few weeks in Venice to broaden my artistic education, while existing on pizza, peaches and cheap wine, before driving my ancient Ford back to my parents' house, with my gaze now fixed on a life in diplomacy.

Chapter 3

Into the Arab World: Learning Arabic, the 'Spy School' and Gulf Tribal Disputes

In late August 1960 I presented myself at the Personnel Department of the Foreign Office, which was housed in a grand house in Carlton House Terrace, for my initial interview. My first question was whether I could defer my entry into the Service for a year in order to take up the French Government scholarship I had been awarded at the Science Po Institute of the Sorbonne. The suave middle-ranking officer interviewing me, whom I had already encountered on the entrance examination, asked what I was proposing to study there. Well, I said, I was thinking of studying the French position on the Common Market (which had recently been established by the Treaty of Rome).

'Oh, come on, old boy', came the reply, 'everyone knows that that's not going to work. It would be better for you to come in straight away and learn a difficult language'.

Swallowing my disappointment at this brisk rejection of my plans, I considered the options he offered: Chinese, Japanese, Thai, Persian,

Photo: the author with Sheikh Rashid Al-Maktoum, Ruler of Dubai, 1963. The Sheikh had a dynamism which laid the groundwork for Dubai's future prosperity.

9. MECAS, the Foreign Office's Middle East Centre for Arabic Studies in the village of Shemlan in Lebanon: all efforts to rid MECAS of its persistent reputation in the Arab world as being a 'school for spies' were undermined by the unmasking of George Blake's double life. (Photo: author)

Russian or Arabic. I made one of the most pivotal decisions of my life without undue hesitation: Arabic. I was attracted not only by the glamour of many of the wide selection of posts in which Arabic was spoken – ranging from Morocco, via Egypt and Lebanon, to the Persian Gulf – but also by the fact that, at the time, Britain still played a major role in the region (in spite of the Suez debacle of four years earlier). I also felt that there was more chance of penetrating the mind-set of the Arabs, followers of another Abrahamic religion, than peoples further to the east. Finally, the Arab world was not too far away.

The decision meant that I would start my career by learning Arabic at the Middle East Centre for Arab Studies (MECAS) in Lebanon. But first came the month-long introductory course for my intake of eighteen or so new entrants into the Administrative Grade.

The course was a well-constructed mixture of teaching us the essentials of the job, interlaced with talks by eminent former, or practising diplomats, politicians, academics and others with a broad perspective on Britain's role in the world. We learned a lot. One dynamic former ambassador, Sir Humphrey Trevelyan, who had served in a number of tough spots, advised us that the important thing was to talk to as many, and as great a variety of, people as possible. So, for example, apart from cultivating the country's elite, if one was being trailed by secret policemen, find a way of engaging even them in conversation.

*   *   *

A few weeks after the end of the course I was off to Lebanon to learn Arabic. Landing at Beirut airport, I remembered that I had been there before on that eventful flight to Singapore to join my regiment. Then, the air had been heavy with the scent of orange blossom from the surrounding orange groves. I had marked it down as a place to which I would like to return. And now here I was.

MECAS was a Foreign Office establishment, the only one that aspired to being commercial, by taking in fee-paying students in addition to British officials. These might, for example, be businessmen or oil-men, missionaries, journalists or private individuals, as well as officials of other governments, such as Japan.

The Centre had been set up in Jerusalem after the war and the first chief instructor had been a future Israeli foreign minister, Abba Eban. In the late fifties it had moved to Lebanon. A tiresome issue had resulted when it was decided to situate the Centre in a mixed Maronite/Druze village, Shemlan, in the hills above Beirut, rather than in the Chouf, the fiefdom of the Druze leader Kamal Jumblat, who had lobbied for it. As a result, the story was put about that the Centre was a 'spy school', which was how it became known throughout the Arab world – in spite of the Centre's valiant efforts to convince the world that it was a purely academic establishment, which it was. As for any other walks of life for which they may have provided training ... I couldn't possibly comment.

The Centre's purpose-built building in Shemlan was modern, light and airy. From it one gazed down at the airport below, adjoining the Mediterranean. The director was Donald Maitland (later Sir Donald), a small and brilliant man with prodigious energy. It was he who had devised the syllabus, grammar and word list, together with James (later Sir James) Craig, the foremost Foreign Office Arabist of his generation, and my future boss in Dubai. The instructors, who showed great patience with our efforts to learn the language, were mostly Palestinians or Lebanese.

The course was demanding. We tried to commit the unfamiliar vocabulary to heart with the aid of cards, on which we wrote the English word on one side and the Arabic equivalent on the other. MECAS students could be spotted strolling along the streets of Shemlan, and even down in Beirut at the weekends, intently turning over their word cards and mouthing silently. But if it was hard for us British students, imagine how much harder it was for the Japanese who first had to learn English as they went along in order to follow the lessons.

When the Christmas holiday came round, four of us decided to spend it in the obviously most suitable places, Jerusalem and Bethlehem. Jerusalem at that time (before the Israeli victory in the Six Day War) was divided by a Green Line between the Israeli side and Arab East Jerusalem which, together with the West Bank, was under Jordanian control. We stayed in the Dom Polski, a hostel run by elderly Polish nuns which was reputed to have the best food in town.

On Christmas Night we took the bus to Bethlehem to join the throng of pilgrims. The Anglicans held a midnight service in a court-yard of the Basilica of the Holy Nativity, by kind permission of the Orthodox Patriarch. At the conclusion of the service, conducted by the Anglican Archbishop in Jerusalem, he turned to the white-bearded Patriarch and invited him to say a few words. The Patriarch blessed us and, with a beatific smile, pronounced what were probably his only English words, 'Merry Christmas'.

On another excursion from Shemlan, I travelled down to southern Jordan for a first visit to the legendary 'lost' city of Petra, the rose-red city 'half as old as time'. Among our group was William Lancaster, son of Osbert, the cartoonist, who, before joining the MECAS course, had done some digging there with the archaeologist Peter Parr. We had Petra virtually to ourselves – which is not the experience of any tourist today! With William as our guide, we were able to explore that fasci-nating site from end to end. In fact, we did it so thoroughly that when we trudged back up the valley at the end of the day, I was exhausted. The glass of mint tea that we were offered in a Bedouin black tent on reaching the village of Wadi Mousa was life-saving, and my first taste of Bedouin hospitality.

*   *   *

On the MECAS course we were taught classical Arabic, which is the literary version, and that heard on the radio. Everyday conversational Arabic, on the other hand, varies greatly from Morocco to the Gulf. A key moment in the course came after about five months with the so-called Language Break, when the students sallied forth into the Arab world for a month, to learn to adapt their classical Arabic to everyday use. The Centre arranged for most students to stay with families in the surrounding countries, who knew what was expected of them. I chose, not entirely sensibly, to strike out on my own.

My plan was to stay for a bit in the legendary Baron Hotel in Aleppo, in Syria, and see where that led. The hotel, which had been patronised by Agatha Christie and Lawrence of Arabia among others, was run by Toto Mazloumian, an Armenian in a double-breasted blue blazer, who spoke impeccable English.

For a few days I delighted in wandering in the ancient souk of Aleppo – from where merchants would embark in times past on the journey along the Silk Road to China. In the evening I would sit on the hotel terrace drinking beer, eating pistachio nuts and watching the crowd in the street below. But the opportunities for using my Arabic in a more than cursory way were frustratingly limited. I gave up and asked Toto if he could find me a local family to stay with.

The family he found were very welcoming, but the snag was that they preferred speaking French to me rather than Arabic. And the daughter of the house insisted that we go out in the evening to one of the many open-air cafés, hung with coloured lights, to dance. All very pleasant, but still not doing much for my Arabic. So, after a few more days of this, and a side trip across the Turkish border to Antakya (ancient Antioch), via the ruined basilica where St Simeon the Stylite stood on top of his column for twenty-eight years, I bade the family good-bye and made my way down the coast back to Shemlan, where the office arranged a ticket for me to fly to Cairo to try my luck there.

In Cairo I explained my dilemma to Anthony (later Sir Anthony) Parsons, the Head of Chancery in the embassy. He regretted that he was unable to help. Any Egyptian family he introduced me to, he explained, could, in view of the strained nature of Anglo-Egyptian relations since the Suez crisis, be in trouble with the authorities. Once again, I was on my own.

I tried a spot of tourism, a train journey to Karnak and a carriage ride around the Valley of the Kings. My co-passenger was a German dentist. I found that German and Arabic had become confused in my head, so that when I tried to talk German to my companion it was Arabic which came out, to his evident bemusement.

The last stop in my, now desperate, quest to speak colloquial Arabic was Alexandria. There I put up in a cheap hotel, on the basis that no-one there would speak anything but Arabic. This was true, but unfortunately they seemed not to be particularly keen to talk to me. I visited the (rather miserable) zoo and identified the Arabic names of all the animals but there wasn't much feedback from them. Finally, I did what you should always do when feeling lonely in a foreign city: I went to the Anglican church on Sunday.

At the end of the service I was approached by a smartly dressed Egyptian Coptic lady and her daughter. She said that I looked lonely, which I did not deny, and invited me to lunch at the Yacht Club. One thing led to another and the upshot was that I spent the last week of the Language Break staying with them, very agreeably, at their villa on Alexandria's famous Agami beach.

One conversation of that week, almost certainly not in Arabic, has stuck in my mind. I mentioned that, when I had been at Oxford the previous year, the books that everyone was reading, particularly young ladies sitting at open windows on summer afternoons, had been Lawrence Durrell's *Alexandria Quartet*. The family's reaction, to my surprise, was vitriolic. In the books, they said, Durrell had betrayed confidences about a Coptic plot, which he had used as a background theme running through the *Quartet*. This had led directly to the arrest of Copts whom my hosts had known. Durrell, in their view, had been inexcusably irresponsible. I have never been able to get at the truth of their outburst.

Back at Shemlan at the end of the Language Break, with a better understanding of some of the surrounding countries, but only marginally improved spoken Arabic, I found that the Centre's repudiation of its reputation as a 'spy school' was about to suffer a reverse. The Foreign Office students on the course had been briefed in London in advance that a fellow student on our course was a member of MI6 under Foreign Office cover. His name was George Blake.

We had found George a pleasant colleague, usually smartly dressed in a blue blazer, who seemed to have successfully endured a seriously unpleasant captivity during the Korean War after the North Koreans briefly captured Seoul, where Blake had been posted as an MI6 agent. He was not pure British, having a Dutch mother and a Spanish-Jewish father, who had British nationality. His wife was the highly presentable daughter of an admiral and their boys, Anthony, James and Patrick, were at prep school in England. George was very good at Arabic. But he was also quite difficult to penetrate.

Thinking back after George had returned to London, to face interrogation, I remembered a convivial dinner in Beirut of a dinner club,

10. George Blake, to become known as an infamous spy, was a fellow student at MECAS. He was called back to London to be interrogated, leading to his arrest, trial, imprisonment and notorious escape to Moscow. (Photo: author)

which William Lancaster and I had set up to enable course members to enjoy a sample of the city's restaurants. Being only recently down from university some of us had embarked on an undergraduate-type discussion on the meaning of communism. During the entire evening George had remained silent.

The Director of MECAS, then John Wilton, called the Foreign Office students into his office one morning in 1961. He told us, with curious wording, that 'a man called George Blake' had appeared before magistrates at the Bow Street magistrate's court, charged with offences under the Official Secrets Act. When the details came out later we all felt personally betrayed.

Blake was sentenced to a record forty-two years in gaol for espionage, but escaped from Wormwood Scrubs after five years, with the complicity of an IRA fellow-prisoner. He managed, with difficulty, to make his way to East Germany and then the Soviet Union, where he lived, in a dacha outside Moscow until his death at the age of 98. He never expressed any regret over the fate of the numerous agents he had betrayed.

I have followed the Blake case with interest over the years, talked to people in the know and seen the various TV programmes made about it. My personal hunch is that his turncoat act had less to do with his 'brainwashing' by the Soviets after he was captured in the fall of Seoul to North Korean forces (although his Marxist convictions seem to have been genuine), or, as he claimed, his shock and disgust at the American bombing of the North Korean villages, which he witnessed while in captivity, than to his condescending treatment at the hands of some of his superiors in MI6, who considered him 'not one of us'. But whatever the real reasons, he will have taken them to the grave on his death in Moscow on Christmas Day 2020, at an advanced age – unrepentant to the end.

Blake turns up again later in my story in connection with the celebrated Cold War spy tunnel in Berlin.

* * *

Towards the end of the MECAS Advanced Course, in January 1962, the Foreign Office students were called in to the Director individually to be told of their postings. I was to go to Dubai as Assistant Political Agent. 'Where's that?' I asked. 'Don't be ridiculous' replied the Director, 'go to the Political Agency in Bahrain and they'll put you on your way'.

At the Bahrain Agency, sweating through lunch with the Political Agent, Peter Tripp, I encountered the hot and humid Gulf climate for the first time – and found that I was wearing a suit that was much too warm. Also located in Bahrain was the office of the Political Resident (the senior British official in the Gulf), the highly experienced Sir William Luce. Luce was away at the time so my first meeting with him, my overall boss, was postponed. When it eventually took place, he congratulated me on having landed a job which was quite unlike that of a Third Secretary in an embassy, 'and none the worse for that'. He was absolutely right.

The Gulf States at the time existed in a kind of time warp. Apart from Kuwait, which had just gained its independence, they were British Protected States which meant that they were not colonies, since they were responsible for their own domestic affairs, but Britain was responsible for their security and for their external representation. Nor were other states permitted resident diplomatic representatives in them, although Kuwait was starting to spread its wings in that area.

These exclusive arrangements dated from the nineteenth century, when Britain had been concerned above all to preserve the security of its links to India, and keep out competing European powers. The Royal Navy had been called upon on occasion to suppress what were considered to be threatening pirate activities (although the southern Gulf States, the main adversaries, rejected this interpretation, and claimed to be acting legitimately to protect their interests).

In 1903, during one such naval intervention, Lord Curzon, Viceroy of India, sailed into the Gulf and summoned the sheikhs onto HMS *Argonaut*, where he held a kind of Durbar, lying off Sharjah. He addressed the sheikhs, with many high-flown rhetorical flourishes, on the undoubted benefits of being under Britain's protection. The relationship between Britain and the Gulf sheikhdoms, which had been originally designed to give British India defence in depth from hostile approaches, had proved to be mutually beneficial in the different circumstances of the twentieth century.

For the sheikhdoms, in my time security meant, in practice, protection from the Shah's Iran, which, by now becoming flushed with oil money, harboured pretensions to being the regional super-power and which also had outstanding claims to three islands in the southern Gulf that came within the jurisdiction of the southern Gulf Arab sheikhdoms. Given the strategic importance of uninterrupted oil flows from the Gulf, Britain took its protection role very seriously. It was exercised through the Political Resident in Bahrain and the Political Agencies, reporting to him, in Doha, Bahrain, Abu Dhabi and Dubai. On matters affecting the UK's responsibilities (in effect protecting British interests) the Political Residents and the Political Agencies had the last word. But this did not extend to controlling the sheikhdoms' internal affairs, which was in the hands of the Rulers. Here the UK's role was advisory – though in the full expectation that any advice would be followed.

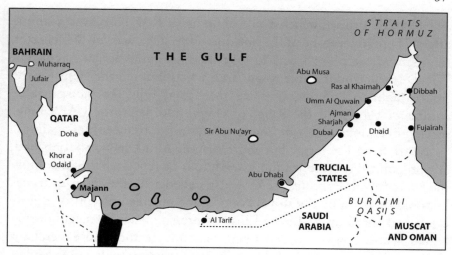

The Trucial States was a group of sheikhdoms which came under British Protection following a series of exclusive treaties signed with Britain between 1822 and 1894 until its dissolution in December 1970 and replacement as the United Arab Emirates (UAE) the following year.

During my time in Dubai the British position was set out clearly in a message from the Political Resident, Sir William Luce, which was read to the 1963 Trucial States Council (the annual meeting of the Rulers) in the following terms:

> It is the belief of Her Majesty's Government that each country in the Middle East should be left to choose its own road to salvation, free from outside interference.

The message was a response to the threat which Arab nationalism was at the time considered to present to Britain's exclusive position in the Gulf. The main vehicle for this was the Egyptian radio station *Sawt al Arab* (Voice of the Arabs). The Egyptian leader Gamal Abdel Nasser was riding high after the Anglo-French debacle at Suez, and the skilful oratory of his broadcasts (as I had been able to judge when listening to them at MECAS) had a powerful effect on his Arab listeners.

✳   ✳   ✳

Such was the political weather pattern when I took the weekly Gulf Air Viscount flight from Bahrain to Sharjah to embark on my first posting.

The Sharjah airport, which doubled up as an RAF base, was a simple affair. There to meet me at the bottom of the steps was Ian Winchester, the man whose place I was to take as Assistant Political Agent. Ian Winchester introduced me to an Arab who mounted the steps for the return flight to Bahrain. This was Mehdi al-Tajir, the indispensable commercial fixer for the Ruler of Dubai and, later, the UAE's long-serving first ambassador in London. I never got to meet him again.

Apart from the large, but more distant Abu Dhabi, Sharjah had, at one point, been the leading sheikhdom of the Trucial States (now the United Arab Emirates, or UAE), so called after the series of truces imposed on them by the Royal Navy in the nineteenth century. But its creek had silted up and it had lost its pre-eminence to neighbouring Dubai, whose creek provided a better anchorage and whose merchant class was busy creating its future prosperity under the dynamic leadership of its Ruler, Sheikh Rashid al-Maktoum.

The other, smaller, sheikhdoms spread out along the coast to the north of Sharjah were Ajman, Umm al-Quwain and Ras al-Khaimah. The smallest, Fujairah, lay on the eastern side of the peninsula, on the Batinah coast. The sheikhdom becoming the richest, due to its nascent oil development, was Abu Dhabi. There were two Political Agents in the Trucial States, in Dubai and Abu Dhabi.

Winchester and I drove across the desert the six miles to Dubai, bisected by its picturesque creek, harbouring *dhows* from all points in the Arabian Sea (see Colour Plate 2). The Political Agency's compound lay on the far side of the creek, and there was no bridge at that stage. One crossed by taking the Agency's *abra*, or ferry, to the landing stage outside the compound, which consisted of a few low buildings housing the office, the Political Agent's house, a bungalow which was to be mine, some outhouses and a tennis court (a recent addition, courtesy of the Ministry of Works in London). Over it all flew the Union Jack on a tall flagpole.

The Political Agent, James Craig, welcomed me warmly. He was not the usual Foreign Service officer of the time. A Liverpudlian with a strong attachment to Scotland, he had been an academic teaching Arabic at Durham University before taking the MECAS post as Chief Instructor, which had established his reputation. He had been persuaded to join the Foreign Office as a late entrant. The Arabic language, indeed language generally, was among the most important things in his life. Arabs were always in awe at his command of their language.

This did not make him a dry pedant. Far from it. He had a warm nature and a good sense of humour, although he was quick to pounce on loose thinking. In Dubai he was accompanied by his wife, Margaret, and their three sons. The family atmosphere they created in the Agency took the edge off what could have been a lonely bachelor existence for me.

Craig explained the nature of our role at the Dubai Agency. We were there to advise and guide the Rulers in their dealings with the wider world, help with development and assure security. This last task was done in co-operation with the Trucial Oman Scouts, the British-officered levies, based in Sharjah, with outposts around the sheikhdoms, which kept in close touch with the tribesmen and dealt with any trouble.

Even as a young newcomer to the game of diplomacy, I was quick to understand that the dynamics behind our role in the Gulf – beyond the rhetoric – was fed by the hard-headed, rational decision-making which saw Britain's role in the region as essentially defensive, aimed at keeping stability in the Gulf and preserving the exclusivity of the Treaties – in other words to keep out, for as long as possible, competitors and threats from potential adversaries such as the Soviet Union, or actual but ambitious allies such as Iran.

In Dubai there was a police force led by the British Chief of Police, Peter Lorimer. Individual Rulers kept order in their own sheikhdoms, but could appeal to the Agency for help if necessary. Since the British Government was answerable for the Rulers' actions at the United Nations the Agency kept a close watch that human rights were not being infringed, for example by prisoners being kept in inhumane conditions.

The Rulers had jurisdiction over their own nationals and the British Government, and hence the Political Agency, had jurisdiction over all non-Arabs. This was exercised in Her Majesty's Court for the Trucial States (Dubai). Criminal trials in this could be time-consuming work and Craig normally delegated this to me. In fact, one of Craig's first instructions to me was to try a drug-smuggling case coming up in court the following day.

And so I found myself, after a short but intensive study of the Indian Penal Code (derived from British India), sitting in judgment on a rather woebegone Pakistani accused of importing a large quantity of hashish, which was on display just below the judge's bench, the fumes from which were in danger of clouding my judgement.

11. When acting as Political Agent I would have dealings direct with Shaikh Rashid bin Sa'id al Maktoum, the dynamic Ruler of Dubai. The hat perched on my knee was worn to add gravitas! (Photo: author)

The prosecution was conducted by Lorimer, the Police Chief. Since the accused had no lawyer to put his case – although he had the right to one – cross examination of the witnesses fell to me, the judge.

To cut a long story short, my first case did not go well. It was a clear-cut affair and I duly found the accused guilty and gave him a prison sentence. He appealed. The appeal was heard by a 'proper' judge, Sir John Wyatt, a former Attorney-General of Kenya, who flew down from Bahrain for the purpose. To my chagrin he upheld the appeal and released the prisoner.

When I remonstrated with Sir John afterwards, he told me in a kindly way that, although the prisoner's guilt was not in doubt, he was obliged to uphold the appeal because I had not recorded the proceedings in the initial trial in sufficient detail. To help me to do better thereafter, he arranged for me to spend a couple of weeks in Doha, Qatar, to learn from the professional British lawyer stationed there, who was Sir John's number two on the Persian Gulf Court. After that my judgments tended to go unchallenged.

In practice, court work did not take up much of my time and I was free, among other duties, to roam the Trucial States calling on the Rulers, particularly to make formal calls at one of the two Eids (religious festivals coinciding with the end of Ramadan and the annual pilgrimage to Mecca). These were colourful affairs with dancing and chanting, much firing of guns and feasting.

Sheikh Rashid of Dubai was the Ruler with whom we were most involved. He was a remarkable man. A tall, alert figure with a sharp mind and a natural authority, he was already making great strides in developing his sheikhdom. Dubai's progress was founded on the entrepot trade passing through its bustling creek and the entrepreneurial spirit of its merchant community – many of whom were of Persian descent. It also depended on Sheikh Rashid's shrewdness, his choice of good advisors (with our help over recruitment) – mostly, but not all, British – and his willingness to take their advice, once a mutual feeling of confidence had been established. One of his closest local advisors was Easa Saleh al-Gurg, who combined his Nasserist sympathies – which were the orthodoxy of the day – with a strong friendship for Britain. He was later a long-serving UAE ambassador in London, where, with his wife Soraya, he was an active and energetic member of the diplomatic scene.

Both James Craig and his predecessor, Donald Hawley, had succeeded in winning Sheikh Rashid's confidence. The Ruler would occasionally drop in at the Agency in the afternoon, away from the public scrutiny of his *majlis*, for a quiet word with the Political Agent. He admired Craig's command of Arabic. His own Arabic, uttered through teeth firmly clamped on a small clay pipe, was almost impossible for me to follow. Even Craig had difficulty with it, as I later heard.

Even in the short two years that I spent in Dubai, Sheikh Rashid's vision for his sheikhdom – which would be carried on after him by his son Sheikh Mohamed bin Rashid – was beginning to take shape. Plans were under way for the Free Port at Jebel Ali and dry dock. The futuristic skyline of today's Dubai, and its envied role as the financial centre of the Gulf, and much more, is due in large part to the solid foundations for growth laid by Sheikh Rashid and, it should be added, the disinterested guidance of a number of British officials and dedicated professional advisers. Among them were Bill Duff (financial advisor), Eric Tulloch (water), Neville Allen (civil engineering), John Harris (architect) and Jack Briggs (Police Chief after Lorimer).

The next largest sheikhdom in our bailiwick was Sharjah. The Ruler of Sharjah, Sheikh Saqr bin Sultan, was a very different character from Sheikh Rashid. A man of some education, he was fond of poetry and the cultivation of roses. On his return from his annual summer holiday in Scandinavia it was his practice, so it was said (I never actually saw one), to produce a slim volume of erotic verse describing his experiences.

Sheikh Saqr could be very charming, but he found himself deposed a year or so after my departure. This could happen if a Ruler's family decided unanimously that he should be replaced. They wrote a letter to the British authorities to this effect. Since those authorities had come to harbour suspicions, with evidence to support them, that his Arab nationalist sympathies were making him a channel for the potentially troublesome intrusion of Egyptian influence, it was decided to take action. He was called to the Political Agency to be given – strange as it may sound in today's world – the unwelcome news and, escorted by the Scouts, to a waiting plane to be flown into exile.

As for Abu Dhabi, the largest sheikhdom, it was the responsibility of a separate Political Agent, Colonel Hugh Boustead. He was a legendary figure, who had enrolled in the Royal Navy in the First World War. Not finding it to his taste, he had deserted and joined the Army instead, winning the Military Cross in France. He had to be given a pardon for desertion before going to the Palace to be decorated with the MC. He had also, for good measure, commanded the Camel Corps in Sudan, helped to restore the Emperor Haile Selassie to his throne in Ethiopia and taken part in the 1933 Everest Expedition.

I took an early opportunity of driving across the desert to call on Colonel Hugh. I found him a delightful old-world personality. He was frustrated at the state of his relationship with the strong-willed, and deeply reactionary, Ruler of Abu Dhabi, Sheikh Shakhbut bin Sultan Al-Nahyan. This had been knocked off course by the British Government awarding an island, which was disputed between Abu Dhabi and Qatar, to Qatar, while Boustead had happened to be absent. Sheikh Shakhbut felt that Boustead had failed to protect Abu Dhabi's interests. Their relationship never recovered although, as Boustead had pointed out to the Sheikh – as recorded in his, Boustead's, memoirs, *The Wind of Morning* – it was his own fault for being too proud to get lawyers to present his case to the boundary commission.

Boustead himself had not wholly adapted to Foreign Office ways and one was liable to find a confidential intelligence report stuffed behind the cushion in his sitting room. In the late afternoon of my first visit I announced that I had better be getting back to Dubai. Colonel Hugh gave me a doubtful look.

Sure enough my Land-Rover, driven by Gambar, our best Agency driver, sank up to its axles in the salt marsh (*sabkha*) which one had to cross in those days before the existence of the present six-lane highway, and which became impassable when the tide was in. I had to squelch back to the Abu Dhabi police post and get a lift back to the Agency, to be greeted by Colonel Hugh with the words 'Ah there you are, old boy, I thought you might be back. Stay the night. Dinner's in half an hour – dead fish as usual.'

The Rulers of the two diminutive sheikhdoms immediately north of Sharjah, Ajman and Umm al Quwain, were both elderly gentlemen whose grey beards gave them an air of serene wisdom. I spent some two weeks in the company of the Ruler of Umm al-Quwain in the mid-summer of 1963 when James Craig instructed me to take part in a boundary commission, under the Ruler's chairmanship, to resolve a border dispute between Sharjah and Fujairah which had broken out at the village of Dibbah on the peninsula's eastern coast.

The definition of frontiers between the patchwork of territories that made up the Northern Trucial States was at that time a relatively recent preoccupation of the Rulers. Indeed, it made little sense. The tribes owing allegiance to the respective Rulers had their traditional areas for grazing their goats and wells for watering their camels, although disputes were not uncommon. The picture had, however, been drastically changed by the prospect of the discovery of oil (not yet a reality) and the promise of seemingly untold wealth which it held out.

To address this increasingly burning issue a political officer of the Agency, Julian Walker, had been set to work a year or two previously to define the frontiers and draw up a map. This he had done with great skill, and excellent spoken Arabic. The work had involved conducting painstaking interviews with all concerned to try to establish the traditional rights associated with particular wells or trees or other features. Even when the map was drawn up and accepted by all the Rulers, Walker's work was not over. Each year he would return to the Trucial States, from wherever his current post happened to be, to resolve whatever disputes over his map had arisen since his last visit.

The Dibbah dispute between Fujairah and Sharjah was urgent and could not await Walker's next visit. Shots were being exchanged

12. Accompanying Sheikh Saqr bin Mohammed al Qasimi, Ruler of Ras al-Khaimah, on a visit for tea to Ted Morgan, director of the RAK Agricultural Research Centre (on leave at his Hastings home), after lunching with my parents. It was Sheikh Saqr's first visit to the UK. (Photo: author)

between rival groups of tribesmen. The Scouts were concerned that matters could get out of hand. So, off went our three-man Boundary Commission, with an escort of the Scouts, to set up a temporary camp in Dibbah, hear evidence from the tribesmen of the rival sheikhdoms and make a ruling.

We remained there for two weeks, wilting in the August heat. The third member of the Commission was the *Qadi* (judge) of Aden who conducted the questioning of the witnesses very efficiently. They were fine upstanding-looking *bedu* who received their briefing from their Sheikh's representative before entering the tent, plus, no doubt, a little something for their pains. Many conflicting claims were made for every feature of the area. Somehow the Qadi was able to make some sense of all this and eventually suggested a settlement to which the Ruler of Umm al-Quwain, one of our fellow arbitrators, nodded his assent. Equally importantly, the two Rulers concerned in the dispute raised no objections.

Our wise adjudication lasted reasonably well, although there continued to be occasional outbreaks of tension, which probably persist to this day!

One of the sheikhdoms involved in the Dibbah dispute was Fujairah. This was the smallest of the sheikhdoms and the latest to have its independent status recognised. Its Ruler, a short and genial figure with a twinkle in his eye, was known to the Brits, predictably, as 'Fudge'. One of the pleasures of my job was to drive over the central mountains and along dry riverbeds to pay a call on him at the Eid. While waiting for the feast to be prepared we would sit under the stars and I would listen to his stories, told in Arabic. The British, he told me on one occasion, were the cleverest people since they had the best intelligence. There wasn't a fish that laughed in the sea, he said, without the British hearing about it.

The sheikh with whom I had the most consequential dealings was the Ruler of Ras al-Khaimah, the most northerly sheikhdom, extending into the mountainous Musandam Peninsula (which largely formed part of the Sultanate of Oman, separate from the Trucial States). Sheikh Saqr bin Mohamed was a Qasimi, from the same Qawasim tribe as the Ruler of Sharjah. They considered themselves the aristocracy of the Trucial Coast. Sheikh Saqr had lost an eye – in a fight, it was said, in which a man had died – and wore a black patch, which made him look suitably piratical.

During my time in Dubai, Sheikh Saqr paid his first official visit to Britain. I happened to be on leave, staying with my parents at their house in Benenden, in the Weald of Kent, where they had moved from Bedford. Hearing of the Sheikh's visit, my father insisted that we should invite him down from London for lunch, on his way to visit the Morgans, the couple who ran the Agricultural Trial Station in his sheikhdom, financed by Britain, who lived down the road in Hastings.

The lunch was memorable. The Ruler arrived with an advisor/interpreter in a London taxi, which must have made a substantial hole in his national budget. In those days, a robed Arab sheikh in dark glasses was a far from usual sight in a Kentish setting. My mother rose to the occasion and Sheikh Saqr pronounced the Kentish lamb to be delicious. After lunch the party, including my girlfriend, drove on down to Hastings to take tea with Ted Morgan and his sister. A vintage day.

*   *   *

My subsequent dealings with Sheikh Saqr, a few months later, were much more serious, and were the highlight of my Gulf posting.

It was in June and July 1963, when James Craig was on home leave and I was in charge as Acting Political Agent. A tribe of hillmen called the Habus, who lived mainly in the mountains above Ras al-Khaimah and who had become enraged at Sheikh Saqr's enclosure of what they regarded as their traditional grazing lands, decided to throw off their allegiance to him. This led to a prolonged dispute which threatened to escalate into a troublesome little mountain war which the Trucial Oman Scouts estimated they would find difficult to control. The following account is based on the dispatch I wrote at the conclusion of the affair to Sir William Luce, the Political Resident in Bahrain, and to the Foreign Office – the first dispatch of my diplomatic career!

In addition to their grievance over enclosures, the Habus, who numbered about 4,000, were complaining about Sheikh Saqr's generally repressive attitude towards them. For good measure they also launched a claim for independence within defined borders. Sheikh Saqr initially affected to treat the matter as a little local difficulty, caused by a handful of troublemakers. If he could arrest them, he said, there would be peace.

We began with a two-pronged approach. The Habus at this stage were ready to fight for what they saw as their rights, with the support of tribal allies and the discreet backing of the Ruler of Fujairah. The Political Resident covered this base by sending a carefully worded message to the Ruler of Fujairah saying that he was following developments with interest. This caused the Ruler to back off. I meanwhile wrote to the Ruler of Ras al-Khaimah telling him of our concern lest the Habus unrest led to fighting, encouraging him to settle the matter peacefully, and offering our good offices to facilitate a settlement.

Matters then took a turn for the worse when news came in that the Habus had impounded a lorry which Sheikh Saqr had sent into the hills to collect stones for building purposes. They had turned away the driver and coolies but were hanging onto the lorry. Sheikh Saqr responded by sending a war party into the hills. It had opened fire on the Habus in an effort to retrieve the lorry, which it had succeeded in doing. We subsequently heard that machine-guns had been used, and that it was a miracle that no-one had been killed.

Although the Scouts, who had brought about a ceasefire, were patrolling the area to keep the peace, the mood among the tribesmen was darkening and the Habus had been assured of support by a neighbouring larger tribe, the Shihuh, who were famous for the little axes which they were wont to plunge into the heads of their enemies.

Politically, there was also an unwanted complication. The Ruler of Fujairah had received a letter from the Sultan of Muscat and Oman (the great power in the region), asserting his own sovereignty over the Habus. Fortified with this, Fudge was once again playing an equivocal role. Sir William Luce had to send him another warning letter.

On 7 July I drove along the coast up to Ras al-Khaimah determined to sort the situation out. But first, remembering the classic imperial solution for resolving such problems, I tried to send for a gunboat, to lie offshore as a show of force and awe to persuade the tribesmen to desist. There was an RN force in the Gulf whose commander, the Senior Naval Officer Persian Gulf, based in Bahrain, rejoiced in the acronym SNOPG (pronounced *snopjee*). Unfortunately, a telegram came back from SNOPG that there was no gunboat available.

I found that Sheikh Saqr was no longer so relaxed about the situation and he asked that the Scouts should continue to patrol to prevent major trouble. I pointed out to him that his sledge-hammer tactics with his machine-guns (and where had he got them from?) had gravely exacerbated the situation and that it would now be more difficult to bring the Habus in for talks. But he promised to see them if they came in.

I then went up into the Musandam hills with a Scouts escort and, with the help of the company commander, Major Wilson, met the hard-core tribesmen at a place called Qara Harf. We squatted in a stone hut – Major Wilson, the Agency's Arab Advisor Ali Bustani (as interpreter) and me. In came a growing number of tough-looking tribesmen, some stripped to the waist, poorly armed, argumentative and a little frightened, but sincere in their grievances and desperately anxious for just treatment. They were people used to walking barefoot on the scorching stones under the noon-day sun and, at the end of a meal, putting the bones of the animal they had just eaten in their mouth and howling like dogs.

With such people negotiations were not easy, but we made good progress. To begin with, they trusted us, and even wanted to appoint me their sheikh in place of Sheikh Saqr, to represent them to him. I side-stepped the honour. More seriously, they insisted that whatever line they took should be cleared first with the Ruler of Fujairah whom they talked of, to my consternation, as being their rightful sheikh. We agreed on a further week's truce while they elected their representatives, decided on their policy and cleared this with the Ruler of Fujairah. I returned to Sheikh Saqr and the conditions of the truce were agreed upon, once I had convinced him that I was not taking Fujairah's side.

A week later I was back in Ras al-Khaimah, together with the invaluable Ali Bustani and John Rich from the Political Residency in Bahrain who had been sent by my boss, Sir William Luce, to keep an eye on things. It was an extraordinary day. Sheikh Saqr had brought in the respected sheikh from Bakha, an Omani enclave further up the coast, as a mediator. We lunched with Sheikh Saqr and impressed upon him yet again the need to come to terms with the Habus by meeting them halfway. Rich gave him a message from the Political Resident lending weight to this advice. Fortunately, I had been able to persuade the Habus to turn up, with a Scouts escort – although they had previously sworn never to come to the 'man of blood' (Sheikh Saqr) in his own town. This was achieved by trading on the trust they had in our good offices, and my personal guarantee of their safety.

In the late afternoon the serious business of discussion began in the Palace, which was actually a modest desert fort built around a central courtyard. It now houses the Ras al Khaimah Museum, which contains many interesting exhibits from the period. But on that day there was no conference table. Instead there were several separate points of negotiation, inside and outside the Palace: Sheikh Saqr and the Sheikh of Bakha were at, or ambled around, different locations within the Palace, while I was stationed strategically to monitor and receive messengers as they plied between us. My main concern was to prevent the matter hardening into a frontier dispute with evidence being produced on either side, and extraneous players such as the Sultan of Muscat and the Ruler of Fujairah joining in the fun.

Both the Habus and Sheikh Saqr came round to accepting this view, although there remained a few tribesmen at the end of the day (possibly in somebody's pay) who were still muttering about frontiers. The Sheikh of Bakha turned out to be a helpful mediator whom the Habus accepted. Possibly it was because of him, or possibly because Sheikh Saqr realised at last that he had no alternative course of action – at all events, after several hours of discussion a settlement suddenly appeared.

It was a better one than we had dared to hope for. The Ruler declared that he was ready to listen to the Habus's grievances and to take on himself the full duties and rights of being their sheikh. After some final pressure from Ali Bustani on my behalf, the Sheikh Saqr, the Sheikh of Bakha and the Habus themselves all reached agreement.

The terms of the agreement, which were fleshed out subsequently, provided for the Habus to have free access to Ras al-Khaimah again. The gardens in the disputed area were to be parcelled up, and those Habus who wished to own gardens were to be given them, and to be given help in buying pumps. Other wells were to be improved and to be declared common wells for the use of all the tribesmen.

At the end of the day, the talks concluded with a medieval and possibly unique ceremony. The Ruler sat in his majlis with me on his right-hand side. He held out his hand and the Habus approached in small groups and placed their hands on his, to swear allegiance. He, for his part, swore to listen to their grievances and to judge them impartially. 'Your young men', he declared, 'shall be as my sons, and your old men shall be as my father, and I shall judge between you with justice and wisdom as before.'

On this note of reconciliation I climbed back into my Land-Rover for the drive back down the coast to Dubai. Sir William Luce later forwarded my reporting dispatch to the Foreign Office with the comment 'I consider that Burton handled this difficult situation very competently and that the successful outcome was largely due to his efforts.' As a still raw 26-year-old I greatly valued these words of praise, particularly coming from such a distinguished public servant.

* * *

On a lighter note, life in Dubai was simple but agreeable. The main problem was the lack of female company. The British community was small. On one occasion relief seemed to be at hand when I was swimming at the beach, as was my habit, on a sweltering mid-summer afternoon. Suddenly a vision appeared about fifty yards away. What seemed to be a beautiful European-looking girl alighted from a Land-Rover taxi, undressed to her swimwear and plunged into the sea. Once I had convinced myself that this was no optical illusion, I followed in pursuit. She was indeed real – and she explained that she was an Australian who had come ashore from the ship lying off-shore for a swim.

I took a hard line. No Australian was allowed into the Trucial States, I explained, without a visa. However, the situation could be resolved, because it so happened that I was the person who issued visas. So, if she would come back with me in my Land-Rover it could all be sorted out. We must have been back in my bungalow for a full five minutes before the door flew open and the half dozen other British bachelors in Dubai tramped in. 'We saw you,' they said. Well, we had a party before sending her back to board her ship – with a visa – having enjoyed an afternoon of merriment in our barren summer.

*   *   *

The Trucial States which I left after two years, in the summer of 1964, were of course very different from the United Arab Emirates of today (the creation of which was brokered by Sir William Luce). It still had echoes of its past. Britain had abolished slavery in the nineteenth century, and it had been outlawed from the beginning throughout the British Protected States in the Gulf. But, in practice, a feeling of insecurity over their status lingered on among some long-term retainers who might not be aware of their rights.

To provide them with comfort, albeit unnecessarily, the Political Agency had been in the habit of issuing anyone who applied with an impressive-looking document called a Manumission Certificate. Beneath two crossed Union Jacks, a flowery text proclaimed that the holder was for ever free. In spite of its appearance the document had no legal force, but that did not lessen the faith that the holder would place in its potency. Occasionally a holder of such a certificate, now tatty with age, would come into the Agency compound for sanctuary and cling to the flagpole, until they were escorted inside to my office to be given a replacement certificate. They left happy.

Visiting Royal Navy ships would fire a seven-gun salute to the Political Agent when he sailed out of the creek on the Agency launch to greet them – and even I, if I was acting PA, was entitled to the same! The Political Resident bore the sonorous title of *ra'ees al-khaleej*, or Head of the Gulf.

The wonder is that the transition to full independence, about which the States were nervous at the prospect of losing British protection, was effected with so little trouble. The threat to the established order came less from Arab nationalism, which by the end of the 1960s had lost much of its appeal following the Arabs' humiliation in the Six Day War, than from Iranian claims to three disputed islands in the Gulf, Abu Musa and the Greater and Lesser Tunbs. Iran occupied the islands on the same day that the United Arab Emirates came into existence, and Britain ceased to be responsible for their protection. And so it remains, to the UAE's strong and continued mortification.

I left the Trucial States in the confident expectation that the apparent anachronism of the sheikhly system could not long survive in the modern world, against the wind of Arab nationalism. I was of course wrong. But I could scarcely be expected to predict that the sheikhs would survive and prosper – fuelled by massive oil revenues – whereas it would be a fading Britain which would fail to last the course.

The story of the UK's withdrawal from the southern Gulf is one of the most embarrassing in the annals of our imperial decline. Faced with recurrent economic problems and balance of payments crises, in the late sixties the government decided it could no longer afford a military presence east of Suez. But initially the southern Gulf was made an exception, and a Foreign Office minister, Goronwy Roberts, was despatched around the Gulf States to reassure the Rulers that Britain's commitment to their defence remained unaffected. Within a year, however, the government had reworked its calculations and found that its commitments in the Gulf would also have to go. The hapless Goronwy Roberts was again dispatched to the region to break the news. The reaction of the Rulers was one of shock. There was even a suggestion at one point that they would take over the costs of the British military presence, which would have been the ultimate humiliation. Britain, in the person of Sir William Luce – its last great proconsul – then devoted its attention to bringing into being a successor state, once it had ceased to be the protecting power. The proposal was that this would be a federation comprising the seven Trucial States, plus Bahrain and Qatar. The latter two sheikhdoms, or emirates, decided not to take part. Of the Trucial States, Ras al-Khaimah also initially wished to be excluded but was eventually persuaded of the advantages of joining.

The resulting United Arab Emirates, with the highly respected Ruler of Abu Dhabi, Sheikh Zayed, as its first president, and the dynamic Sheikh Rashid of Dubai as vice-president, was a success from the start, which more or less coincided with the largely Abu Dhabi-driven burgeoning oil wealth, allowing it to play a notable role on the world stage. Britain's role in the creation of the UAE was crucial, and in no small measure enabled by the relative peace and stability which the preceding Trucial States had guaranteed in the region.

* * *

Contemplating the extraordinary skyline of today's Dubai, nostalgia for the old days, although tempting, would be as misplaced as a longing to get back to Roman London. The only common features are the bustling creek and the *abra* ferry on the Dubai side which still departs from beside Captain's Store. As for the Persian wind-towers, architectural features from the Iranian desert cities of Yazd and Kerman which used to funnel cool air into a house in a boiling summer, they are now non-functional architectural add-ons that inappropriately surmount some skyscrapers.

There have, of course, been bumps along the way. Dubai, particularly under the leadership of Sheikh Mohammed bin Rashid, has not been short of ambition, as can be seen, for example, in the Palm Island developments. But occasionally this has led to economic overreach, and some spectacular property crashes, which have forced it to turn to Abu Dhabi (the paymaster of the UAE) for support. The most egregious example is the Burj al Khalifah, which, when it faced insolvency, had to bailed out by Abu Dhabi and took the name of its royal family as a result. Furthermore, Dubai's achievements are built not least on the contribution of the thousands of expatriate professionals attracted by its generous wages and laid-back lifestyle. The labour force, drawn from poorer Arab countries, the Indian sub-continent and elsewhere has to accept fairly basic living and work conditions as the price for the higher wages than could be expected back home.

But these are features which Dubai, once the small fishing and trading port which I have described, together with the other emirates, shares with all the other oil-rich states of the Arabian Peninsula. As regards what may be going on beneath the surface, I am not in a position to comment, still less to form a judgement, having left the coast more than fifty years ago. My own instinctive feeling is one of astonishment at what the Emirates (as they now are) have become in the intervening years since my service there in the early sixties: the massive free port of Jebel Ali, the dry dock, the iconic hotels and Palm Island, as well, of course, as the Burj al-Khalifah, the tallest building in the world. The Emirates airline, which grew out of the simple airport where I used to greet Sheikh Rashid on his return from hunting trips abroad, is now the world's biggest. And the airport itself is on the way to becoming the world's busiest. Dubai's role as a financial, travel and leisure hub in the Middle East is a tribute to the vision of its rulers.

In moments of reflection, we might also consider some realities within which to contextualise the UAE phenomenon. There can be no question that the massive oil wealth of the UAE, almost entirely through the resources of Abu Dhabi, has contributed enormously to the prosperity of the county. Its leadership, including the sheikhs of all the UAE components, but most prominently the Rulers of Abu Dhabi and Dubai, have made dramatic strides in building up the countries' economies by encouraging tourism, providing financial services, and creating travel hubs for business and tourist movements between North America and points east.

The downside of this story is that given the tiny indigenous populations of the country – under 1 million UAE-born citizens – the dynamic of the countries' growth, while planned by its apparent visionary leaderships, has actually been produced by migrant labour from management levels to labourers on building sites. The net effect of this is that – barring some very capable elites – the real productive contribution to the development of the UAE has been generated by expatriate professionals and business people from other Arab countries, the Indian subcontinent and Europeans who manage everything. And it is the Asian guestworkers from India, Pakistan and South East Asia who make up the countries' small traders, low-tier administrators and manual labourers – many of whom, it should be added, live in quite dismal conditions.

For me the Trucial Coast will always hold memories of hunting for rock oysters on the shore of Ajman, swimming off the Agency's launch in the bay of Ras al-Khaimah, tribal dancing at the Eid, hunting with falcons at dawn for Macqueen's bustard, the beauty of the desert and coastal landscape and, above all, the warmth of the people. I was sad to leave, but eager for the next chapter.

Chapter 4

Diplomacy at Home and Abroad: Marriage Despite Opposition, the Iraq and Iran Desks, Sudan and on to the Six Day War

I returned from the Middle East in 1964 on board an Italian ship, the *Esperia*, sailing from Beirut to Marseilles. It was a comfortable and relaxing experience. Regrettably, the option of joining, or returning from, a post by ship was withdrawn by the Foreign Office under a combination of budgetary pressure and a fall in the cost of air travel. As long as it lasted, it was a civilised way of adjusting gradually to the changes in one's life.

Back in London I found myself sharing digs in a fashionable address in Eaton Place with two other bachelors, one of whom was my old friend from Oxford and MECAS, John Coles, who rose to become the Permanent Under-Secretary and Head of the Diplomatic Service. The flat belonged to Sir Ian Scott, who had been John's ambassador in Khartoum, the posting from which he had just returned. The only

Photo: My marriage to Henrietta created the ideal personal and diplomatic partnership – after a rocky bureaucratic opening.

disadvantage was that it was on the fifth floor and there was no lift. However, it was very spacious and the lack of a lift kept us fit.

In the Foreign Office I was assigned to the Iraq desk in Eastern Department. It was a high-powered department headed by Willie Morris, later ambassador to Ethiopia, who sadly died young. There were also two future ambassadors to China, including my immediate boss, Percy (later Sir Percy) Cradock, as well as David (later Sir David) Hannay, who went on to be a Companion of Honour and a member of the House of Lords as Lord Hannay of Chiswick.

Some traditions from an earlier age still lingered on. The telegrams were noisily distributed around the building in tubes propelled on wires, like bills and money in an old-fashioned department store. The rooms were heated with coal fires. More senior officials frequently wore striped morning trousers to the office. And the informal custom still persisted of members of the department coming together twice a day for a short coffee break or afternoon tea. This sounds unduly leisurely, but was actually quite useful in enabling a cross-fertilisation of ideas to take place between officers covering different parts of the region.

Eastern Department encompassed the Levant on the west: Israel-Palestine, Lebanon, Syria and Jordan. This part of the department dealt with the Arab-Israel question, which was not at the time (the 1960s before the 1967 Arabi-Israeli War) a particularly active issue. The other half of the department, under Percy Cradock as assistant head, comprised Iraq (my desk), Iran, Afghanistan and CENTO – the pro-Western grouping of Turkey, Iran and Pakistan which was set up to provide a sort of Middle Eastern counterpart to NATO, and to contain the forces of Arab nationalism. It was originally known as the Baghdad Pact, but with the demise of Iraq's pro-West monarchy in 1958 a change of name seemed advisable.

The Iraq desk provided plenty of interest. The country had been formed, after the First World War, by bringing together three provinces in Mesopotamia of the defeated Ottoman Empire, within frontiers arbitrarily drawn on a map by Winston Churchill (as Colonial Secretary), while attending the Cairo Conference in 1923. The Emir Faisal, who had played a leading part in the Arab Revolt against the Turks – with the support of TE Lawrence (Lawrence of Arabia) – had been installed as king. The country became formally independent, with the end of the British Mandate, in 1932, although British influence had remained strong.

The brutal *coup d'état* in 1958 had brought down the Hashemite royal house, a branch of the same family as the Jordanian royal family, and cost the lives of the 23-year-old King Faisal II, his uncle, Crown Prince Abd al-Illah, and the long-serving Prime Minister, Nuri Es-Said, who was captured and executed after trying to escape dressed as a woman. The coup ushered in a republic, marked by recurrent further military coups with leaders to a greater or lesser extent anti-Western, and a succession of bloodthirsty strongmen, who would culminate a few years later with Saddam Hussein (no relation to King Hussein of Jordan).

In spite of the recent nationalisation of the Iraq Petroleum Company, in which British Petroleum had a major interest, relations with Britain were business-like, if not particularly cordial. Arms sales were, as so often in the Middle East, a sensitive issue. I became familiar with the arguments determining the issue of an export certificate, which never seemed to vary, however insistent a new government was in claiming that it was operating an ethical foreign policy. Doubts about a particular weapon's end-use were frequently trumped by the argument that, if we did not sell it, some other country would, and, more tangibly, that a number of industrial jobs were dependent on the sale.

In Eastern Department I was particularly fortunate to learn the skills of Foreign Office drafting from Percy Cradock, a brilliant man with an incisive mind. One of my tasks – twenty-eight years before Saddam Hussein's invasion of Kuwait – was to draft a weekly paragraph on any discernible increase in the threat to Kuwait from the Iraqi side of the border between the two countries. I would take my offering to Cradock for checking before it went on up the line. To begin with, Cradock's pen would hover ominously over almost every word as he clarified the meaning, removed any unnecessary verbiage and tightened the argument. After a few months I was delighted, and relieved, to find that the paper passed Cradock's scrutiny virtually unscathed, and I began to feel that I was becoming a proper Foreign Office drafter. This was an invaluable part of my training.

Years later, in 1993, when Sir Percy Cradock had become the Foreign Affairs Advisor to Margaret Thatcher, I reminded him of our weekly monitoring of Iraq's intentions towards Kuwait. He fiercely rejected my teasing suggestion that he had taken his eye off the ball when Saddam Hussein had invaded Kuwait in August 1990, and countered that he had advised the Prime Minister to take up the threat of an invasion urgently with President Bush – which she had done, but, unfortunately, only after the invasion had taken place!

After about a year on the Iraq desk my colleague in the same room who dealt with Iran left to join the Department for Overseas Development and I moved across to take over the Iran desk. It was a time when the Shah was riding high and British policy was mainly concerned with keeping him sweet, particularly with arms sales in mind. This could be a somewhat humiliating process. There was one occasion, it was said, when the Defence Secretary had to position himself at the foot of a ski run in St Moritz in order to catch His Imperial Majesty as he swept down the run direct to his residence, the Villa Suvretta, and seek his agreement to the purchase of British tanks.

Willie Morris called me in after a few months on the Iran desk to tell me that I had been selected to become the Private Secretary to the Foreign Office Minister of State (in Harold Wilson's Government). The minister was a Welsh trade union leader named Walter Padley. He was then succeeded by Fred Mulley, a more heavy-weight minister, who later became Defence Secretary.

*　　*　　*

When I had to leave my prestigious digs in Eaton Square, because our landlord returned to London from Khartoum and wanted his flat back, I joined three other bachelors in a house in Christchurch Street in Chelsea. Shortly afterwards I met the girl to whom I became engaged.

Jindra (pronounced *Yindra*) – who would some years later choose to call herself Henrietta (the version of her name on her wartime birth certificate under the Nazi occupation), in order to avoid having to explain her foreign-sounding name, and tell her life story, every time she met someone new – was a Czech-born, naturalised British subject. She shared a flat with a girlfriend just round the corner from my new digs. The girls wanted to meet the new man in our bachelor house and arranged a dinner party. I was immediately drawn to Jindra (as I have always called her), who had just returned from a holiday with her parents in Cyprus, where they lived.

An only child, she had been born during the wartime Nazi 'Protectorate of Bohemia and Moravia' (now the Czech Republic) in Zlín, the company town of the global shoe manufacturer Bata in Moravia, to the east of Prague. Her Czech parents had left the country in 1946 after the war, as the communists strengthened their grip, and Bata was threatened with takeover. Her father, a senior executive with the company, was offered the chance of developing its operations in several different countries before he decided to settle in Cyprus. The island appealed to him and his wife for a number of reasons, not least the fact that it was a British colony. He set up a shoe factory there, the island's first, and the family became naturalised British subjects.

When EOKA, the Greek Cypriot independence movement, shattered the peace of the island in the 1950s, Jindra, as an expatriate child, faced increasingly unpleasant experiences. On one occasion she had stones thrown at her by some boys while walking home from school. Fortunately, she spoke fluent Greek at the time and was able to shout back at her attackers. Whereupon the boys' mother came out, told them to stop, and apologised, saying that it had been a mistake since they thought she was English. Finally her parents decided, after a particularly ugly incident in which her school bus was held up by armed men, that it was no longer safe for her to remain on the island.

Accordingly, they made arrangements, reluctantly, to send their only daughter to boarding school in England. So, at the age of 13, Jindra found herself trying to adapt to the chilly surroundings, both literally and figuratively, of Hollington Park School, a traditional girls' school in St Leonards in East Sussex (which no longer exists). She was not happy there, not least because, although her parents had spoken English to her at home in order to help her integrate into the British community in Cyprus, her background marked her out as being different.

By the time of the Chelsea dinner party, when we met, she was in her early twenties and working as a Production Assistant at Independent Television News (ITN). This meant that she was working nights, while I was working during the day. Getting together at the early stage of our courtship proved difficult and we were both wondering whether the relationship was leading anywhere when I managed to pin her down to accompanying me to the national day reception at the Iranian embassy, to which I was invited as the recent Iran desk officer in the FCO. Ardeshir Zahedi, the Iranian ambassador, and the Shah's former son-in-law, was a popular figure on the London social scene at the time, who gave excellent parties.

From that point on, our relationship caught fire, and at Christmas, which was spent with my parents at their house in the Kent village of Benenden, I proposed – and, to my great joy, was accepted.

The story then turned sour. Foreign Office rules at the time were that any officer had to report an intention to marry a non-British-born spouse. In the case of Americans, West Europeans and Commonwealth spouses this presented no great problem and the service abounded in such foreign-born wives. But the case of a Czech-born girl at the height of the Cold War was more problematic. Jindra herself was fully aware of the problem, since she had been turned down for a job at SHAPE, the Supreme Headquarters Allied Powers Europe, when she was studying in Paris, and even one with BOAC, on these grounds.

So, I duly reported my engagement to Personnel Department, and in due course it was approved, which I did not think unduly strange, given that Jindra had been naturalised British since childhood, her family had cut most of their links with Czechoslovakia and her parents, as refugees from communism, were the last people to feel any sympathy for it.

The blow fell a mere three weeks before our wedding date, by which time all the arrangements had been made, invitations sent out and presents had started to arrive. I was called in by the unsympathetic head of Personnel Department to be told that my case had been reviewed and, in view of the security risks involved, I would have to resign from the Service if the marriage went ahead.

This threw me into the deepest of depressions but I was determined to fight the decision on the basis that, although our case fell on the wrong side of the existing rules, it was unjust not to take into account the particular facts surrounding it, so that the actual risks could be properly assessed. Jindra, for her part, was determined that my marrying her should not be an impediment to my diplomatic career. The wedding was therefore cancelled, she returned the engagement ring, resigned from ITN and flew back to her parents in Cyprus, who were patient and supportive of their daughter throughout.

My parents, on the other hand, thought that calling off the wedding was no bad thing. There were family tensions, but my father sportingly came to the Foreign Office and saw the Permanent Under-Secretary (PUS) to add his weight to my case. The matter was complicated by unwelcome coverage in the press under the heading 'The Diplomat and the Blonde', sparked by an unhelpful leak by a supposed friend.

I was fortunate in one respect. My office, as a ministerial Private Secretary, was close to the heart of the Foreign Office, and I was known on the network of Private Secretaries. This helped me, although my rank was the modest one of a Second Secretary, to get a personal hearing from the head of administration, who rejoiced in the title of Chief Clerk (to whom Personnel Department reported) as well as from the PUS. Both were reasonably sympathetic and my case was referred up to the Foreign Secretary himself for a final decision.

This was Michael Stewart, the Labour MP for Fulham (where I now live). I shall always be grateful to him that he agreed to see me in his imposing office overlooking St James's Park not once, but twice, in the course of the 1966 election campaign. My argument was essentially that it was a matter of trust. I had been trusted up to this point in my career – why could that trust not continue?

The case against me was that the (admittedly active and unscrupulous) Czech Intelligence Service might try to exert pressure on me by making life uncomfortable for Jindra's relations in Czechoslovakia. My reply to this was that her parents had kept only tenuous contact with their family back in the country apart from with Jindra's ageing grandmother. It seemed hardly likely that the Czechs would work on her. And if they did, I could surely be relied upon to report any approach.

These arguments seemed to strike home. On my second interview with Michael Stewart he told me, to my great joy, that it had been decided that my marriage could go ahead. There would, however, be certain conditions imposed on my progress in the Service. One of these was that I could never serve behind the Iron Curtain, particularly in Czechoslovakia. Another involved a reduction in the level of my security clearance. This was a serious matter, in that it could have greatly reduced the number of posts in which I could expect to serve.

Suffice it to say that my career ended with me as Her Majesty's Ambassador to the Czech Republic in Prague, after the fall of communism, as this story will recount. The obstacles fell away and the wheel eventually, and elegantly, came round full circle.

*   *   *

I flew to Cyprus in the summer to bring back my bride, and to meet her parents Joseph and Jindra Hones, who welcomed me warmly. We were married, a year after the original date, on 1 April 1967. We are still married, more than fifty years later.

Immediately following our wedding, rather than being allowed a period at home, which would have been normal, we were sent on our first overseas posting together – to Sudan. We felt that we were bound for a kind of exile as the flight to Khartoum flew for hours over featureless desert, until, almost miraculously, a great brown-coloured city, spread around the confluence of the White Nile and the Blue

13. General Gordon's last stand in Khartoum in 1885: the imperial moment was captured in this iconic painting by George W Joy showing a suitably defiant Gordon, before being cut down by the Mahdists. The image was indelibly associated with Britain's then ambitions in the Arab world and Africa. (Photo: author)

Nile, came into sight beneath us. This was to be our home for the next two years.

As a boy, I had been a keen reader of the GA Henty's colourful adventure stories of Britain's imperial history in the nineteenth century. Sudan was the setting for one of the best: *With Gordon to Khartoum* was the story of General Charles Gordon's epic defence of the city against the besieging army of the Mahdi until he was cut down on the steps of Khartoum Palace, shortly before the arrival of the relieving force sent from Egypt – to the fury of Queen Victoria, when she heard the news.

At the time of our arrival, Sudan had been independent since 1955, having previously been an Anglo-Egyptian Condominium (under the joint rule of the two countries). Two years later a military strongman, General Abboud, had seized power but had lost it after a coup in 1964. Neither of these convulsions, happily, had involved bloodshed. In fact, Sudan was experiencing a period of parliamentary democracy.

The political scene was a kaleidoscope of competing parties. The leader who attracted most interest in the West was Sadiq al Mahdi, the Prime Minister. Oxford educated, with a tall commanding presence, he was a descendant of the same Mahdi Mohammad Ahmad whose uprising against Anglo-Egyptian rule in 1884–85 had brought about General Gordon's doom. His followers had eventually been defeated by an expeditionary force under General Kitchener at the Battle of Omdurman in 1898, in which Winston Churchill rode in one of the last cavalry charges in British military history.

14. Sayyed Sadiq al Mahdi, Prime Minister of Sudan at the time of our arrival. Oxford educated, and descended from the Mahdi of Khartoum fame, he fell from power shortly afterwards. (Photo: author)

Sadiq al Mahdi's party, the *Umma*, had been founded by his grand-father Sayyid Abdurrahman al Mahdi, one of the grand old men of Sudan, known to the British as SAR. It was now split between a faction headed by Mohammed Ahmed Mahjoub, which wanted Sudan to become an Islamic state, and his own faction, which was politically secular and believed in promoting economic development – also as a solution to the rumbling discontent in the non-Arab south of the country.

Shortly after our arrival, Sadiq al Mahdi, whom many Sudanese considered an inspirational leader, was outmanoeuvred in an internal power struggle and was replaced as prime minister by Mahjoub – who happened to live opposite us on our road.

Apart from these two, the other main political leader was Ismail al Azhari, a veteran from the time of independence, who occupied the largely ceremonial role of president, but remained both popular and influential. There was also an active Sudanese Communist Party, and a Muslim Brotherhood following.

* * *

My job in the embassy, as Second Secretary in the political section, was Information Officer, dealing with the local media. This involved scanning the press on a daily basis for stories and comment of interest to improve the embassy's understanding of the internal Sudanese scene, plus evidence of the material sent from London being put to use – and hopefully having some influence in the active propaganda war taking place (particularly against Soviet bloc embassies). I also cultivated the principal newspaper editors and tried to make them sympathetic to British policies. This was best done by calling on them in the evening armed with a bottle of whisky and not leaving until it was finished. My training in the Officers Mess of the Rifle Brigade helped me to survive this work ritual.

As one of the only two Arabic speakers among the UK-based staff, my duties also included analysing the Sudanese political scene and advising the ambassador, a distinguished former Colonial Service officer named Sir Robert Fowler, who had no previous experience of the Arab world.

If the thinking behind my posting to Khartoum had been to choose a place where security issues were unlikely to arise, it proved to be rather wide of the mark. One of the first things that happened was that the embassy's archivist was recalled to London and charged with an offence under the Official Secrets Act. It turned out that he had been copying files and passing them to the Soviet embassy in return for money.

The official concerned had fallen for the attractive wife of a British Council colleague on the ship out to Sudan. In Khartoum he had found the costs of having an illicit affair, and keeping it from his wife. This had strained his finances and the Soviets, spotting this, had been only too happy to provide an additional source of income. A very different, low-key, kind of traitor in comparison with George Blake. I never heard how much damage had been done. Khartoum was not at the front line of the Cold War although the communist powers were all represented and were looking for any opening.

Among them was the Czechoslovak embassy. On arrival at post, my wife and I were told to give it a wide berth, for obvious reasons. But when the Prague Spring happened in August 1968 – the brief period when Alexander Dubček tried to introduce 'communism with a human face' into the country – there was a change of tack, and we were encouraged to chat to Czech diplomats, to judge their reaction to events. But after Brezhnev engineered the invasion of Czechoslovakia by Warsaw Pact forces, this came to an abrupt end and the instructions reverted to normal.

An amusing sequel was that the Foreign Office reacted to the Warsaw Pact invasion of Czechoslovakia by instructing that posts should be represented at the lowest feasible level at the forthcoming receptions at all Soviet missions to celebrate Soviet Army Day. In Khartoum my wife and I were sent as the embassy representatives. Our welcome at the Soviet embassy was distinctly frosty: the ambassador barely greeted us and, it seemed, waiters had been instructed not to bring us any refreshments.

But we had become friendly with the amiable Sudanese Chief of Staff, General Mohammed Idris. On seeing our plight, he summoned waiters to stand beside us with trays of champagne and vodka, and dishes of caviar and other delicacies, and not to move unless instructed. The fury of the ambassador and his staff was a sight to behold.

*   *   *

Within weeks of our arrival, the embassy was put to a severe test by the outbreak of the Six Day War between Israel and the neighbouring Arab countries. This followed a demand by the Egyptian leader, Gamal Abdel Nasser, couched in his usual aggressive rhetoric, for the withdrawal of a UN buffer force protecting the Straits of Tiran, the opening into the Red Sea which at its other end led to the Israeli port of Eilat. The Israelis chose to interpret Nasser's rhetoric at face value as a serious threat to blockade Eilat, or undertake some other attack, so they launched a pre-emptive strike. This took the form of a stunning dawn raid on the Arab air-force bases, destroying the bulk of their aircraft on the ground.

Unwilling, or unable, to live with the shame of such a humiliating setback, the Arab governments thereupon claimed that the attacks had been launched by the US Air Force and the RAF. This 'Big Lie', as we called it, had severe consequences for us and the Americans. Firstly, the mob flooded onto the streets of Khartoum denouncing the western 'imperialists' and heading for our embassies. Since the British embassy was on the third floor of the Shell Company building, one of the few high-rise buildings in the city, we were not particularly vulnerable, and I watched from the balcony as the mob headed round the corner to the Americans, whose defences proved adequate to the task.

Secondly, and more seriously, the Sudanese government, which had hitherto not been especially strong supporters of the Arab line, decided that in this case they should demonstrate solidarity, and followed the lead of the Arab front-line states in breaking off diplomatic relations with Britain and the US.

This was hugely tiresome, due to the constraints it imposed on the embassy's work. After a short interval Sir Robert Fowler had to return to London, seen off by the whole embassy at the airport. Happily, he was, unusually in the case of a break in relations, able to return to post about ten months later, after a delicate negotiation. Diplomatic relations are easy to sever, but not so easy to restore, since face has to be saved on both sides.

The rest of the embassy staff remained, but the Union Jack was lowered over the embassy building and the Residence, and we became the British Interests Section of the Italian embassy, coming under the nominal supervision of the Italian ambassador, Signor Puri Purini. In practice we carried on much as before, with the embassy counsellor, Norman Reddaway, in everyday charge.

After the conclusion of the war, which led to the total defeat of the Arab forces and the Israeli occupation of Jerusalem, the Sinai peninsula (Egypt), the West Bank (Jordan) and the Syrian Golan Heights, the Arab League convened a summit conference – in Khartoum.

Since we were no longer in diplomatic relations with the Sudanese government we had no direct access to the conference venue and were reduced to reporting the proceedings as best we could by monitoring the media and talking to our contacts. To get a feel for the event I went out into the street and mingled with the crowd to watch the Arab leaders drive into the city from the airport. Among them was a figure of particular interest, the newly appointed leader of the Palestinian Liberation Organisation, Yasser Arafat. I was to come to know him many years later, as well as King Hussein of Jordan.

The Six Day War was the first time that the Israel–Palestine question had impinged on me directly. Although the Palestinians I had encountered as instructors at MECAS, and during my Christmas break in Jerusalem and the West Bank, had given me a feeling for their plight, my reaction to the war was essentially to take the Israeli side. It was clear that it had been provoked by Nasser's aggressive behaviour, and it was hard to feel anything but satisfaction that it had left him much reduced in standing.

But the Israelis were to remain sensitive about having fired the first shots. About five years later, a minister of state at the Foreign Office, Lord Balniel, called on the Israeli Prime Minister Golda Meir. He was accompanied by James Craig, my boss from Dubai days, by then head of the relevant FCO department. In the course of the meeting Mrs Meir asked, in challenging tones, who had started the 1967 war. When Lord Balniel said nothing, Craig replied 'You did.' Mrs Meir furiously denied this and launched into a tirade about Nasser's provocation. Craig, for his pains, found himself the lead story in next day's *Times* (following Israeli briefing) for his unacceptable intervention.

Their losses in the war did not reduce the Arabs' natural inclination to defiance. The outcome of the conference was a resounding declaration, which came to be known as the Khartoum Declaration, that there would be 'No Peace, No Negotiation and No Recognition of Israel'. The Three No's. The Arabs' need to cover their wounded pride was understandable, but in this way they painted themselves into a corner and rejected the path towards an accommodation with Israel opened up by the careful wording of UN Resolution 242, drafted by Britain. That Resolution called for Israel to withdraw from 'occupied territories' (left deliberately vague) in exchange for a 'just and lasting peace'. The Resolution thus gave birth to the concept of 'land for peace' which was, and in my view remains, the only basis for a durable peace in the region.

If the Arabs had accepted it and acted on it at the time, they would have enjoyed a large measure of international support, and the Middle East could have been spared decades of conflict and human misery.

It was not to be. The Three No's froze the problem for the next seven years – not to mention leaving fifteen ships rusting at anchor in the Great Bitter Lake south of the Suez Canal – until Nasser's successor as Egyptian president, Anwar Sadat, had the courage to fly to Israel in the wake of the 1973 'Yom Kippur' war and take the first step towards peace. He paid for it with his life, falling to an assassin's bullet at a military parade in Cairo in 1981.

After my instinctive reaction to the Six Day War, my more considered view of the Israel-Palestinian question, which lies at the heart of the Middle East's troubles, was that it was a profoundly tragic confrontation, arising from the competing claims of two ancient peoples to a single piece of land. Both sets of claims are rooted in history. The appalling Jewish experience in the Holocaust did not, however, in my view, give the Zionists a prior claim to that land.

The Palestinians, on the other hand, have passed up many opportunities for peace. And Britain cannot escape its share of blame, due to the contradictory promises it made to both sides during and after the First World War: offering the Arabs independent kingdoms in order to encourage the Arab Revolt against Turkey, and then, with the Balfour Declaration, promising the Zionists a national homeland in Palestine. Conflict between the two sides thereby became tragically inevitable. Ascribing blame to one side or the other is essentially pointless.

This remained my view throughout my diplomatic career. It occasionally set me apart from my Arabist colleagues in the Service, many of whom tended to be wholehearted supporters of the Palestinian cause.

On a lighter note, we gave a party in our Khartoum garden during the conference for the British and American journalists covering it. In the middle of the conviviality we saw through the hedge that the road had been unexpectedly illuminated with TV lights outside the house opposite of Prime Minister Mahjoub. The next thing that happened was the arrival, in successive convoys of cars, of the Egyptian leader,

Gamal Abdel Nasser, and King Faisal of Saudi Arabia. Our party emptied, as the journalistic guests rushed across the road to see what was going on.

In due course they returned in a high state of excitement. The news was that the two leaders had proceeded to reach an agreement over the North Yemen civil war, in which they had been supporting the two opposing sides in the conflict. Our guests enquired admiringly how we had known that this was to happen. We passed it off nonchalantly as the kind of thing one acquired a feel for in diplomatic life.

The background was that the war in Yemen, the most populous country in the Arabian Peninsula, had been going on since 1962, when the newly crowned Imam, Muhammad al Badr, of the Matawakkilite Kingdom of North Yemen, had been deposed in a military coup by revolutionary republicans under the command of Abdullah al-Sallah. The Imam had escaped to Saudi Arabia, from where he had raised support among the Shi'i northern tribes to regain his throne. The fighting escalated rapidly into a full-scale civil war. The Imam was supported militarily by the Saudis – but only up to 1965 – as well as by Jordan and Israel; Britain also gave covert support – after all Nasser, whose nationalist regime was backing the Sallah coup, was still seen in London as a destabilising thorn in Britain's side.

Nasser had supported the republican side with as many as 70,000 troops and weapons. However, Egypt's losses in the Six Day War had forced him to re-assess his commitment to Yemen, and the deal forged with King Faisal that evening, under Sudanese chairmanship, was the trigger for a gradual pull-back. Nevertheless, the war ended in 1970 with a republican victory, leading to the formation of a new government containing some royalist elements, but not the royal family.

Life generally in Khartoum at the time was very agreeable. We found it easy to make friends with the Sudanese. A particular friend (to this day) was Fadel Abdurrahman al-Mahdi, one of the most respected of the Mahdi's descendants. One of my first duties in the embassy was to attend a commemorative event in Omdurman on the anniversary of his father's death. It was an impressive sight: a veritable sea of white-robed Ansar (as the Mahdi's followers are called) gathered to hear speeches in his honour.

Khartoum's very isolation brought the expatriate community together, and there was a vibrant social life. But entertaining at home had its problems. Since only the most basic foods were available in the shops, most of our provisions were imported by air from Kenya. An order would arrive two weeks after it had been made, so advance planning was essential. For a few months the situation became even more complicated when the refinery in Port Sudan which produced the cooking gas blew up. All the cooking, including for large dinner parties, then had to be done on primus stoves. Good training for a newly minted diplomatic wife!

The main drawback was the climate. From March through to November one discomfort after another was visited upon us like the plagues of Egypt. Summer nights provided no let up from the daytime heat. The rainy season was followed by a period of dust storms, known as *haboobs*, which in turn was followed by more rains, turning the dust into mud. As soon as I saw a *haboob* approaching, from my office in the Shell building, I would ring home, so that my wife could close all the windows and shutters to keep out the dust. Even so, it managed to penetrate into the fridges, which were situated in an inside corridor with no windows.

15. A sketch by Jean Reddaway of the *Melik*, the flagship of the Blue Nile Sailing Club. The ship had originally sailed up the Nile as General Kitchener's gunboat to the Battle of Omdurman (1898), its Gatling gun making it a weapon of mass destruction of its day. (Photo: author)

There was an especially grim season of flying blister-beetles. Brushing them away did not prevent a blister forming – and wherever your hand next touched your body would erupt in another blister. There were also occasional plagues of locusts for good measure, stripping the foliage from gardens and farms. These were countered, ineffectively, by standing in the middle of the garden and banging on a tin tray.

The saving grace was that if you survived the summer months, the winter, by contrast, was a delight. The temperature was ideal and there was no better place to play sport. In addition to indulging my lifelong passion for tennis I acquired a sailing boat and joined the Blue Nile Sailing Club.

All the boats were of the same steel-hulled design, Khartoum One-Design. The club's flagship was a famous vessel moored by the bank of the Blue Nile, the *Melik*. It had been the gunboat accompanying Lord Kitchener's force when he had sailed up the Nile from Egypt to defeat the dervish army at the Battle of Omdurman. With its front-mounted Gatling gun blazing away at the enemy lining the riverbank it was, in effect, the 'weapon of mass destruction' of its day.

As our flagship, the *Melik* now fulfilled a more peaceful role. The club existed for its races during the sailing months of mid-December to the end of February. They were started and controlled from onboard. Afterwards, there was an excellent bar. To be competitive in the races one had to spend long hours in advance working on one's boat's hull, by sandpapering and painting, to make it go faster through the water. I also brought out a new set of sails from England.

The main difficulty was to master, not only the currents, but the usually light and changeable wind, which could leave one becalmed in the middle of the great river. This was a critical factor when the fleet raced down the Blue Nile to its confluence with the White Nile, and then up the White Nile for our annual regatta at a broad stretch marked by what was known as Gordon's Tree. If the wind died on you at the confluence you could in theory drift off downstream towards Egypt. Once one arrived at Gordon's Tree, care had to be taken to avoid infection from the *bilharzia* beetles lurking in the mud through which one had to wade to reach one's dinghy.

All this was great fun. The winter months in Khartoum were not to be missed and the multinational expatriate community made the best of them, with boat trips on the river and lengthy Sunday lunches at their spacious villas in Khartoum North. The British club, called the Sudan Club, still occupied a prestigious site beside the Blue Nile and its spacious lawns contained echoes of past glories. The weekly quiz night was a popular feature. Each of the other national communities had its own club. One New Year's Eve we planned to drop into the Greek and Italian clubs before ending up at the Sudan Club. This was not a success, and we saw in the New Year in a traffic jam.

We would often end the evening, and catch up with Sudanese friends, in an informal setting, at the Gordon Music Hall, a Khartoum institution presided over by Jimmy Kirk, a Hungarian expatriate. The whisky flowed and the conversation was good.

*   *   *

Our tour of duty in Khartoum lasted for two years. Towards the end of our first year our first child was born, Samantha, or, as we called her, Samantina. We decided that she should not be born in Khartoum, but rather in Cyprus, in the British Military Hospital in Dhekelia. This lay in one of the Sovereign Base Areas on the island which meant that legally it counted as being just as English as Kent, and no UK citizenship issue could therefore arise for the child in the future. The other advantage was that my wife would be with her parents, who lived on the island, and she would have their support.

The disadvantage was that I would have to remain at my job in Khartoum. I therefore did not see Samantina until a few weeks after her birth, when she arrived off a plane from Cyprus, via Beirut, with her mother – accompanied by my father, who had stopped off in Cyprus on his way to visit us in Khartoum. Like any father, I was overcome by Samantina's beauty. But I was also surprised to see that she was still yellow with jaundice; although it is not uncommon in a baby immediately after birth, it should have gone by this stage. The hospital in Dhekelia had said, however, that there was nothing to worry about.

When the jaundice nevertheless persisted, we consulted a distinguished British professor of medicine lecturing at Khartoum University, Professor Morgan. He advised that it was serious and that we should take the baby back to Great Ormond Street Hospital in London. My wife flew home with Samantina without delay, and I followed shortly afterwards.

My wife, together with my father, met me at Heathrow with the shattering news that Samantina had been diagnosed with a congenital liver condition, *biliary atresia*, or the absence of a bile duct. The consultant at Great Ormond Street, Mr Norman, warned that she could not be expected to live beyond about four months, with two years as the absolute maximum (she actually lived until only two days short of her second birthday). He added that we might be approached about a liver transplant, but it was only performed in one hospital in Texas and, at that stage, was highly experimental. He did not recommend it. After much discussion and heart-searching, we decided against this course.

So, we returned to Khartoum with our sick baby and for the rest of our time there tried, with all our love, to make her as comfortable as possible. By good fortune we were able to find a motherly Ethiopian nanny, Hanusu, who, with great patience and devotion, held Samantina comfortingly to her bosom and remained with us throughout her life, even when we were transferred to Paris.

We were now living in a dark tunnel, trying to sustain our suffering child, and each other, with our love. But we were faced constantly, as we looked at other children of her age, with the pain and anguish of realising that we would be losing her. Due to the oppressive heat of Sudan we frequently wondered whether she would make it through the day. My wife took her for long drives in our Land-Rover, which helped to alleviate her suffering. It was a terrible time.

*   *   *

When I was called in by my ambassador (who had now returned to Khartoum), after two years at post, to be told that my next posting would be to the embassy in Paris, it was the fulfilment of my heart's desire. Paris was, in my view, the most prestigious post, charged with furthering Britain's most historically charged and fascinating bilateral relationship. Also, the prospect of spending some years in that glorious city, which we had last visited during our honeymoon, was enticing for us both. We started to pack.

But before we finally took the plane, after overcoming the bureaucratic assault course of obtaining all the necessary documentation, Sudan still had a mystery in store. On our final evening in the country we attended a drinks party in the garden of our Military Attaché's house. Somewhat to my surprise I was approached by a senior Sudanese officer named Khaled Hassan Abbas, whom I had come to know, with a strange request.

He asked me rather solemnly to come to his office at 11 o'clock the following morning as he had something to tell me. Perhaps he thought, wrongly, that I was a member of MI6. I explained that this was impossible as the following day was our final departure from Khartoum. He persisted, saying that it was very important. I repeated that we were leaving – the two of us and the baby, plus the nanny and the cat. I asked whether I could suggest that one of my embassy colleagues call on him instead. He said no, and turned away.

One week later, far off in my parents' village in Kent, I opened the paper to see that there had been a *coup d'état* in Khartoum. An army colonel named Jaafar Nimeiri had placed his tanks in front of the President's palace, seized the radio station and toppled the government. Unlike previous changes of regime in independent Sudan this coup had been bloody and many lives had been lost. President Azhari himself apparently met a gruesome end.

My military interlocutor of a week previously had become the number two in the new regime, vice-president and Minister of Defence. I never found out what he would have told me in his office that morning. And if it had been a tip-off about the impending coup, I shall never know how HMG would have handled such incendiary information. Such mysteries make a diplomatic career worthwhile.

Chapter 5

Paris and Britain's Path to Europe: From the Heath–Pompidou Summit to the Queen's State Visit (via the Cannes Film Festival)

O ur arrival in Paris coincided with what would prove to be a key moment in the post-war relationship between Britain and France, following the departure from the political scene of President de Gaulle.

Our immediate impression, however, coming direct from Khartoum, was something of a cultural shock. The Swinging Sixties were in full swing. The austere head-to-toe white *gallabiyas* worn in Sudan were replaced by Mary Quant and her mini- and even micro-skirts. A contrast, but one that took a bit of getting used to.

We took over the apartment rented by the embassy for my predecessor, James (later Sir James) Adams, on the top floor of an apartment building in the fashionable Eighth Arrondissement, just off the Avenue Georges V. At one end of the avenue lay the Champs-Elysées. At the other was the River Seine and the Place de l'Alma.

It was easy to give directions on where to find the flat by mentioning that it was just around the corner from the famous Crazy Horse Saloon. To enter the courtyard one had to pass the lodge from where the formidable concierge, Mme Gravet, kept a severe eye on visitors, and on us.

The apartment was wonderfully situated but sparsely furnished. The owner, a very senior functionary in the Banque de France, had a number of daughters. When one of them was to be married, which seemed to occur with striking regularity, he or his wife would be found standing unannounced in the hall selecting which item of furniture should be removed to furnish the bridal home. Somewhat incongruously I had to take the rent in a brown envelope on a monthly basis to the back door of the Banque de France and hand it over to a porter.

The *quartier* contained some of the most famous French couturiers, such as Balenciaga, Courrèges and Christian Dior. There were also a number of excellent bistros and an enticing charcuterie with irresistible dishes in the window, as well as all the other traditional local shops which give Paris its unique character. We were very happy there.

Charles de Gaulle, the great national leader who had dominated the French political scene since the end of the war, and established the Fifth Republic, had recently retired to his home at Colombey-les-Deux-Eglises, having been defeated in an (unnecessary) referendum.

His resignation followed the national convulsion of 1968 when, as in the United States, Germany and elsewhere, students (allied to the trade unions) demonstrated violently against the established order. For a time, something approaching anarchy reigned in Paris. The Science Attaché at the embassy told the story, for example, that he had paid a routine call at the ministry which contained France's nuclear secrets to find the building virtually unguarded and even the office of the official, with whom he had an appointment, deserted.

My appointment at the embassy was as First Secretary in the Information Section. This involved working, under the Information Counsellor, to influence the Paris media to take a favourable view of British policy; a colleague, Kim Isolani, covered the regional press. At the time of my arrival the Information Section was in the doghouse. The embassy was reeling from the aftermath of a serious spat in Anglo-French relations known as the Soames Affair, taking its name from the recently appointed ambassador, Christopher Soames (later Lord Soames).

Soames was a politician, rather than a career diplomat. Only 47 years old at the time of his appointment to Paris, he had been Member of Parliament for Bedford from 1950 to 1966 (where my parents had been among his supporters) before losing his seat in the General Election of that year. During those sixteen years his political career had been highly successful, including acting as Parliamentary Private Secretary to his father-in-law, Sir Winston Churchill. He joined the Cabinet as Minister of Agriculture in 1960, in which role he collaborated closely with Edward Heath in the first (unsuccessful) negotiations on Britain joining the EEC in 1961 and 1962. When he lost his Bedford seat, Soames had been considered very much a rising star.

On the retirement of Sir Patrick Reilly from the Paris embassy, the Labour Government, with Harold Wilson as Prime Minister and George Brown as Foreign Secretary, had made the surprising decision to appoint Soames, a heavyweight Conservative (in every sense of the word), in his place. Britain's relations with Europe, and with France in particular, seemed to be stuck, after the second French veto of December 1967, over its accession to the EEC. The thinking was that Soames, with his formidable political and social skills, his love of France and, not least, his much-admired wife Mary, Churchill's youngest daughter, at his side, was the man to break the log-jam.

Soames's mission did not get off to a good start. The story of the 'Soames Affair' was subsequently recounted in a well-researched paper, 'Embassy to France, An Account of Anglo-French Relations 1968-1972', on which I have relied, by Sir Alan Campbell, an experienced diplomat who was serving at the embassy at the time.

When Soames formally presented his credentials to General de Gaulle at the Elysée Palace they held a brief talk in the course of which de Gaulle said that he detected some 'movement in Britain's attitude towards continental Europe', which he found welcome, and promised to pursue this at a further and more leisurely discussion. The follow-up discussion took place on 4 February 1969, also at the Elysée Palace, in a conversation *à deux* of more than an hour before and after lunch. De Gaulle said several interesting things which appeared to constitute a new approach.

He started by speaking somewhat disparagingly about the present Community of the Six and of the NATO organisation, deploring the tendency of European countries other than France to be unduly dependent on the United States. As regards the EEC, he said that if Britain were to join, it would become something entirely different from the present organisation. It would be more in the nature of a Free Trade Area, with provision for an exchange of agricultural products. This might be no bad thing. However, in such an organisation the biggest countries would have to exercise greater influence if it were to work properly.

He then suggested confidential bilateral talks between Britain and France to discuss the way in which a truly independent Europe might be organised. These talks would cover economic, monetary, defence and political problems with a view to reconciling any differences of concept. Finally, he said that if the British Government thought this a good idea, they might care to propose it and the French would be willing to respond positively.

On returning to the embassy Soames made a careful summary of what the General had said and telegraphed it to London. Then, mindful of previous occasions when British and French records of important conversations had differed, and especially since there had been no note-taker present, he decided to take the unusual course of having his record checked for accuracy by the French side. He duly left a copy of his report to the Foreign Office with the General's most senior official who promised to show it to the General. Back came a message via the French Foreign Minister, Michel Debré, a few days later, that the General had seen this record and had no comments to make on it. Debré confirmed that it had been completely accurate.

Subsequent developments in the Soames Affair, which were a classic example of the pitfalls besetting the conduct of the bilateral relationship between Britain and France, can be summarised briefly. The British Government was suspicious of the motives underlying the General's approach, feeling that bilateral Anglo-French talks could be seen as cutting across its policy of joining the EEC without seeking any fundamental modifications. But its immediate concern was whether or not to tell the German Government, with which Prime Minister Wilson and Foreign Secretary Michael Stewart were due to hold talks, of the General's thinking.

Unfortunately, the Germans were given an account in Bonn before the French were told that this was to happen. The French were furious at this discourtesy, which was made worse when the press briefing issued on the British side – which had been prepared on a contingency basis in case of misleading briefing from the French side! – clumsily used the emotive word 'directorate' in describing the General's suggestion that the bigger countries should exercise greater influence in a future European association.

Soames was summoned to a frosty interview at the French Foreign Ministry to be upbraided on the way the British Government had handled the matter – although there was no suggestion that he personally had acted in bad faith. There were sore feelings on both sides of the Channel, heightened by the press in both countries going into nationalist overdrive in attacking the other.

Emotions had barely cooled when I arrived three months later to take up my post in the embassy's Information Section. One or two of the key British correspondents in Paris were barely on speaking terms with us. As for the French press, which was largely of a Gaullist persuasion, it felt reinforced in its conviction that Britain was not a suitable partner in a European framework. It was a highly inauspicious background to my doing my job.

Fortunately, the political cards in France were then reshuffled. Just a month after our arrival in Paris the presidential election following de Gaulle's departure produced a clear victory for his long-standing Prime Minister, Georges Pompidou. A cautious, pragmatic banker and politician with a provincial background, he had a brilliant intellect. He had been a faithful supporter of the General and was not aiming at any substantial change in his foreign policy. But the new faces in his government were an encouraging portent of a more open mind on British accession to the EEC. In particular Maurice Schumann, whom he appointed as Foreign Minister, had lived some years in London, spoke admirable English and had a very wide circle of British friends and acquaintances including politicians of all parties.

The happy outcome of these changes was a thawing of relations between the embassy and the Quai d'Orsay, the French Foreign Ministry. We then began to move forward on the ambassador's policy of preparing the ground for a renewed attempt to join the EEC. This was the embassy's priority task and the Information Section had a key role to play in it.

*   *   *

In the domestic arena, our Paris tour started with the happiest of events. The consultant at Great Ormond Street Hospital had told us, when giving us the appalling prognosis on our first child, Samantina, that we should not delay in trying for another child. My wife had arrived in Paris heavily pregnant, and a few weeks later we had a bumpy drive through the cobbled Paris streets to the fashionable maternity clinic favoured by the embassy, the Clinique du Château de Belvedère, where she gave birth to our son, Nicholas. We drove along the same route two years later for the birth of Amanda.

Our great happiness was nevertheless clouded by Samantina's illness. Due to her missing bile duct she was still only the size of a baby, although now aged 16 months, and in distress for much of the time. But she slept peacefully on her daily trips in her pram to the Tuileries Gardens, pushed either by my wife or the ever-patient Hanusu, the Ethiopian nanny whom we had brought with us from Sudan. Inevitably crises, when they occurred, came during holiday weekends when the doctor was not available. She died in the following January, just two days before her second birthday (the consultant had said that this was the longest she could expect to live). She is buried in Maidstone Cemetery, near my parents' home at that time.

* * *

The American embassy near our own, was the scene for an unforgettable occasion shortly after our arrival. I joined the crowd watching the first moon landing live on a giant screen set up in the embassy garden. No-one with any imagination could have remained unmoved by the sight, although our Science Attaché tried to question at the morning meeting next day whether it was worth the expense – and received short shrift on the grounds that, if nothing else, it was an organisational achievement of staggering proportions.

These morning meetings in the embassy were a daily challenge for me as Press Secretary. My daily routine was to walk before breakfast to the kiosk on Place de l'Alma, near our flat, to buy all the French and British daily papers. Having scanned through them over breakfast I would drive to the embassy in the rue du Faubourg St Honoré to prepare a summary of the main points relevant to the embassy's work, in time for the meeting. This was received by a well-informed and critical audience, since each person around the table had their particular expertise. The meeting was chaired by the Minister at the embassy, the hugely experienced Michael (later Sir Michael) Palliser, who went on to be Permanent Under-Secretary at the Foreign Office, after being the first head of the UK Representation to the EEC following our accession. Nothing missed his attention. I eventually found a sure way of drawing him away from some omission in my summary by quoting an economic newspaper, *Les Echos*, which was the only one I knew he did not normally read. He probably realised what I was doing but he was graciously forbearing.

My job had unquestionable advantages. It was my enviable duty to take influential French journalists out to lunch at some suitably enticing restaurant in order to convince them of the merits of Britain joining the EEC. Many were sceptical. The feeling among those with a Gaullist inclination was that Britain, with its strong links with the USA, its currency bound in with its residual empire through the sterling balances, its dependence on food imports from New Zealand and Australia on the other side of the world rather than the continent, and its mind-set as a global trading nation, was fundamentally different from its European neighbours, and would be an uncomfortable fit in the Community

These were not easy arguments to counter, because they contained much that was true. Britain was being asked to pay a high price for having missed the bus by not having joined the Community when it was formed. To take just two examples: Britain, as a massive importer of its food, largely from Commonwealth countries, was bound to be disadvantaged by the EEC's nascent Common Agricultural Policy, which was designed to penalise imports and subsidise domestic producers. Secondly, our traditional fishing areas around our shores would have to be shared with our new continental partners,

In the end I would fall back on pointing out that Britain believed in keeping the rules, and this would be the case once we were inside the EEC. Anyone walking down Pall Mall in London, I observed, would be struck by the fact that we were a nation of club members. It was a basic principle that once you were elected to a club, you abided by the rules. So would it be when we joined the Common Market.

This line of argument was greeted with polite scepticism, which would have been much greater had we ventured into the deeper waters of the argument about sovereignty. In the Europe of the Six it was France under de Gaulle that was the guardian of national sovereignty in the face of the idealists inspired by Jean Monnet, the founding father, who dreamed of an integrated Europe which would be attained, like the outcome of a game of Grandmother's Footsteps, at the end of a long process of small steps. The dream of 'ever closer union' was embedded in the Treaty of Rome. But, as long as the Community was dominated by Gaullist France, there seemed to be not much cause for Britain to worry about its final destination.

However, with the departure of the General, and the fading of his influence, there was greater reason to worry. What I glossed over with my lunch guests was that Britain approached this central issue from a different standpoint from that of its continental neighbours. Apart from its long history as a nation state – a history only to be compared, as de Gaulle once commented to the equally tall Dutch Foreign Minister Joseph Luns, with that of France and the Netherlands among the original Six members – Britain's approach was shaped by its continuing global role and by its contrasting wartime experience. Uniquely among European countries, other than the neutrals, it had not been defeated or occupied, let alone an aggressor in the war, but had emerged as one of the victorious powers. It would hardly have been diplomatic to have laboured the point to one of my French lunch guests.

Jumping ahead, it was not long after our accession to the EEC in 1973 that the British people were asked whether they wished to have second thoughts about our membership. Only two years after our entry, Harold Wilson, who had defeated Edward Heath in the election fought on the basis of 'Who Governs Britain?', in the wake of a divisive miners' strike, put the issue of our EEC membership to a referendum. The issue of sovereignty played little part in this, in spite of the eloquent efforts of Peter Shore and Tony Benn on the Labour side, and Enoch Powell for the Conservatives, to thrust it to centre-stage. That happened only later, when the momentum towards integration in the newly formed European Union of the 1990s, particularly the moves towards economic and monetary union, made it impossible to gloss over.

Fortunately, well before the 1975 referendum I was back in London and did not have to face any quizzical interrogation from my erstwhile Parisian journalistic lunch guests on my claims of my countrymen's virtuous approach towards membership of a club. However, Wilson did at least ensure that the country firmly endorsed that membership, unlike David Cameron who lost the critical second referendum of 2017, having failed to make a convincing case out of the advantages that membership had brought to the United Kingdom over the preceding forty years, even when balanced against some loss of sovereignty.

Back to my time-line. The issue of Britain's EEC application had suddenly come to the top of the agenda when Edward Heath won the 1970 General Election. The outgoing Labour Government, Harold Wilson's first administration, had not let up in its efforts to promote the cause, particularly under the energetic minister for Europe, George Thomson (later Lord Thomson of Monifieth). Wilson himself had become convinced that membership of the EEC was the right course for Britain, and Thomson had even taken advantage of lulls in his election campaign in Dundee to prepare for the opening of negotiations in Luxembourg at the end of June. But after the electors had given their verdict it was not he but a Conservative minister, Anthony Barber (later Lord Barber of Wentbridge), who made the opening statement on the UK's application on 30 June.

It was now that the Paris embassy, under the larger-than-life Christopher Soames, came into its own as the tip of the spear for prising open Britain's path into Europe. France was the key country in the EEC and Britain stood no chance of being accepted as a member unless France, under President Pompidou, could be persuaded not to stand in the way.

But the first ten months of the negotiations for Britain's entry into the Community, and that of the other candidate countries, Denmark, Norway and Ireland, were frustratingly slow. Most of the time was taken up with the Six coordinating their own position while the candidates twiddled their thumbs. One cardinal point that they insisted upon was that the candidates accept whatever the Six had already agreed upon, the so-called *acquis communautaire*.

For Britain this meant that the discussion of the most difficult issues – Community finance, New Zealand butter, Commonwealth sugar and fisheries – revolved around the details of how the UK would adapt to EEC practice during a transitional period. The greater issues, such as the future policies of the enlarged Community, and the evolution of its institutions, were not addressed in that forum. As far as the UK and France were concerned, they had to wait until the historic Heath–Pompidou meetings in Paris in May 1971.

Before that occurred, the major event in Paris was that General de Gaulle died, on 9 November 1970. He had lived in carefully guarded seclusion since his retirement, so that the impact on the nation was less than it might have been. On the political level the French government may have felt a twinge of relief that, as it approached the prospect of Britain joining the EEC – which the General had twice vetoed – the possibility no longer existed of a sonorous repudiation emanating from Colombey-les-deux-Eglises.

The General's death was marked with a solemn Mass at the cathedral of Notre-Dame, attended on the British side by a delegation headed by the Prince of Wales and Prime Minister Heath. As the attendant press officer, I accompanied the delegation to the cathedral and managed to find a strategic spot, standing beside a pillar, to view the proceedings. During the drive back to the embassy after the ceremony, it was striking that the loudest cheers of the Parisian onlookers, thronging the rue de Rivoli, were reserved for Anthony Eden, the wartime foreign secretary and a long-standing friend of France.

The embassy's preparations for the vital confrontation between Heath and Pompidou to address the French block on Britain joining the EEC were a classic example of successful diplomatic groundwork for a meeting of national leaders. Knowledge of the preparatory contacts, conducted by Soames on the British side and Pompidou's chief advisor, Michel Jobert, on the French side, was kept within the tightest circle. This was in order to avoid cutting across the ongoing negotiations between the UK and the EEC in Brussels, and also so as not to commit the two principals to the meeting taking place until there was a large measure of agreement on the outcome.

Eventually, Heath flew to Paris for two days of talks with Pompidou on 19 May 1971. The talks were on a one-to-one basis with only interpreters present. Since the sole UK interpreter at the talks was the embassy minister, Michael Palliser – who was completely bilingual in French – we were fortunate to get a privileged briefing in the embassy, after the event, on their progress.

At the conclusion of the two days of meetings – from which, amazingly, not a word had leaked out of what was going on – a major press conference took place in the Salle des Fêtes at the Elysée Palace, which I attended. Old hands wondered whether there was any significance in the fact that the chairs pointed in the opposite direction to that when de Gaulle had pronounced his two vetoes on British entry in the same room.

The two leaders explained in turn that their talks had been constructive, and outlined the main lines of the progress made. The dramatic moment came when President Pompidou, having explained that the essence of the talks had been on the general conception of Europe and its prospects, continued:

> Many people believed that Great Britain was not, and did not wish to become, European, and that she only wanted to enter the Community in order to destroy it or to divert its purposes. Many people also believed that France was ready to use any pretext to place finally another veto on the entry of Great Britain.
>
> Well, ladies and gentlemen, you see before you this evening two men who are convinced that neither of these things is true.

This was the truly historic, and heady, moment when many of those present realised that, barring accidents, Britain's accession to the European Community was assured.

The story behind the story, as Michael Palliser told us at an embassy meeting later, was that Pompidou's main objective had been to secure Heath's agreement to do nothing to impede the completion of the establishment of the Common Agricultural Policy. He had urged Heath that he had nothing to fear from this, since the dynamic nature of British industry would more than compensate for any disadvantages arising from it for the UK. Unfortunately, as time would show, British industry, at least in the early years before the Thatcherite revolution and the curbing of the unions, failed to fulfil its side of the bargain!

It is a curious fact, or rather an observation of mine, that when the British economy is doing well, the French economy is usually not, and vice versa. There was no doubt that, at this particular time, Britain was performing poorly – beset by labour problems and indifferent political and industrial leadership – whereas France was experiencing a kind of economic miracle. The difference between the two countries' economic performance was epitomised, in my eyes, by the reception given the UK Chancellor, Anthony Barber, when he came to Paris for talks with his French opposite number. This was a rising young centrist politician by the name of Valérie Giscard d'Estaing, later to become President of France. Barber had to mount the stairs in the Finance ministry to be greeted by the tall Giscard at the top – who towered over him, like Louis XIV at Versailles, with an almost palpable air of condescension.

Not that many other visiting British politicians, in my experience, fared much better with their French counterparts. They had a tendency to think that the best approach was to get on a matey basis, preferably using first names. This rarely did the trick, since the French are more formal. Nor did cracking jokes – which do not translate well – or the use of obscure allusions which meant little to non-British interlocutors go down well. French politicians are no less innately competitive than British ones – frequently more so.

The two nations clung to outdated stereotype images of the other. For the British, the French were represented by an onion seller on a bicycle, with a striped vest and a beret. The French still viewed the British through the prism of a book, *Les Carnets du Major Thompson*, the humorous journal of a starchy Englishman living with his wife in France, and finding the French very peculiar, although, since it was written by the French author Pierre Daninos, it was really a take on French eccentricities seen through fictional British eyes. They were shocked when this traditional, and upright, figure was elbowed aside, during our time in Paris, by the advent of the less appealing British soccer hooligan.

The arguments for and against Britain's entry into the EEC were aired, for the French public, on a popular weekly current affairs TV show called *À armes égales*. The format was that the opposing champions on either side of the chosen topic would each muster some supporters and prepare a short film in advance. There would then be a debate, after which the French public would vote on the winner.

Invited to suggest a British champion for what would be a unique cross-channel debate, Soames put forward the name of Roy Jenkins, a leading Labour pro-European. The lead on the French side was the formidable former Foreign Minister, Maurice Couve de Murville, who was no friend of Britain's. To help Jenkins prepare, and be briefed on the French angle, Soames instructed me to cross to London to act as his advisor. This went well, and on the night of the debate Jenkins argued a good case, although he was distracted at one point by a shrill attack from his right flank by a eurosceptic Labour MP, Annie Kerr – whom the BBC, in their quest for balance, had placed near him in the London studio audience – shouting 'Roy, you're a traitor to the cause!' As a thank-you, Jenkins invited me to an enjoyable and well-lubricated dinner at Brooks's Club.

Britain finally joined the Community on 1 January 1973. Now back in the Foreign Office, I was invited to raise a glass of champagne to toast the event in the office of John Robinson, my immediate boss and one of the key members of the UK negotiating team.

* * *

On a lighter note, I was given the assignment, on two consecutive years, of being the official UK delegate to the Cannes Film Festival. At that time the Festival would invite government representatives for the countries which had films in the main competition, whose function was mainly to collect the Palme d'Or if their country's film won. For my wife and me, it was a unique opportunity to move for a short time into the glamorous world of the big screen. We headed for the Côte d'Azur.

The British film industry's presence at the festival was co-ordinated by the Film Production Association of Great Britain, who made a big effort in 1970 to raise its profile. This included bringing out a booklet, 'Seventy-Five Years of British Films', featuring a discussion on the creative perspective for 1970 with contributions from, among others, producers John Schlesinger (*Midnight Cowboy*) and Leon Clore

16. Henrietta and me with our ambassador, Christopher (later Lord) Soames, at the Cannes Film Festival. Attending the festival turned out to be one of the unexpected pleasures of our posting in France. (Photo: author)

(*Morgan: A Suitable Case for Treatment* and *The French Lieutenant's Woman*). Leon's wife Miriam was the editor.

The Clores, whom we came to know well, presided over a daily lunch buffet on the British Beach which was resoundingly popular with the Brits, and not to be missed. Back in London they entertained stylishly in the penthouse flat of their house in Tite Street, in Chelsea. We spent many convivial evenings there in later years, at what was, in effect, their salon for the film world. The cast ranged from the director Karel Reisz, actors such as David Warner, the writer David Mercer (who wrote the script of Leon's film *Morgan*), critics including Alexander Walker (*Evening Standard*) and John Russell Taylor (the author of a number of film biographies) to, on one occasion, the Duke of St Albans. Conversation was stimulated by Miriam's propensity for outrageous remarks and Leon's excellent cellar.

We were accommodated, by the Festival, at the splendid Carlton Hotel on the Croisette, a short walk from the Palais des Festivals where the main film showings took place, and the main hub of activity, with film deals being discussed in every corner.

In my first year at Cannes the British entry was John Boorman's *Leo the Last*. At the gala party after the showing he and I had a row. I objected to what seemed to me his criticism of all things British (in reality he was probably just winding me up), and I walked out of the building in high dudgeon. Only then did I remember that the party was at a location some distance from the town and I had to return inside, ignominiously, to order a taxi! Boorman left Cannes but returned at the end of the Festival to collect the Best Director Award. He graciously sent me an apology.

The next year the British entry (though not in the main competition) was Christopher Miles's *The Virgin and the Gypsy*, based on a DH Lawrence story. This time the uneasy relationship between the film world and diplomacy was tested by Ambassador Soames's decision to visit the Festival in person. All went well until, once again, the post-showing Gala Party. At the height of this, the actress playing the Virgin, Joanna Shimkus, jumped onto a table to do a flamboyant dance. Someone persuaded the ambassador, sportingly, to join her on the table top. I desperately, but vainly, tried to stop the photographers from taking pictures, so as not to compromise his future political career. More effectively, the film's producer saved everybody's blushes by buying up the negatives.

*   *   *

Living in France is a bracing experience intellectually. The Cartesian manner of thinking imposes a rigour in debate usually absent on this side of the Channel. At a Parisian dinner-party one could not expect to get away with observations about the weather or the latest TV. The knack, I learned from a more senior member of the embassy, was to enter with a prepared, and provocative aphorism, to get one off the mark in the conversationally challenging environment. Needless to say, women were expected to look stylish.

But France is also about its distinctive culture and its quality of life, not least its food and drink. In Paris our favourite restaurant was Chez André, on the rue Marbeuf, round the corner from our flat. Hugely popular, it took no advance booking. Everyone had to queue for a table, even such film stars of the day as Alain Delon and Jean-Paul Belmondo. On one occasion, André pointed out with glee that the claimant to the throne of France was sitting near our local butcher. But the wait was usually not too long, and the food and atmosphere were so good that no-one minded.

We would also occasionally go clubbing – dancing the kazachok, the dance of the moment – at such fashionable discos as Régine's and Chez Castel. The evening would conclude with listening to cool jazz featuring Joe Turner, who had made his name singing the Blues with Count Basie, at a bar on the nearby Avenue Pierre 1er de Serbie.

We took every opportunity to explore the country. I have already mentioned our forays to the Côte d'Azur for the Cannes Film Festival. We also spent a summer holiday there, when Nicholas was a toddler, renting a small villa with a garden on Cap d'Antibes. We spent a glorious few weeks swimming at the local beach, shopping in Antibes market, and exploring on most afternoons in the hills above. The only bad episode was returning on one occasion to discover that we had been burgled in our absence, by one of the many criminals who abounded in that playground of the rich.

Another summer holiday was spent in a villa beside Lake Annecy. The inspiration for this came from seeing a film by Eric Rohmer called *Le Genou de Claire*. The film itself, billed as a moral tale, was pretty tedious, consisting of endless advice to the conflicted middle-aged hero on how best to seduce the teenage Claire, with whose knee he had become besotted. But the film's setting, around Lake Annecy, was superb, and made a wonderful backdrop to our holiday.

The cinema played a large part in our life in Paris, where we had the good fortune to live just a ten-minute walk from the Champs-Elysées with its abundance of cinemas. The films we saw there, in all their variety, best expressed, I felt, the particular genius of French culture. From the vulnerability of a young woman discovering love (Jean Seberg in *Bonjour Tristesse*), the timeless elegance of Catherine Deneuve in *Belle de Jour,* to the frenetic energy of Jean-Paul Belmondo in *À Bout de Souffle*, and the realism of the numerous police thrillers starring the gravelly voiced Jean Gabin and Jean-Louis Trintignant, they all had an immediacy which made them stick in the memory. The haunting musical scores of Michel Legrand certainly helped. Of more recent products of French cinema, the ones which have made the most impact on me have been Claude Berri's *Jean de Florette* and *Manon des Sources*, a realistic saga of revenge in rural France which can be compared, not too fancifully in my view, with Dumas' *Count of Monte Christo*.

On one occasion in Paris I almost changed the course of modern French history. Driving in rather a hurry along rue Marbeuf towards the embassy, I caused a pedestrian to leap for safety to the pavement. When I looked guiltily in the mirror I saw that it was François Mitterrand, the recently elected leader of the Socialist party, who went on to enjoy two successive terms as President of France. I recognised him because, a week or so earlier, I had attended a lunch at which he had spoken to the foreign press corps to outline his thinking on transforming France. It was an occasion which highlighted the difference between the average British and French politician. Mitterrand's address was on a high intellectual level, following a clear logical argument in stylish French. At about the same time Bernard Levin wrote a stinging attack on him in *The Times* on the grounds that he was taking great pains to gloss over his role in the collaborationist Vichy regime during the war. Surprisingly, this raking up of his past proved to be an isolated occasion, which was not, as far as I was aware, repeated.

In contrast to the British obsession with the Second World War, the French were still uncomfortable about it. The trial of Klaus Barbie, the so-called Butcher of Lyon, where he was the Gestapo chief who had been responsible for the death, among many others, of the resistance hero Jean Moulin, re-awakened bitter divisions which lay not far beneath the surface. The more recent Algerian war was an even more contentious subject. Gillo Pontecorvo's powerful film *The Battle of Algiers,* released in 1966, was refused a showing on television for years and could only be seen in the cinema. It offers an explanation for the problems France is encountering with the alienated communities in the suburbs surrounding its main cities to this day.

In spite of France's proclaimed democratic ideals, including *égalité* – and the fate of the *aristos* faced with *madame guillotine* – it was noticeable that class played a scarcely less prominent role in society than in Britain. On one occasion we attended a dinner party where the guests included the Prince Napoleon, a claimant to the French throne, as well as the foreign minister, Maurice Schumann. When the time came to go into dinner it was comic to see these two representatives of the old and new order going through a charade of bowing to each other to be the first through the door, before each then pushing to be the first through, in order to claim precedence, and ending up by squeezing through together in a less than dignified manner.

On another occasion, the golf club I belonged to, Saint-Nom-la-Bretèche, staged the first major golf tournament in France, the Prix Lancôme. The eight top golfers of the year were invited to compete, including Gary Player, Arnold Palmer and Tony Jacklin. To my delight, Jacklin emerged the winner in a thrilling conclusion. Rising to present the prize, the Club Chairman announced with great satisfaction that the event had finally proved that golf in France was no longer a game for 'the rich, the privileged and the old'. When the applause had died away, I remarked to a friend that these were noble sentiments, particularly coming from someone who was an 80-year-old millionaire, and a marquis.

*   *   *

The climax of my time in Paris was the state visit to France by the Queen and the Duke of Edinburgh in May 1972. This was the first of what turned out to be four state visits by the Queen with which I was to be involved during my career. All state visits are important symbolic events, reflecting the nature of the enduring links between the two countries concerned. This one marked the birth of a new relationship between Britain and France after the years of wary sparring during de Gaulle's presidency and his two vetoes on Britain joining the EEC. Both countries agreed that it should be memorable.

17. The Queen with President Georges Pompidou at the Palace of Versailles during her historic state visit in 1972, which reset the bilateral relationship prior to the UK's entry into the European Economic Community. (Photo: author)

The care and sheer hard work that went into the preparations were impressive. The first task was to decide on the non-routine aspects of the programme and agree them with the French. The Queen's Private Secretary, Sir Martin Charteris, came out to discuss it. He was accompanied by William Heseltine, the Queen's Press Secretary who was in charge of all the media aspects, and with whom we in the Press Section would be working. At a meeting in the ambassador's drawing room decisions were taken on such matters as the use of the Royal Yacht for the Queen's departure, and where she would visit outside Paris.

At this meeting, at which I was the most junior person present, I rather rashly piped up to make a proposal. How would it be, I suggested, if, in the course of her drive through the centre of Rouen to join the Royal Yacht in order to sail down the Seine back to Britain, the Queen were to make some symbolic gesture at the memorial to Joan of Arc – such as placing a wreath – which would be seen as a burial of the hatchet, and applauded throughout France? This youthful effusion was greeted politely, but brushed aside as being somewhat over-imaginative. I have always wondered, however, whether the French

Government might have had the same idea. When the Rouen visit took place, it replaced the mayor, a prominent centrist opposition politician and former presidential candidate named Jean Lecanuet, with the Prime Minister Jacques Chaban-Delmas who accompanied the Queen during the drive. When the carriage passed the Joan of Arc memorial, he drew her attention in the opposite direction, to admire the gargoyles on the cathedral. The moment passed.

The twin highlights of the Paris part of the visit were a magnificent evening at the Palace of Versailles, where a gala opera performance was followed by a state banquet. The fountains played, illuminated in different colours, the Hall of Mirrors was lit by candlelight and the champagne flowed. An unforgettable night.

No less unforgettable was the gala dinner and ball given by the ambassador at the residence on the final evening in Paris. The Prince of Wales also attended.

What was not known at the time was that another reason for Prince Charles's joining the royal party was an altogether sadder one. The Duke of Windsor, who lived with the Duchess in a villa in the Bois de Boulogne, was close to death. It had been arranged that the Queen and Prince Philip, together with Prince Charles, would call at the villa after attending the races at Longchamps in order, in effect, to take their leave of him. However, it was considered essential that the public did not learn the true nature of the call, to avoid casting a dark shadow over the state visit.

This meant that the press arrangements for the call had to be handled with great discretion. On the preceding evening, the French had laid on a reception for the press of both countries covering the visit in the restaurant of the Eiffel Tower. My boss, the Press Counsellor Bill Harding, and I spent much of the evening negotiating with the press to form a small 'pool' of TV and still photographers who would cover the event and make their material available to the rest of the media. The reason for the huge interest was that the visit was expected to provide a unique picture of three generations of British monarchy – the Duke of Windsor, the Queen and Prince Charles.

Except that it was not to be. After the Longchamps races – a jolly occasion – everyone drove to the Bois de Boulogne villa. The pre-arranged media pool reported to us for their briefing. I then broke the news that, unfortunately, the Duke was suffering from a nasty cold and would be unable to come out for the Royal Party's departure

1. Ras al-Khaimah (now in the UAE): the small town and creek, nestling below the Musandam Peninsula mountains, arguably has the most attractive landscapes of the Emirates and succeeded in preserving some of its original authenticity.

2. The Political Agency launch, with its flag flying, proceeding down Dubai Creek to the sea in 1964, to greet an RN ship lying offshore. The Creek was then, as now, a bustling commercial waterway.

3. Allied Kommandatura: the UK representatives are on the right, with the author second from the end, and the British Commandant on his left. The American and French representatives are on the other side of the table. The photograph on the right on the end wall is of the Soviet representative who walked out in 1948, never to return.

4. The Wall opening at the Brandenburg Gate: the family braving the rain at the official opening ceremony which had been delayed by reports of the fall that day of Ceaușescu in Romania on 22 December 1989. (The Ceaușescus were to be executed three days later, on Christmas Day.)

5. The ceremony of lowering the Allied flags outside the Allied Kommandatura building for the last time on the eve of German and Berlin reunification, October 1990.

6. Signing the Golden Book of Berlin after seven years in the city, watched by Henrietta and Mayor Diepgen and his wife. On the right is the formidable Hanna-Renata Laurien (known as Hanna the Grenade), the presiding officer of the Berlin Parliament.

7. The Queen, during her state visit, unveils the Henry Moore sculpture that adorned the garden of our Residence in Prague. Shortly after the ceremony, the sculpture – which had been on loan to the Embassy – had to be returned to England, somewhat to our dismay.

8. Savouring the moment before hosting, as ambassador, my last Queen's Birthday reception in Prague, after thirty-seven years in HM Diplomatic Service.

18. The Queen, Prince Philip and Prince Charles during the 1972 state visit to France, bidding farewell to the Duchess of Windsor after calling on the Duke, who was gravely ill, at their villa in the Bois de Boulogne. His absence deprived the media of their coveted historic shot of three generations of British monarchy. (Photo: author)

– particularly in view of the chilly and overcast weather. At this point the clouds parted, the sun shone through and the photographers expostulated that surely now it would be all right. To their disappointment I stuck to my story about the nasty cold. Only the Duchess appeared, to wave off the royal party on their departure. To an observer such as me, there was nothing in the body language of the group to suggest the real significance of the occasion. The relationship between the Duchess of Windsor and the royal visitors, seen from a distance, seemed to be lacking in cordiality, which was scarcely surprising given the sombre nature of the occasion and the long history of strained relations since the Abdication. Prince Charles looked particularly glum.

Only one journalist, the long-standing Paris correspondent of the *Evening Standard*, Sam White, smelled a rat. I later apologised to him for the deception, which had been necessary.

About two weeks after the end of the Royal Visit the Duke of Windsor died. The large number of Parisians who came to sign the book of condolences at the embassy was testimony to the regard in which he was held there. An RAF aircraft flew to Paris to carry the coffin back to England for interment in the grounds of Frogmore House in Windsor Great Park, where he was joined in due course by the Duchess.

A few weeks later our family of four, with Gino the Sudanese cat, in a newly purchased trendy Renault 5, also drove out of Paris to return to London, at the end of a fascinating posting of almost four years. We had been more than fortunate with our timing, being part of an embassy team performing at the top of its game at a key moment in the long history of Anglo-French relations. Those of us who served in Paris at the time look back on the Soames embassy as a golden period, in which we were lucky to have played a part.

Chapter 6

Science and Technology in the Foreign Office, then Back to the Middle East: Lebanon, Jordan and Israel

The Foreign Service is two types of career in one. When serving abroad the task is to get to know and report on the country and its leading personalities as fully as one can, and to promote British interests. People skills are at a premium. Back in the Office the emphasis is on the clear presentation of policy options to ministers, which demands different talents. The much-mocked, but undeniably glamorous cocktail circuit lifestyle is replaced by the more mundane daily routine of a Whitehall civil servant. But the interest of the subject matter means that there are many compensations.

On returning to the Foreign Office from Paris in July 1972 I became the assistant head of a department dealing with, not this time a specific country or region, like Eastern Department (on my previous home posting), but with an eclectic mixture of subjects under the heading of

'Science and Technology'. Those which particularly engaged my attention were policy on outer space and the environment.

Environmental diplomacy was a new area which had been kick-started by the UN Conference, recently held in London, on the Prevention of Marine Pollution by the Dumping of Wastes at Sea. Policy was being driven by the formidably energetic Martin (later Sir Martin) Holgate in the Department of the Environment, who was to become well known and internationally honoured as a distinguished environmentalist and biologist. As regards the nascent formation of an EEC environment policy, Holgate had been quick to point out that it was not always suited to particular British circumstances.

For example, in the EEC context, measures to clean up European rivers, which flowed through a number of different countries, required the setting of common standards. These tended to be more demanding and inflexible than were needed to regulate Britain's single-country rivers. Holgate's argument that, instead, a 'best-endeavours' regime would better meet the UK case, was an early example of our approach to shared EEC problems tending to set us apart.

On the other hand, I feel that the UK being made to conform to European standards in other areas of environmental policy, such as the cleanliness of our beaches, was one of the great benefits of being a member of the European Community.

On Environment policy the Foreign Office was not the lead department, but made an input into the Whitehall debate, as necessary, to ensure that the foreign policy implications were fully taken into account. Similarly, with space matters, the lead lay elsewhere, in this case in the Department of Trade and Industry.

Space was one of the first subjects to cross my desk. There was a crisis in European space policy (which fell outside the remit of the EEC), largely caused by the UK's controversial decision to cancel the Blue Streak rocket launcher on which the European space research programme depended. The UK position was that maintaining an independent European launch capability was expensive, when procuring a cheaper alternative from the USA was a perfectly viable option. This cut little ice, with the French in particular. To sort this out a one-day European Space Conference was convened in Brussels in December 1972. The leader of the UK delegation was the dynamic new Industry Minister, one Michael Heseltine. I was attached to the delegation as his FCO advisor.

It proved to be a remarkable day. Firstly, being December, there was fog in the Channel so that, in the classic phrase, the 'continent was cut off', this being a generation before the Channel Tunnel, with the consequence that our delegation arrived in Brussels late. We were armed with firm instructions to oppose any further UK involvement in a launcher programme, but to promote opportunities for the burgeoning UK satellite industry, and to press for the creation of a European Space Agency, on the lines of NASA.

On arrival, we were greeted with the cheerful news that everything had been arranged in our absence, on the following lines. All the European countries, whether in the EEC or not, would be invited to take part in a new French-led European launcher, to be known as Ariane. There would also be general participation in a German-led space laboratory project. This was to be a re-usable science laboratory for use on the US space shuttle.

Heseltine firmly rejected both propositions and insisted that the discussion start again at square one. He made clear the UK opposition to any contribution to a launcher programme, and was sceptical, but slightly less so, over involvement in the space laboratory. He then placed on the table a British proposal for the establishment of a European Space Agency (ESA), as a counterpart to NASA. Countries were free to join its programmes, when agreed, on a voluntary basis. He made it clear that we would expect the new agency to develop a satellite programme, in which the UK had a particular interest.

After much hard bargaining these proposals were unanimously accepted, but only once Heseltine had secured agreement on the telephone from a reluctant London to our making a nominal contribution towards Ariane, which, it was agreed, would be a key programme of the agency. The outcome of the conference was, in effect, the birth of a European space programme.

After a successful day's work the delegation went out to dinner in a Brussels restaurant. I was left in admiration of Michael Heseltine's negotiating skill, as well as the force of his personality.

The decision on setting up a European Space Agency had the happy consequence that I travelled frequently to Paris over the following months to take part in the talks on its terms of reference and constitution. So frequently, in fact, that my wife was in the habit of giving me a food shopping list of items to bring back from our favourite Paris shops – including even our butcher – as if we had never left!

If space was something of a European success story for the UK, I found that the general attitude towards the EEC in Whitehall was sceptical, if not hostile. John Robinson, deputy to Sir Con O'Neill, was engaged in the thankless task of trying to persuade Whitehall generally that our accession meant that new rules applied, and that departments had to learn to be more community-minded (*Communautaire*). The reception he encountered was usually frosty.

Later, another important area of the department's work was the supersonic airliner, Concorde. The Labour Party had won the 1974 election with a promise to cancel three major projects in its first week in office: the Channel Tunnel, a third London airport at Maplin Sands and Concorde. The first two were duly given a death sentence, although, of course, the Channel Tunnel project was revived, and became a reality, in the next decade. When it came to cancelling the supersonic airliner Concorde, whose development was at an advanced stage, the department felt duty bound to point out that its construction was based on a treaty with France to bear the costs on a 50/50 basis. If we pulled out, we could possibly be liable to pay a huge amount in compensation to the French.

This intervention saved the Concorde project. Legal advice was sought from the government's legal advisors. When this was produced, coming to the conclusion that a liability for compensation could not be excluded, the government got cold feet, and the project to build that beautiful aircraft – for better or for worse – went ahead. Personally, I was delighted, since I felt that Concorde was a major technical achievement and a source of pride to the country.

Securing overflying rights for Concorde – with its problematic sonic boom – from other countries was another matter. India, for example refused them, on the understandable basis that it was being asked to accept a noise problem for its population living under the flight path, which the UK was not prepared to inflict on its own citizens. This refusal had fatal consequences for Concorde's profitability on Far Eastern routes.

The United States was no less obdurate over granting landing rights at its airports. It required a major lobbying exercise before its resistance to landing at New York and Washington was finally overcome. Without this agreement the project would not have been viable. The US attitude was essentially viewed as sour grapes, that it had failed to develop a supersonic airliner of its own to rival Concorde.

With our lengthy tour in Paris I had become bilingual in French, and, back in London, I was sometimes called in to interpret for the Prime Minister, Edward Heath, when he was entertaining French VIPs, both at No. 10 and Chequers. Normally this was straightforward, but on one of these occasions, a dinner for President Pompidou at Chequers, I found myself almost embarrassingly at a loss. After dinner I was called over to interpret between the President and the Governor of the Bank of England, who were discussing the merits, or otherwise, of a 'crawling-peg' exchange rate system. I had never heard the term before and cast around with increasing desperation, as interpreters do, to think of a suitable circumlocution. I cannot have been too far off the mark because the next day, to my huge relief, there was no run on the pound.

I enjoyed Science and Technology Department and was stimulated by the diversity of the subjects it dealt with, particularly when, in the latter stage, my head of department was Jimmy (later Sir James) Mellon, who had a refreshing and untypical approach to the work, allied to a sharp mind, which made him fun to work with.

19. Interpreting in French for Prime Minister Edward Heath at 10 Downing Street.
He was in fact more interested in the topic under discussion than this picture suggests.
(Photo: author)

*   *   *

After this two-year London interlude the family set off to return to what had become a turbulent Middle East. My posting was to the embassy in Amman, Jordan, in the middle-ranking job of Head of Chancery (a coordinating role similar to that of an adjutant in an army battalion) and Consul. Before taking up the post the plan was to stop off for a month in Lebanon on the way, at the Foreign Office Arabic language school, MECAS, to refresh my Arabic.

To reach Lebanon the family (Nicholas was now six, and Amanda four) drove down through France to Genoa in order to board a ship of the Italian Adriatica Line, the *Ausonia*, to sail to Beirut. We arrived on board with little money due to my inability to master the pre-euro Italian currency. The Office had issued me with 'subsistence' funds for the journey and booked a hotel room in Genoa ahead.

Unfortunately, we arrived in Genoa in pouring rain and late, after the long drive, and failed to find the hotel where we had our reservation. In desperation I managed to find a hotel which, although somewhat grand in appearance, seemed to have reasonable rates. I was too tired to be alerted to my mistake by the gold taps in the bathroom. When I came to pay the bill, after a very comfortable night, I realised to my horror that I had miscounted the number of noughts in the price of the room, denominated in old lira. The bill took the bulk of our remaining subsistence money and meant we had a somewhat austere crossing to Beirut.

Returning to MECAS, in the mountain village of Shemlan, looking down on Beirut airport, I found that outwardly little had changed in the intervening twelve years. But there was a discernible new edginess in Lebanon following the recent expulsion of the Palestine Liberation Organisation (PLO) from Jordan to Lebanon. This grew more acute during the month I spent in Shemlan brushing up my Arabic. On 13 April 1975 a bus containing some Palestinian fighters was attacked by a Christian militia in the coastal city of Sidon, leaving a number of them dead. In retrospect this proved to be the incident that sparked the Lebanese civil war.

The febrile atmosphere in Lebanon was brought home to us in a frightening way just before the family left for Jordan. The first of April was our wedding anniversary and my wife and I drove down to Beirut to dine in a restaurant and dance in the famous Cave du Roi nightclub.

For our return drive up into the mountains I chose a back route, a quiet country road winding up through mountain villages and olive groves. It was after 3am and there was no other traffic on the road.

Suddenly, to our consternation, we saw a file of armed men coming down the road towards us. They signalled to us to stop, which we did. The leader came round to the driver's side of the car, ordered us to lower the window and poked his gun in. But since we had a UK-style right-hand drive car, it was my wife, rather than me, whom he confronted. My knees were knocking together but my wife, who had grown up in Cyprus during the EOKA troubles, remained amazingly calm.

'Good evening, is there anything we can do for you?' she asked. Clearly put off his stride by her reaction, the fighter replied, in perfect English, 'Please turn off your head-lights and do not turn them on again until we have gone some distance past you.' 'All right,' said my wife, 'is there anything else?' 'No, thank you' was the polite reply. We did as he had asked, and only resumed our journey, considerably sobered, some minutes later.

Next day we learned what a close shave we had had. We were told that, on the same road, a UN official had been travelling with his girlfriend when they were similarly intercepted by an armed group (possibly the same one). He had reacted angrily, with the dire result that he was pulled out of the car and tied to a tree. His girlfriend had then been raped in front of him, and finally he had been shot.

Once we arrived in the Jordanian capital, Amman, the ambassador, Glencairn Balfour-Paul, who was himself on the point of departure, kindly accommodated us for a few days in his residence before we moved into our own accommodation. This was a house perched on a steep hillside, overlooking a valley, across which we gazed at another of Amman's many hills. It boasted a covered veranda on which we and our friends would sit on many an evening, gazing at the sunset shading the valley below from pink to purple, the lights gradually coming on, and the tinkling of the bells as the goatherds brought their flocks in for the night. We were very happy there.

Jordan, during our two and a half years in the country, enjoyed a rare period of tranquillity in its often uneasy history. But it did not seem like that at the time of our arrival. There was an edginess over security, dating from the expulsion of the PLO three years earlier in an operation that became known as Black September, after the month in which it took place. Sensing the mood, and mindful of our encounter with the fighters on the Lebanese mountain road, my wife, after listening to the alarming reports on the BBC World Service every morning, was even reluctant, for a few weeks, to set about unpacking our heavy baggage, in case we were forced to make a sudden departure.

Her caution seemed to be justified when, shortly after I had taken up my duties in the embassy, there were sounds of gunfire and military helicopters clattered overhead flying in the direction of the Intercontinental Hotel, a few hundred yards down the road. The telephone rang. It was the BBC in London saying that they understood that an attack was taking place on the hotel, and could I please tell them what was going on.

There was indeed an assault in progress by a group of armed terrorists, for which Black September later took credit. They sprayed bullets around indiscriminately in the hotel lobby, causing a number of casualties, before being eventually overcome by the Jordanian special forces. Their objective was, presumably, to demonstrate to the Jordanian authorities that their violent ejection of the PLO had not been forgotten and would be avenged.

The raid certainly had the effect of tightening security in Amman. But its essential futility was shown to me a few weeks later when I happened to be laid up in the King Hussein Medical Centre for a minor operation. In the adjacent room was a Palestinian-American orthopaedic surgeon who recounted to me that he had been in the hotel lobby at the time of the raid and had sustained a bullet wound in one leg. He was on a visit to Jordan from the United States with his daughter, whom he had wanted to introduce to his homeland, or as near as he could get to it. The bullet in his leg, fired by fellow Palestinians, had severed the sciatic nerve. He feared that his career as a surgeon, required to stand for long periods in order to perform operations, might be over.

*   *   *

Serving in Jordan, a front-line state, brought me, for the first time, face to face with the reality of the Arab-Israeli dispute, the central problem in the Middle East. British diplomats regularly found themselves on the back foot on the issue when confronted with the Balfour Declaration, which the Arabs blamed for creating it. This was a letter which Arthur Balfour, the British Foreign Secretary, wrote to Lord Rothschild in

1917, in which he stated that the British Government viewed with favour the establishment of a Jewish National Home in Palestine. He continued, crucially, 'provided this did not prejudice the civil and religious rights of the other inhabitants of the country'. That meant the Palestinians themselves, who were the indigenous inhabitants.

In other words, the British were backing both sides, in a way which the Arabs considered to be an act of breath-taking cynicism.

Granted a Mandate by the League of Nations in 1922 to govern Palestine, Britain found itself with the unforgiving task of presiding over the inevitable conflicts its policy had created between the rising tide of Jewish immigrants – particularly after the rise of the Nazis in Europe and the subsequent Holocaust in the Second World War – and the Palestinian inhabitants. The Mandate ended with the creation, by the UN, of the State of Israel in 1948, and the departure of British forces.

Aside from its Mandate over Palestine, Britain created the emirate of Transjordan, to the west of the Jordan river. This was done by a stroke of Winston Churchill's pen (as Colonial Secretary) during the Cairo Conference which he convened in 1922 to settle the frontiers in the Middle East following the defeat of the Ottoman Empire. The new emirate was handed over to the Emir Abdullah, one of the sons of the Hashemite Sharif Hussein of Mecca, as partial recompense for Britain's failure to honour its promise to him of support for Arab independence, in exchange for his launching of the Arab Revolt against Ottoman domination (an issue which led to the bitter disillusionment of TE Lawrence, Lawrence of Arabia). This promise, also, had been overtaken by Britain making a parallel agreement with France (known as the Sykes–Picot Agreement of 1916) to divide up the region between them. Another of the Sharif's sons, the Emir Faisal, was given the throne of Iraq, another creation of the Cairo Conference.

After the creation of Israel, and the immediate war between it and the Arab states that followed, the Emir Abdullah's army – the Arab Legion, led by the British general Sir John Glubb, who became known as Glubb Pasha – was the only Arab army to stand its ground against the Israeli forces, holding onto the West Bank and East Jerusalem. These territories were then incorporated into the Hashemite Kingdom of Jordan, which gave Abdullah, and then the young King Hussein when he succeeded his grandfather, the responsibility for upholding the Palestinian cause. This responsibility was subsequently contested

20. A roadside poster of the Jordanian branch of the Hashemite dynasty. From the left, Sharif Hussein of Mecca, King Abdullah I of Jordan, King Talal (whose reign was short), King Hussein and King Abdullah II. The legitimacy of the royal lineage and its continuity have always been a key feature of how the Jordanian leadership presents the country. (Photo: author)

with the loss of those territories to Israel in the Six Day War, and the creation of the Palestine Liberation Organisation.

It was this bitter rivalry between the King and the PLO for the right to speak for the Palestinians which had led to the PLO's expulsion from Jordan in the events of what came to be known as Black September.

King Hussein's main objective, at the time of our arrival, was to regain control of the West Bank and East Jerusalem, which he had forfeited in the Six Day War of 1967. He had managed to keep Jordan largely out of the recent 1973 Yom Kippur war which had restored a measure of Arab pride – due to the Egyptian successes in the opening stage (if not thereafter). It had opened up the possibility of a disengagement of Egyptian and Israeli forces in the Sinai Peninsula. The Americans, in the person of the secretary of state, Henry Kissinger, were engaged in trying to broker a successful outcome, through a process of shuttle diplomacy.

There was also a peace plan of sorts on the table known as the Allon Plan, named after the Israeli Deputy Prime Minister, Yigal Allon. This was intended to address the bigger question of a 'just and lasting' settlement of the Israel-Palestine dispute over the West Bank under Israeli occupation, by returning 90 per cent of its territory, and 95 per cent of its population, to Jordanian jurisdiction. But King Hussein rejected the plan, preferring to stick to UN Resolution 242 including the statement that territories cannot (legally) be acquired by force, which is the basis for international non-recognition of Israel's right to build settlements on the West Bank.

A major complication then arose, from the King's point of view, when the Arab states agreed at a summit in Morocco that the PLO (rather than Jordan) would henceforth be the 'sole representative' of the Palestinian people.

This meant that the prospect of the Israelis agreeing to an interim agreement over the West Bank disappeared, since they did not recognise the PLO and would not negotiate with it. Furthermore, if they did unilaterally renounce a measure of control over the West Bank, it would not be the Hashemite Kingdom of Jordan that would benefit. This left King Hussein effectively on the side-lines and depressed at the turn of events.

The King nevertheless remained a trusted interlocutor for American politicians and British ministers. His survival against all the odds, allied to his strong links with Britain and America and his disarming personality, made him a highly regarded figure in London and Washington. Much later, his standing in the West would be tarnished, for a time, by his backing of the Iraqi leader Saddam Hussein (no relation) when he invaded Kuwait in 1991. Margaret Thatcher was infuriated by his stance. He owed his eventual rehabilitation to the Queen, who nominated him to take the Sovereign's Parade at Sandhurst in her place. After his death in 1998 the King was accorded the unique honour (for a Muslim leader) of a Memorial Service in St Paul's Cathedral, attended by the Prince of Wales.

*   *   *

Closer acquaintance with the Arab-Israeli dispute produced conflicting thoughts in me. Firstly, I did not depart from the conviction I had formed when in Sudan at the time of the Six Day War, that the problem arose from the tragedy of two ancient peoples contesting over one piece of land. It was inappropriate to attribute blame to one side or the other for the existential conflict in which they found themselves.

On the other hand, it was difficult when faced with the reality of the plight of the Palestinians, whether in refugee camps or living under Israeli occupation, not to feel sympathy for their lot.

The main Palestinian refugee camp in Jordan lay in a valley a few miles north of Amman. It was large, but long-established and well run by UNRWA, the United Nations Relief and Works Agency. Broadly, Jordan treated the refugees well and they were allowed to work in the economy. Nevertheless, visiting the camp, and hearing the harrowing stories – oft repeated – of what the refugees had left behind in their homes, in Haifa or Jaffa or wherever, was touching. They refused to give up the dream of returning to them one day. This is the reason why Yasser Arafat did not agree with the terms offered by Israel at the Camp David Summit brokered by President Bill Clinton in 2000, which did not recognise the right of return of the refugees. For this, he was widely blamed for the failure of the summit.

Our friends were both Jordanian and Palestinian, sometimes both in one family. For example, Laila, the sister of one of our best Jordanian friends, had been recently widowed when her Palestinian husband, who was serving in the Jordanian army, had been killed by an unhappy stroke of chance in the Jordan valley. He had been the only casualty when a random bomb dropped by the Israeli air-force, in retaliation for an attack by some Palestinians across the Jordan river into the West Bank, had killed him. The life of a widow in the Arab world is not easy, and Laila faced many difficulties.

Her late husband had had two maiden aunts who lived together in a house just outside the Damascus Gate in Jerusalem. The sisters were artistic and produced beautiful miniature watercolour paintings of the flowers of the Holy Land. They were also indomitable in their rejection of the Israeli occupation. They resisted all offers by the Israeli authorities to move them elsewhere, even with suitable compensation. They also refused to post any letters to avoid giving revenue to the Israeli-run postal service. We called on them for tea on our occasional visits to Jerusalem. It was impossible not to admire their iron resolve.

We saw things from the Israeli side and had the opportunity of hearing their point of view on another of our visits to the West Bank and Israel. Crossing over the Allenby Bridge (now the King Hussein Bridge) over the river Jordan, even with all the necessary documentation, was never a straightforward business. On this occasion the Israeli border authorities refused to believe that I was a British diplomat because I was not carrying a diplomatic passport (the reason being that the UK, uniquely among countries, refused to issue them to its diplomats for fear of parliamentary criticism that they were undemocratic, until compelled to comply with general EU practice on the subject many years later). Eventually, a UN official became aware of my heated altercation with an Israeli immigration officer and intervened to enable us to go through.

Once in Jerusalem we presented ourselves to the British Consulate-General – which was independent of the embassy in Tel Aviv, mirroring the position that the Israeli occupation of East Jerusalem (and the West Bank) is not recognised in international law. They lent us a Land-Rover, which enabled us to travel around. Apart from Jerusalem itself, where we stayed (as on all our visits) at the delightful American Colony Hotel, we drove to Bethlehem and Hebron in the south. The latter town contained the Tombs of the Patriarchs and was a regular flashpoint of tension between Jews and Muslims, owing to the site being sacred to both religions.

Journeying to the north of the country we stayed the night beside Lake Tiberias (the Sea of Galilee). From there we rather unwisely ventured up onto the Golan Heights, which the Israelis had captured from Syria in the Six Day War. It was only when some Israeli soldiers waved us frantically to stop that we realised that we were driving through a minefield! We retreated very slowly and gingerly, with their guidance.

A highlight of our tour was a dinner given for us in the coastal town of Jaffa by a young member of the staff at our Tel Aviv embassy (all embassies accredited to Israel, until the advent of President Trump, were located in Tel Aviv, pending international agreement on the status of Jerusalem). He had invited an eclectic selection of Israeli politicians and journalists. As the evening wore on, the discussion, particularly over the situation on the West Bank and in Jerusalem, became increasingly animated. Since I was not posted in Israel, I felt I could speak my mind freely.

When I vigorously criticised Israeli actions in the Occupied Territories, the response of the Israelis was equally full-bloodied, focusing on the alleged iniquities of British policy towards the region over the years. But at the end of the evening both sides managed to calm down, and we parted friends. In fact, the Israeli guests remarked that they had not enjoyed such a frank discussion for a long time.

In Amman we followed developments in the civil war which had flared up in Lebanon with close attention. There was an alarming incident involving the family when my wife flew with the children to Beirut, to take a connecting flight to Cyprus to stay for a few weeks with her parents there. As they were waiting for their flight, Beirut Airport, for the first time, came under mortar fire. Hearing this on the radio, back in Amman, I was beside myself with anxiety.

I should have had more confidence in my wife's resourcefulness. When the firing started, most of the passengers in the terminal had taken refuge under the tables. She did not, and she noticed that a solitary plane had landed and was taxiing to the cargo area. Deciding to try her luck in getting the pilot to take her and the children to Cyprus, she ran to it across the tarmac, accompanied by a solitary British journalist, the only other passenger prepared to take the risk. Together they managed to persuade the pilot to take them, but only them, together with the children.

When she returned to the terminal, she could not resist breaking the news of the offer to the other passengers. The pilot was appalled when the whole group turned up, but he managed to squeeze them all in and took off for Cyprus. That must have been one of the last planes to leave Beirut before the civil war closed the airport.

When we left Jordan, after two and a half years, we felt that it had been a highly enjoyable posting for the whole family. We had spent Easter holidays by the sea at Aqaba, snorkelling in the Red Sea, with its pristine coral reefs, and water skiing. We had driven out, some afternoons, to the well-preserved ruins of the Roman town of Jerash, to search for baby tortoises to take back to our garden. We had paid many visits to the remarkable site of Petra – the 'rose red city, half as old as time' and the ancient capital of the Nabataeans – on one occasion camping there overnight under the stars. We had ridden on camels in the Wadi Rum – captured so memorably in David Lean's film *Lawrence of Arabia* – and sung songs around the campfire in that extraordinary landscape.

Most vividly of all, we had spent many weekends with our best Jordanian friend, Mamdouh Bisharat, at his farm in the Jordan valley by the river Yarmuk, looking up at the Golan Heights. The children had learned to dive off the Roman column standing in his natural swimming pool, fed from a nearby warm sulphur spring. On the hills above lay the ruins of Umm Qais, one of the ten towns of the Roman Decapolis, from where, according to biblical tradition, the Gadarene Swine had rushed to their doom.

We were leaving with memories to treasure, and many dear friends. It was therefore with mixed feelings that we flew across the Arabian desert to our new posting in Kuwait.

Chapter 7

Kuwait: Observing the Islamic Revolution Next Door in Iran

The second part of my five-year tour in the Middle East – my last, as it turned out – was a transfer to the embassy in Kuwait in May 1977 on promotion to Counsellor and Deputy Head of Mission (DHM).

Kuwait was then considered, at least in its own estimation, as the pre-eminent Gulf state. It presented a contrast to Dubai, my first posting at the other end of the Gulf, not least due to its arresting twin water towers. It was more advanced, politically, economically and culturally, and played a significant role on the world stage.

Kuwait's standing rested on its huge oil reserves, and its status as one of the first oil producers in the Gulf. Kuwait was also the lowest cost producer; the oil pumped out of the ground ran downhill under the force of gravity, it was said, with some exaggeration, into the waiting tankers. Bahrain's production was modest by comparison, and that of the southern Emirates, although expanding fast, had not

Photo: The Kuwait towers – elegant and modern – symbolised Kuwait's drive into the contemporary world.

yet reached comparable volumes. Dubai's role as the financial hub of the Gulf was still a distant ambition. The Kuwaitis saw themselves as being, in a way, top of the class; its National Assembly, for example, was a gesture towards democracy, even if it made little impression on government polic. A Kuwaiti could rest comfortable in the knowledge that he, or she, had drawn a winning ticket in the lottery of life.

Kuwait City was also on a different scale from other Gulf cities, and was well planned. The centre was surrounded by concentric circles of roads, known as Ring Roads, each one a substantial dual carriageway. There were at least six of these. The Ring Roads were divided into districts by spoke roads of the same size, with each district having the same facilities such as a school, shopping centre, playground, and so on.

After a long relationship, dating back to a treaty in 1899 between the Kuwaiti ruler, Sheikh Mubarak al-Sabah, who came to be known locally as Mubarak the Great, and the British Crown, Kuwait had achieved full independence in 1961. Although at that point Britain had relinquished its responsibility for guiding the Emir on external and internal affairs, in that year it had rushed troops to Kuwait in the boiling summer to deter Iraq from any aggression, at a time of heightened tension between the two countries. Some of my military and diplomatic colleagues on the MECAS Arabic course had also been drafted in, on liaison duties.

I found that relations with Britain, although cordial, were not as special or privileged as they had been in the southern Gulf. Following the ending of the exclusive treaty relationship, the major powers were all represented diplomatically, and Britain was merely one among many. But our position was underpinned by our continuing to provide military training to the Kuwaiti forces through the Kuwait Liaison Team.

And there was a living reminder of the close relationship of the past in the person of Dame Violet Dickson, the widow of Colonel HRP Dickson, an outstanding and long-serving Political Agent, who was greatly respected in Kuwait, and continued to live there in retirement. It was a joy to visit Dame Violet, who lived in the former Agency, to which she and her husband had returned on his retirement (now a national museum and Cultural Centre). There, in one of the few remaining traditional old houses, near the seafront, one could experience something of the feel of Kuwait in the old days. Dame Violet presented us with a copy of her late husband's seminal book, *The Arab of the Desert*.

The embassy was also situated on the seafront, near the water-towers which were the iconic image of Kuwait. It was an imposing brick building with a concave façade, which seemed rather out of place until one learned the unlikely explanation (which may be apocryphal).

Construction of the embassy began in 1932 according to the designs of Robert Tor Russell, the chief architect of the Government of India, and his team. They were engaged at the time in building New Delhi, including four buildings destined for the four sides of the Connaught Circle, a major roundabout at the centre of the city. The story went that, as this project proceeded, officials were puzzled that the architectural drawing for one of the buildings had disappeared. After a search, the embarrassing truth emerged that the missing plan was being used for the construction of the Kuwait embassy. Be that as it may, Russell did discuss with HRP Dickson the merit of including an unusually wide curved balcony, to catch the sea breezes. This is the embassy's best feature.

My ambassador, on arrival, was Sir Albert Lamb, better known as Archie Lamb, a dynamic, commercially minded diplomat, and an old Gulf hand, who was on the point of departure. Before leaving, he briefed me on the important contract he had been nurturing for the purchase of some fast patrol boats by the Kuwaitis for their navy. The key figure on the Kuwaiti side was the Defence Minister Sheikh Sa'ad al-Abdullah al-Salim al-Sabah, who was in favour of the deal. The British manufacturers were confident the contract was about to be signed. Lamb urged me to watch developments closely after his departure.

It turned out to be a sorry tale, and an object lesson in not taking matters for granted. The day after a party we attended to celebrate the contract, although it was still not signed, the Amir, Sheikh Sabah al-Salim al-Sabah, died. Sheikh Sa'ad became Crown Prince under the new Amir and vacated the post of Defence Minister. The British firm involved wrongly thought that the changes in the country's leadership would not affect the deal for the patrol boats, and went back to Britain for a Christmas break.

When they returned everything had changed. In their absence, their European rivals had managed to get the contract put into the melting pot and had turned it round in their favour. The contract was lost.

Our new ambassador, (Sydney) John Cambridge, was a bachelor. It therefore fell to my wife to make the numerous courtesy calls on the Sheikh's wives which custom required, particularly at the Eid. My duty, on those occasions, was to call on the senior male members of the royal family, which filled day one of the Eid, followed by calls on the top merchant families on the second day. This arrangement reflected the division of power in the commercially minded city-state.

One could detect, at the time, a latent uneasiness in the country over the threat from Saddam Hussein's Iraq to the north – the same threat that it had been my task to monitor in Eastern Department in the Foreign Office twelve years earlier. The Kuwaitis dealt with this by following a simple foreign policy of being friendly to everyone. This worked reasonably well and, during our two-year posting in the country, relations with Iraq were smooth.

*   *   *

It was from another direction that the storm clouds began to gather. We returned from our summer leave, a year after our arrival, to learn that a prominent Shi'i cleric in the Iraqi holy city of Najaf had been thrown out of Iraq by the Baghdad government – which had a largely Sunni complexion – for having an undue influence with the country's majority Shi'i population, and for generally being a nuisance.

This was the Ayatollah Ruhollah Khomeini, the Iranian cleric whose followers were preaching insurrection in neighbouring Iran. The Shah had pressed the Iraqis to expel the Ayatollah and they had obliged. Initially he had come to Kuwait and sought asylum there, but the Kuwaitis had refused him. He then flew on, to be given political asylum in Paris, from where he issued the taped messages which, back in Iran, fatally undermined the Shah's authority and prepared the way for the Islamic Revolution. Arguably, had he been left to fulminate from Najaf things might have turned out differently. But over in Paris his novel and effective method of communicating with his supporters in the Tehran bazaar enabled him to grab the attention of the world's media, which helped to strengthen the revolutionary momentum.

In the embassy we naturally followed the unfolding events across the Gulf intently. We also found ourselves becoming a staging post for those seeking to reach Tehran from Britain, as the air links became increasingly uncertain. One of these frustrated travellers was Sir John Graham, who staged through for a week or so on his way to take up his appointment as the new British ambassador in Tehran.

Another visitor using Kuwait as a staging post was the former Foreign Secretary George Brown. He was being employed by a UK newspaper to cover developments in Tehran, and also, he would have us believe, to provide a steadying influence on the Shah, who was rapidly losing his grip. Unfortunately, there was no way for him to complete his journey. This meant that for a week we had him as our guest (in the absence of the ambassador, who was on leave).

Fortunately, by this late stage in his life George Brown's fiery temperament, which had been legendary, had somewhat calmed down. I found him fascinating to talk to over dinner, particularly on the subject of his mediation in the Arab-Israeli conflict in the aftermath of the Six Day War, and his passionate espousal of the cause of Britain in Europe. It was a privilege to discuss the twin issues which had dominated my earlier postings in Sudan and Paris with someone who had played such a pivotal role in both.

At the end of the week a prominent British businessman in the UK solved George Brown's transport problem by sending a private plane to take him on to Tehran. This was just as well because he was clearly becoming frustrated. I never discovered how he got on there, but the Shah went into exile shortly afterwards.

A memorable feature of our tour in Kuwait was our family car. We had passed on our Vauxhall estate to my successor in Jordan on leaving, judging it to be unsuited to the rigours of the desert. We felt that what was needed in Kuwait, with its wide roads, extreme heat and practically free petrol, was a comfortable American car, with seriously good air-conditioning. We found it in the parking lot of a second-hand car dealer, named Beshir. It was a magnificent, silver and red, Oldsmobile 98, covered in sand, which exemplified the popular saying that Kuwaitis changed their car as soon as the ashtray was full. It fulfilled all our dreams.

But unfortunately, a year later, it was the cause of a fraught experience in the desert. We planned to drive back to Jordan for a few days, to see old friends there. Our route took as along the Tapline road, which followed the line of the oil pipeline from the Gulf oilfields to the terminal on Syria's Mediterranean coast. Before setting forth we took the car to Beshir to service it and make sure that everything was in order. As it turned out, he slipped up badly by draining the transmission fluid and failing to properly replace it.

All went well for the first day (although I felt that something was not quite right) and we stopped, as planned, to sleep for the night in the desert under the stars, beside the car. We had two small children in the back, Amanda and her friend Alisdair, who seemed to subsist only on boiled eggs. We had been told that the trick was to pour petrol in a circle around our sleeping area, to keep out the scorpions and other unwelcome intruders. Unfortunately, the petrol ran out before the circle was complete, leaving a small gap. Sure enough, we woke in the night to find that we were under invasion, and had to spend the rest of the night with the children sleeping in the car, and us on top.

Next morning, I realised as soon as I started the car that something was seriously wrong with it. Half an hour later it stopped and the engine steamed. The only thing to do (before the age of mobile phones) was for me to hitch a lift from a passing lorry-driver to his village about twenty miles away in order to arrange for a tow to take us to Jordan – leaving my wife and the children behind in the car.

It was late afternoon when I came back to rescue them, having negotiated a deal with a tow-truck. I need not have worried unduly. My wife had politely turned down several offers of assistance from passing lorries. At the end of a painfully laborious tow, we eventually arrived in Amman late in the night, exhausted, but relieved to have survived the experience, and grateful for the friendliness of all those we had encountered along the way.

Apart from this epic drive, Kuwait did not provide the same opportunities for family adventures as Jordan. The flat landscape only came to life in the spring when wildflowers sprang up in profusion in the desert. The Kuwaitis made the best of them, by setting up family camps in the desert in an attempt to recapture something of the feel of their nomadic origins. But, illustrating I suppose, my father's dictum that any fool can be uncomfortable, they made sure that their tents were luxuriously furnished and they took their home comforts with them from the city, with generators providing the power.

For us, days off were usually spent by the beach, often with Kuwaiti and Palestinian friends. The Palestinian community played an important part in the country. They filled many of the professional jobs, particularly in the oil and banking sectors and the media. But this came to an abrupt end with Saddam Hussein's invasion of Kuwait in 1991. The Palestinians, with Yasser Arafat himself setting the policy, threw in their lot with the invaders, to the fury of their Kuwaiti hosts.

One story that came out of that time was that of a German friend, who headed the Mercedes agency, and found himself as the unofficial leader and organiser of the German community, which had gone into hiding at the start of the occupation. Their whereabouts were betrayed by one of his own senior Palestinian executives, and they were all rounded up. Our friend was held hostage in a chemical works in northern Iraq, until former Chancellor Willy Brandt secured the community's release. The experience permanently damaged his health.

When the Amir and the royal family eventually returned from exile in Saudi Arabia, the Palestinians were given short shrift, losing their comfortable position in the Emirate. Led by Yasser Arafat, they had made the wrong decision in choosing to back the Iraqis and were made to pay for it. Many found themselves no longer welcome in the country.

Passing through Kuwait two years after the invasion, in order to brief the Kuwaitis on talks I had held with the Iranians in 1993 (as recounted in Chapter 12), I learned about the brave and crucial role which the women of Kuwait had played in the resistance to the Iraqis. This had earned them a promise of playing a greater part in the political process after the return of the government, but they were disappointed to find the outcome fall short.

One moment of excitement was a fire which broke out in an oilwell in the huge Burgan oilfield. The chairmen of the Kuwait Oil Company, Ahmed Jaffer, a good friend of ours, had to send for the Texan firefighting company headed by the legendary, death defying, Red Adair to extinguish it. This was no easy task, and involved massive risks. The uncertainties were so great that Ahmed told us that he had had to sign a blank cheque, with no quibbling, before they would take the contract. It was thrilling to meet the team and hear from them the hair-raising stories of their profession, and then to watch them in operation, when they did finally put the fire out.

A highlight of our time in Kuwait was the visit of the Queen and the Duke of Edinburgh in 1979. This was not technically a State Visit. Kuwait was the first port of call on their Gulf Tour on board the Royal Yacht *Britannia*, which took in Saudi Arabia and the other Gulf states and ended in Oman. It was historic, in that it was the first visit by a British monarch to a region where Britain had played such a dominant role, recognising a long-established relationship.

It was also the first time that British protocol had encountered Arab protocol, which also had long historical roots and followed equally formal rules, the foremost of which was the principle of reciprocity. From an early stage of the planning for the visit, this led to a certain awkwardness.

21. The Queen and Prince Philip visited Kuwait at the start of their Gulf Tour in 1979, based on the Royal Yacht *Britannia*. Diplomatic embarrassment was avoided by some deft manoeuvring around the gangway up to the yacht. (Photo: author)

On the British side it was of great importance that the Royal Yacht *Britannia* should be used for the whole of the Gulf Tour, which made sense from many points of view. But the Kuwaitis found it hard to accept that the royal couple would not be accommodated in their own lavishly appointed guest palace, like other official guests, and as the conventions of Arab hospitality demanded. It required no less than a personal letter from the Queen to the Amir to bring them to accept that an exception should be made on this occasion.

Another problem that arose involved me personally. Within the embassy, I was in charge of the arrangements for the visit. The ambassador's involvement in the run-up was limited, for medical reasons, which he found frustrating. So, it fell to me to be summoned by the Kuwaitis after the State Banquet in the Amir's palace on the first evening of the visit. The Amir had greeted the royal couple at the foot of the palace's steps and conducted them into dinner. It had been a glittering occasion.

What, the Kuwaitis asked, would be the arrangement for the Amir's reception on the following night for the Return Dinner offered by the Queen on board *HMY Britannia*? I said I would enquire. The answer was that the procedure was for the guest to go up the gangway, or 'prow' as it was called, to be piped on board and greeted by the admiral. The admiral would then conduct the Amir through the first set of doors, where he would be welcomed by the Duke of Edinburgh, who would accompany him through the second set of doors, to be greeted by the Queen.

When I conveyed this answer to the Kuwaitis their response was emphatic. In that case, they said, the Amir would not come. It was unacceptable that the Queen would not welcome the Amir at *Britannia*'s gangway, as he had welcomed her at the steps of his palace. Gulping, I assured them that all would be well. They made it clear that they would hold me responsible if this was not the case.

On the night of the dinner I was in a state of some trepidation, walking up and down the deck of *Britannia* in my black tie, gnawing my finger-nails. As chance would have it, Prince Philip spotted my plight and asked what was wrong. I explained the situation. 'That's simple', he said, 'how would it be if I went down and greeted the Amir and brought him on board?' 'Sir, you have just saved my life,' was my relieved reply. I was the Duke's devoted admirer ever since.

The evening culminated with the Royal Marines band beating Retreat on the quayside, watched by the guests from the deck of *Britannia*. It was a performance of such perfection that it brought a lump to my throat, and an overwhelming feeling of pride. The Kuwaiti guests were deeply impressed. With the decision to retire the Royal Yacht, without a replacement, the nation truly lost a unique asset for the projection of its values.

Poor Kuwait. The lottery of life had a nasty surprise in store. Twelve years after our departure, the Iraqi leader, Saddam Hussein, mounted his brutal and devastating invasion. His pretext was the allegation that the Kuwaitis were not only keeping the oil price low by overproducing on their OPEC quota, but also stealing his oil, by drilling laterally from their northern oilfield into the neighbouring Iraqi Rumaila oilfield across the border. The issue was not entirely clear-cut. Further confusion arose when the US ambassador in Baghdad, instructed to remonstrate with Saddam Hussein over the build-up of his forces on the Kuwaiti border, left him with an ambiguous impression of US intentions. Iraqi forces poured across the border, and the Kuwaiti government took refuge in Saudi Arabia.

The resulting First Gulf War, which began with Saddam's invasion of Kuwait in August 1990 and ended with his defeat in February 1991, was a resounding success from the military point of view. The largely American and British-led Coalition had relatively little difficulty in overcoming Iraqi resistance in Kuwait. Iraqi forces retreated back in total chaos to their own country, harried by the Coalition in what was called a 'turkey shoot' along the way, leaving a devastated and traumatised Kuwait behind, with its oilwells on fire and its coast polluted.

There has since been much debate on whether the Coalition should have pursued the fleeing Iraqi forces further into Iraqi territory and toppled Saddam Hussein before agreeing to a ceasefire. Its failure to do so arguably led to the Second Gulf War against Saddam in March 2003. It is a tempting argument, but even with the benefit of hindsight, I do not agree with it. Assembling the Coalition, to include even Syria among the Arab countries, had been a significant diplomatic achievement. Its Arab members would certainly have baulked at invading a fellow member of the Arab League, and the Western members would have lost the kudos with the Arabs they had won by liberating Kuwait. Furthermore, it could have led to substantially more casualties, and, as was amply demonstrated after the Second Gulf War, the Coalition could have found it very difficult to extricate itself.

As it was, Western interests received a blow when resentment in some quarters in Saudi Arabia at the continuing presence of US forces in the land of 'the two Holy Mosques' (in Mecca and Medina), lit the spark for the creation of Al Qaeda, led by Osama bin Laden.

We left Kuwait in 1979. It turned out to be the last of my postings in the Arab world. The cumulative experience these had given me of the Arab world had been both enjoyable and enriching.

The years of my involvement coincided with Britain withdrawing from its quasi-imperial role in the Gulf and handing the baton to the United States as the main guarantor of Western interests in the region. For the United States, however, its own interests naturally took priority and, in relation to the Arab-Israeli dispute, the principal cause of regional instability, this meant support for Israel which was seen (thanks to the influence of its powerful domestic Jewish lobby) as its strategic partner. While maintaining a close dialogue with US decision-makers on the subject, Britain generally took care not to cut across America's efforts to promote a peaceful settlement, which meant, unfortunately, that in the Arab world we tended to be seen as its 'poodle', without much of an independent role of our own.

I found this frustrating, which is the main reason why I was glad, on leaving Kuwait, to be moving into other areas of work, unconnected with the Middle East. Nor was I anxious to return, even in a more senior role as an ambassador.

I had, however, been fortunate to serve in parts of the region as diverse as Lebanon, Dubai, Khartoum, Jordan and Kuwait. Nor, as it turned out, was this to be the end of my involvement, which was to reach its fruition thirteen years later, when I became Middle East Director in the Foreign Office.

In that role, I paid two return visits to Kuwait. The first was on my way home from Tehran, where I had been exploring the possibility of getting the Iranians to lift the *fatwa* pronounced by Ayatollah Khomeini on the writer Salman Rushdie. I held talks with senior Kuwaiti officials on the situation in the country following its liberation, and in the region generally. It was sobering to see the suffering which had been inflicted on the country. But it was also inspiring to hear stories of the heroic resistance which some Kuwaitis had put up against the invaders. I visited a house preserved as a memorial to that resistance.

22. The House of Resistance, preserved as a memorial to some Kuwaitis' stand against the Iraqi invasion of their country in 1990. Iraq's seven-month occupation proved a traumatic experience for Kuwaitis. (Photo: author)

The second return visit was when I accompanied the Prince of Wales on a tour of the Gulf, including Saudi Arabia, in 1993 in the wake of his speech drawing attention to the rich and many-faceted contribution of Islamic thinkers, scientists and artists to the world's cultural heritage – which had been most warmly received in the Arab world. This time there was no protocol hitch!

On leaving Kuwait, I was once again bound for the Foreign Office, to head two contrasting departments, in succession.

Chapter 8

From Kensington to the Khyber Pass: The Iranian Embassy Besieged and Travels in South Asia

On returning to the Foreign Office in 1979 I was promoted to head a department that dealt with a clutch of subjects rather than a geographical area. It rejoiced in the title of Maritime, Aviation and Environment Department. The department's role consisted mainly of providing advice to other Whitehall departments which were engaged in international negotiations.

The subject which took up most of my attention was one which did not even feature in the Department's title, counter-terrorism! The main problem at the time was aircraft hijacking, particularly in the Middle East. The leading Group of Seven (G7) countries had addressed the issue at its latest meeting in Bonn, and had issued the so-called Bonn Declaration. This stipulated that any country which

Photo: The Kabul Embassy Residence, since destroyed in the fighting following the Allied intervention, was altogether from a different British imperial experience.

was complicit in an aircraft hijack would have its air services to G7 countries suspended.

We did not have long to wait before the first case arose, requiring attention. A Pakistani (PIA) aircraft was hijacked in flight after leaving Islamabad and flown to Kabul, the Afghan capital. There, with the clear connivance of the Afghan authorities, arms were placed on board, apparently by Murtaza, the terrorist brother of the Pakistani politician Benazir Bhutto. Murtaza had fled to Afghanistan after the execution of his father Zulfikar, who had been overthrown by General Zia-ul-Haq the previous year. The aircraft then flew on, via Damascus where it made a short stop, before it was boarded, and the incident resolved, in one of the North African capitals.

The recently elected Prime Minister, Margaret Thatcher, demanded that the Bonn Declaration be implemented by the imposition of sanctions on the guilty party, as a deterrent to further hijackings. The instruction landed on my desk. The question was, which country should be sanctioned? The one against which the clearest case could be established was Afghanistan, which had fallen under the control of the Soviet Union. Working closely with US colleagues, we started to collect reactions from the other G7 countries (Canada, Japan, France, Germany and Italy).

Afghanistan, at the time, only had air links with the European members of the G7 countries. They, however, showed little enthusiasm for implementing the Bonn Declaration as proposed, not least because the Afghans had just taken delivery of two modern (European) Airbus aircraft. It was only after some heavy top-level pressure that a collective decision was taken. This led to the Bonn Declaration being implemented, for the first time, on 21 July 1981, by banning Ariana, the Afghan airline, from flying to European capitals.

From the Foreign Office point of view, this was a satisfactory outcome to a diplomatic lobbying exercise, with a salutary deterrent effect. But it had an unexpected coda when, two or three years later, I found myself in Kabul, having switched over to head South Asia Department, facing a dilemma, as I recount below, on whether to travel by Ariana myself – hoping that they were unaware of my role in shutting down their European services!

Another strand of the department's counter-terrorist activities was the preparation of contingency plans for use in possible terrorist incidents. It was not long before counter-terrorism ceased to be just a bureaucratic exercise and came to dominate the nation's TV screens.

On 30 April 1980, I was attending a Whitehall-wide inter-departmental meeting to discuss how to handle the media in the event of a terrorist incident, when a note was brought in to the chairman, my Home Office opposite number, Hayden (later Sir Hayden) Phillips. He informed the meeting that the policeman on duty at the Iranian embassy in Prince's Gate had activated his alarm on, apparently, being dragged back within the embassy under compulsion. Contingency arrangements were being activated.

This was the start of the famous Prince's Gate siege, in the heart of London, opposite Hyde Park. The first action in Whitehall was the opening of the government's command centre, known as 'Cobra'. The well-known acronym stands for Cabinet Office Briefing Room A. At that time its existence, which is now common knowledge, was a state secret. I was to spend much of the next five days closeted within it, as the Foreign Office representative at official level (Douglas Hurd, the Minister of State, occasionally attended at ministerial level).

When Cobra initially convened, it was unclear what the crisis was all about. Gradually it emerged that a group from the Khuzestan Liberation Front had seized the embassy, taking hostage all those

23. The siege of the Iranian embassy was brought to a successful climax with the SAS abseiling down the front of the building and storming it. (Photo: © Alamy)

within it, staff and visitors, plus PC Trevor Lock who had been on duty at the door. They were demanding that the UK government secure the release of seventy or so members of their organisation who were being held by the new revolutionary government in Iran. They also demanded safe passage for themselves out of the UK. It was the job of the Foreign Office to make sense of this, and, as part of the Home Office-led response team, to deal with the international ramifications.

Khuzestan is an area of south-west Iran populated mainly, not by Persian-speakers, but by Arabs. They had not accepted the revolution in Iran inspired by Ayatollah Khomeini, and were demanding an autonomous status. The group holding the embassy threatened that unless Tehran released their comrades forthwith they would blow up the embassy.

The details of the siege, and the daring SAS operation which brought it to an end, have since been widely revealed, and I shall not repeat them here. But since it was a significant political moment, which raised Margaret Thatcher's standing in the country at an early stage of her premiership, as well as doing wonders for the global reputation of the SAS, some personal recollections may be in order.

The chair of Cobra was taken by William Whitelaw, the Home Secretary. A former Guards officer with a calm and authoritative manner, he was just the person for the job. He also had sufficient influence with the Prime Minister, who was still feeling her way, and who relied on him, to be able to say to her at the start 'Margaret, you go on down to Chequers, and I will be in contact as soon as we need you.' She did not demur, and went to Chequers, as planned, for the Whitsun weekend. She could not bear to stay away entirely, however, and she turned up unexpectedly at one point during the negotiations to take over the chair and fire off a number of questions, some of which were directed at me, sitting in the Foreign Office chair, not all of which I was able to answer. When I reported this later to Douglas Hurd, his comment was 'She will have enjoyed that!'

I had first met Mrs Thatcher three or four years earlier, when, as the newly elected leader of the Conservative Party, she had visited Jordan as the guest of King Hussein, and I had been detailed to shepherd her around. Still new to the job, she had listened to my briefing, at that stage without penetrating questions! She was now altogether more formidable, and, although newly in office, was clearly in command.

As the negotiations between the police negotiators and the terrorists dragged on, Willie Whitelaw had a bright idea. 'Surely, as Muslims, the terrorists could be made to realise that what they are doing is contrary to their religious beliefs,' he said, turning to the Foreign Office, 'isn't there someone we could bring down to Prince's Gate who would impress this on them, and urge them to give up?'

This led to my holding an embarrassing telephone conversation, within earshot of those in the command centre, with Sheikh Zaki Badawi, the Chief Imam of the Central London Mosque in Regents Park, an eminent Muslim religious leader and highly respected, not just within his own community, but throughout Britain. It went something like this:

Me 'Sheikh Zaki, you don't know me, and I can't give you my name, or tell you where I am speaking from, but it is in connection with the events taking place at the Iranian embassy in Prince's Gate. We wondered whether you could come down there and persuade the hostage-takers that their actions are wrong and that they should give themselves up.'

ZB 'Let me get this straight. You want me to leave my family in the middle of a holiday weekend, go to the site of a highly dangerous terrorist incident that the whole world is watching, stand in front of the building in full view and tell the terrorists to give up? You must be out of your mind.'

I had to tell the Home Secretary that his idea had met with a frosty response. Later Sheikh Zaki and I became friends over lunch at the Athenaeum Club and we laughed over that idiotic exchange. He was appointed an honorary KBE for his work with the Islamic College.

After five days of negotiations, during which the terrorists had grown increasingly frustrated at what they considered (rightly) the delaying tactics of the police, the siege came to a dramatic climax when they pushed the body of one of the Iranian hostages out of the embassy door. After this there could only be one outcome: an assault by the SAS. The police officer in charge formally requested assistance from the military, and the Home Secretary sought and received clearance from the Prime Minister.

As we waited in Cobra for the assault to go in, we nervously watched the TV monitors positioned around the room. It was a surreal moment. The World Snooker Championship invariably took place over the Whitsun weekend. The TV monitors all carried pictures of the calm, mathematical, movement of snooker balls around the table. We, on the other hand, could only guess at what scenes of violence were about to erupt onto the screens in their place.

The coverage that suddenly interrupted the snooker contained images which were among the most memorable of the seventies. The SAS had been preparing meticulously for this moment, reconnoitring the layout in the embassy from plans of the building, briefing released hostages and lowering listening devices down the chimneys. There were also listening devices inserted into the wall from the adjoining building. Ingenious ways were found of creating diversionary noise to mask the necessary drilling, including roadworks and changing the flight path of aircraft flying into Heathrow.

The black-clad SAS unit were seen abseiling down the front of the embassy building, breaking a window and hurling in stun grenades. Black smoke poured out. Shots could be heard as soon as the soldiers made their entrance. It transpired that they had shot five of the terrorists and captured the remaining one. It was a brutally swift and entirely successful operation.

There was jubilation in Cobra as the tension gave way to relief. Not long afterwards the Prime Minister arrived with her husband, Denis. There were gin and tonics all round. After this Willie Whitelaw went on television, with the Commissioner of Police, to tell the story to the nation. In my view he received less credit than he deserved for the successful outcome of the siege, possibly because of the G&Ts!

Full credit, of course, went to the SAS for their part. The two SAS commanders in charge would later, as it happened, be my travel companions in different circumstances. Lieutenant General Sir Peter de la Billière, Director of Special Forces, was a fellow advisor accompanying the Prince of Wales on his tour of the Gulf in 1993; and, in my retirement, Lieutenant General Sir Michael Rose, who commanded the actual assault, was a fellow Guest Lecturer at an event where we shared the podium.

My overall impression was that the Cobra system, which was being tested on an incident of this scale for the first time, worked well during the siege. Furthermore, handling the media in a terrorist incident – which was the very issue we had been discussing when the siege started – had proved indeed to be of central importance. If the media had not been handled carefully, their actions could easily have affected the course of events and created confusion. There were moments at Prince's Gate when this was in danger of happening. For example, there was a TV unit at the back of the building of whose presence we were not aware, and who were in a position to film the SAS unit taking up position on the roof of the building – which would have alerted the hostage-takers, who were monitoring the TV. Someone high up in Whitehall must have called in some favours to persuade it to hold off.

*   *   *

After two years of dealing with Maritime, Aviation and Environment Department's rich tapestry of subjects, I was transferred to head South Asian Department early in 1981, succeeding John Coles, who crossed Downing Street to become the Prime Minister's Foreign Office Private Secretary On a personal level this was a thrill. It meant connecting with the sub-continent, where several generations of my family had served – as soldiers, sailors or policemen – during the Raj. I had never myself been there. My only sadness was that my father had died a few months previously, and I was not able to talk it over with him.

I made plans for the customary familiarisation tour around my new parish, starting with Pakistan and India. In Islamabad I found that the Permanent Under-Secretary-designate (i.e. Head) of the Foreign Office, Sir Antony Acland, was also undertaking a familiarisation tour of the region, prior to taking up his new position. We decided to travel together for some of the way, beginning with a drive with our ambassador, Oliver Forster (soon to be Sir Oliver), up the Khyber Pass to the Afghan border.

On the way there was an amusing exchange between Acland and the high-level Pakistani official accompanying us, who was asking precisely what Acland's new functions would be. Sir Antony began explaining the role of the Permanent Under-Secretary, only to be interrupted by the Pakistani, who turned out to be a fan of the 'Yes, Minister' series. 'Ah, he said, you will be Sir Humphrey!'

On the way back down the pass from Landi Kotal we stopped at a lay-by on the road, to watch the famous weekly train from Peshawar winding its way slowly up the valley below, belching black smoke. Somewhat to our surprise, there was a group of British tourists doing the same thing, who explained in answer to our enquiry that they were a train-spotting club from Scunthorpe!

The next stage of our joint familiarisation tour was to cross the demarcation line between Pakistan and India at Wagah near Lahore. This is the point where splendidly uniformed soldiers from each side compete in performing a ritualised Beating Retreat ceremony each evening, with plenty of choreographed mock aggression, cheered on by their respective compatriots. After crossing, we were met by a car from the High Commission in Delhi, sent to drive us down the celebrated Grand Trunk Road to Delhi.

But first we visited Amritsar, the city whose name is tragically linked with one of the most notorious events of the Raj – the massacre of a large number of innocent civilians in 1919 at the Jallianwalah Bagh by Indian army troops commanded by Brigadier Reginald Dyer. Dyer had ordered his troops to open fire without warning on a sizeable crowd assembled for a religious festival in possible violation of martial law regulations but contrary to all military practice to warn civilians or fire in the air. The actions of 'The Butcher of Amritsar' were widely condemned in Britain as well as India. The official death toll was 397, but Indian estimates at the time were much higher.

Another massacre took place in the city in 1984, two years after our visit. In Operation Blue Star, Prime Minister Indira Gandhi ordered troops to attack the Golden Temple, which had been occupied by Sikh militants. On that occasion 493 civilians were killed in a controversial operation, which led to Mrs Gandhi's own assassination only four months later by two of her Sikh bodyguards, enraged at the assault on their holiest shrine.

As for us, we took off our shoes and socks and were shown round the glorious Golden Temple, built at the end of the sixteenth century, and set in the middle of a man-made pool. It was a memorable experience, not only because of the beauty of the building, or gurdwara, but because of its sense of peace and spirituality. There are entrances from all four directions, symbolising, we were told, its openness to people of all walks of life, and all quarters. All are made welcome.

Another, less tranquil, experience was the drive down the Grand Trunk Road to Delhi. Each moment produced a fresh game of 'chicken' as we hurtled along the crown of the road towards the oncoming traffic and held our breath to see which vehicle would veer off to the side at the last second. We reached Delhi in time to attend the spectacular Republic Day parade, when contingents from each of the armed services, and colourful floats from all the different Indian states, wend their way in a seemingly never-ending procession, from the presidential palace to the India Arch.

The India in which I had arrived, for the first time, was of course very different from the India my parents had left shortly after Independence. The feeling of ordinary people towards the former imperial power was normally friendly, with even an occasional touch of nostalgia for the old days.

But at the political level Indo-British relations (as I had found with Anglo-French relations) were difficult and complex, overlaid by centuries of shared experiences, some positive, but which also included bitter differences, misunderstandings and military conflicts. Some events were viewed through opposite ends of a telescope. What for the British, for example, was the Indian Mutiny in the mid-nineteenth century, was known to the Indians as their First War of Independence. The statues of the British monarchs and administrators of the Raj era had been relocated to a dedicated space in Delhi, Coronation Park, where they had been left in peace.

A major effort was made during my time in South Asian Department to use the spectacular Festival of India, being held in Britain, in order to reset the relationship. It was a cultural feast, including performances by artists such as Ravi Shankar, and a fascinating lecture on the iconography of the Ashoka Chakra, the wheel at the centre of the Indian flag, given by Madam Nan Pandit, Mrs Gandhi's aunt and a highly respected former High Commissioner in London.

Prime Minister Indira Gandhi herself flew to London to inaugurate the Festival. Her visit provided the occasion for a keenly awaited meeting with Margaret Thatcher. The media were agog to learn how the two formidable ladies would get on. Although the relationship was not particularly warm, they developed a healthy respect for each other.

There was an ever-present touchiness on the India side over some perceived condescension by the British. This could be over almost anything, which made it hard to predict. A regular feature at the time was Indian resentment that, as they saw it, we were not doing enough to control the harmful activities of Sikh activists in Britain. The subject of Kashmir was another issue of particular sensitivity, to be avoided above all else – as a later British Foreign Secretary, Robin Cook, found to his cost during a state visit by the Queen in the 1990s.

British influence – or soft power, as it has come to be called – was most effectively promoted by the large British Council centres located in all the main cities, and the BBC World Service, which had a huge audience throughout the subcontinent.

The main focus of the Department's interest in South Asia during my time was the Russian invasion of Afghanistan. Although 'invasion' was a convenient shorthand term, it was not really the right word since the Soviet Union had been invited to intervene militarily by the then (communist) president, Nur Mohammed Taraki, in order to prop up his government against attacks by the Mujahideen rebels. There had then been a rapid turnover of communist leaders and one Babrak Karmal had emerged on top. The United States had opposed the Soviet intervention from the beginning, and had given covert support to the Mujahideen, as had Britain, Pakistan and Saudi Arabia.

Britain had been the first country to identify and support Ahmad Shah Massoud, a tribal leader in the Panjshir Valley (stretching north east from Kabul towards China), who became by far the most effective guerrilla commander in attacking the Russians. He then became the military commander of the forces of the government which uneasily governed the country after the Soviet retreat, but resumed his opposition, from his base in the Panjshir, once the Taliban took over. He was assassinated in an Al Qaeda/Taliban suicide attack on 7 September 2001. Two days later, as it happened, Al Qaeda attacked the Twin Towers in New York.

In order to get a proper understanding of what was going on I made several visits, with a member of the High Commission in Islamabad, to the Mujahideen leaders, who were based in Peshawar, the nearest Pakistani city to the Afghan border. I found them generally to be not very communicative, but always wanting more resources.

On one of these visits I drove via Abbottabad, which had been the HQ, prior to Independence, of my father's regiment, the 5th Royal Gurkha Rifles, and other regiments which comprised the Punjab Frontier Force (known as Piffer). My brother Clive had been born there. Accompanied by Nicholas Adams from the embassy, I visited the Piffer memorial in the town, to take a photograph. I found that there had been a name change over the years and Piffer now stood for the Pakistan Frontier Force – and, unfortunately, it was strictly forbidden to take photographs. We were warned off. Abbottabad later achieved global notoriety as the secret refuge of Osama bin Laden, the leader

24. A gathering of Afghan refugees in Peshawar, Pakistan's North West Frontier Province, while Afghanistan was under Soviet control. Thousands streamed across the border, with many young men eventually returning as part of the Mujahideen resistance to the Soviet presence. (Photo: author)

of Al Qaeda, when he was killed in the successful raid by helicopter-borne US Navy Seals. Since Abbottabad is a cantonment town, it is, frankly, hard to believe that the Pakistani military were unaware of the cuckoo in their nest.

On a later visit to Peshawar I accompanied Lady (Janet) Young, a minister of state at the FCO, on her familiarisation tour of the sub-continent. This included our being received by the president, General Zia-ul-Haq, in his office in Rawalpindi. An urbane, if somewhat chilly figure, he later died in a helicopter crash, in mysterious circumstances.

We also visited a British aid project in Nepal: the construction of an important mountain road between Dharan and Dankuta in the east of the country. Enormous care had been taken to prevent it being carried away by landslides in the rainy season – as tended to happen. Chinese-built roads had been washed away with some regularity. There was a lively reputational competition between aid donor nations in Nepal as to whose road would last best!

Lady Young's tour ended in dramatic fashion. Her party consisted of her private secretary, me (as head of the department) and her husband, Geoffrey. We arrived back in Delhi at the end of the tour, having travelled round the sub-continent on local airlines, which were sometimes rather basic. It was a relief to board British Airways' up-to-the-minute Lockheed 1011 Tristar aircraft for the long flight back to London.

At the time British Airways were running a commercial on TV in which a frazzled couple made their way through a crowded departure lounge populated by scary monsters to finally arrive on board, where they sank back with relief into their seats, to be cossetted by solicitous BA staff. That was the image. The reality was that half an hour into the flight, when the plane had reached its cruising height and breakfast was about to be served, there was a sudden bang and the cabin filled with a choking white smoke.

This was the moment when the emergency procedures I had taken too little notice of over the years suddenly became reality. An urgent pre-recorded announcement crisply ordered passengers to return to their seats and attach the oxygen masks that had been lowered, without delay. To my mounting alarm, the mask above my seat failed to drop. I had to move around to find a spare one dangling over a vacant seat, which I managed to do. The plane then went into a steep dive. The pressure on the ears was intense.

After what seemed like an eternity the plane levelled out. The panic within the cabin began to subside. Only then did the captain come on the intercom, explaining, in the deep and reassuring tones that must be a qualification for the job, that we had suffered a loss of pressurisation at our cruising height, which had necessitated the precipitous dive to a height of 9,000 feet, where it was no longer required. We would be returning to Delhi, he told us, jettisoning fuel along the way (which cannot have been welcome to the inhabitants of Rajasthan below!).

We all breathed an immense sigh of relief. Lady Young was travelling in the First-Class cabin with her private secretary, I was in Club Class and Lady Young's husband Dr Geoffrey Young (who was paying his own way) was in Economy. Since there was room in the First-Class cabin, we were invited to join Lady Young for a reviving glass of champagne. Before long, we landed back in Delhi, shaken but unharmed, with full emergency procedures at the airport and speeding fire engines escorting our plane along the runway.

A message of our return had gone ahead to Delhi and the Rolls-Royce of Sir Robert Wade-Gery, the High Commissioner, was there to meet us and take us back to his residence. But seemingly no-one had told Sir Robert of the cause, and his reception of us was on the cool side – it was a Sunday and his plans for the day had been disrupted. Only after the Youngs had gone up to rest, and I was finally able to enjoy a much-delayed breakfast on the veranda, was I able to explain how relieved we felt to be still alive. After that we spent a pleasant and relaxing afternoon watching a polo match before catching a replacement flight home in the evening.

It transpired that the cause of the near disaster had been a faulty valve in the aircraft door, and that other Lockheed Tristars had encountered the same problem, which could have been fatal.

Although Afghanistan was under Soviet control, Britain continued to do business, at a basic level, with the Afghan government and kept open its mission in Kabul for the purpose, without formally recognising that government – an important distinction. This led to an awkward moment at the conclusion of an adjournment debate in the House of Lords on Britain's policy on Afghanistan. After Lady Young had wound up the debate and the vote had been called, the peer who had asked the final question stood up again and said that he had omitted to ask the minister whether Britain recognised the Afghan government. To my consternation, sitting in the officials' box, Lady Young replied 'yes', and sat down.

Her reply could have caused big embarrassment all round if it had been allowed to stand. It was therefore my task to try to persuade the rigorously correct staff of Hansard, the parliamentary record, that, on this occasion they may not have heard what the minister had said in its entirety. What she had said, I argued to the sceptical shorthand writers, was 'Yes, we continue to do business with the Afghan government'. Happily, they were prepared to accept this.

I looked forward eagerly to my familiarisation visit to the mission in Kabul, one of the posts in the department's area of responsibility. The ambassador's residence was a magnificent and spacious whitewashed building, thanks to Lord Curzon. When he was Foreign Secretary after the Great War he had decreed that, in order to reflect the role of the British empire in the Great Game (of rivalry with Russia for influence in the region), the British Minister in Kabul should be the best-housed diplomat in Asia. And so he was.

I flew into Kabul from Delhi on Air India to stay for two days with John Garner, the Chargé d'Affaires, in that historic residence, guarded by Gurkha soldiers. Calling on officials of the Afghan government was off-limits (because of the recognition aspect), so Garner took me to call instead on friendly diplomatic missions – such as those of the United States, Germany, Italy, France, Pakistan and India – to compare notes on how we saw the situation.

Garner also showed me the sights of the town, including Chicken Street, a long-established market for trade along the Silk Road. There I bought some caviar, the only useful commodity the Russians had brought with them to the country. To my surprise the shopkeeper was happy to accept a cheque drawn on Lloyds Bank of London as payment, explaining that it would be discounted many times before being eventually presented for payment!

As my official visit drew to an end, the weather closed in. For the next few days, there was little to be done. I discovered how the missions I had previously visited actually spent most of their energies – which was to stave off boredom by entertaining each other in a jolly round of rotating parties.

* * *

After I had headed South Asia Department for two years, and enjoyed every moment of them, I was summoned to the Permanent Under-Secretary – my erstwhile travel companion, Sir Antony Acland. He said that the oil company British Petroleum (BP) was looking to have an exchange of personnel at middle management level with Whitehall. The Foreign Office had been invited to put forward a candidate, along with the Home Civil Service, for a policy-related job. Was I interested? I said yes.

The interviewing panel at Britannic House in Moorgate included Robert Horton, a dynamic personality (who was later to become the chairman). It was explained that the job was to head the Policy Review Unit, a small independent think-tank within the company, reporting to the current chairman, Sir Peter Walters. I asked what it actually did. The reply was that it was required to produce 'blue sky thinking', 'thinking the unthinkable' and suchlike.

This sounded fascinating. I was glad to be offered the job shortly afterwards, on temporary secondment from the FCO. When I reported for work on my first day, early in 1983, I found that the vague formulation about the need for blue sky thinking was actually a complete job description. I was faced with a blank page. This was both exciting and daunting. My immediate predecessor had been a top-flight energy economist, John Mitchell. With my generalist background, what could I offer to a company which contained such a wealth of expertise as BP?

Some of that expertise was contained within the Unit (known as POL), which comprised six or eight people from different disciplines, all of them with much to contribute. BP at the time was highly diversified and was formed of eleven different businesses. These ranged from the core businesses of oil and gas production and marketing, and chemicals, to a nutrition business. The big question facing the company was what it should be concentrating on in the coming century, given that, according to some predictions, oil had an uncertain future. There was also an imperative, through diversification, to counter the unpredictable fluctuations in the oil price.

I spent the first few months talking to people throughout the company, trying to understand what it was all about. I visited some of the businesses on the ground, including taking a scary helicopter flight out to the Magnus production platform, the most northerly installation in the North Sea. Oil rigs look impressive edifices when photographed from sea level, but they are less so when approached in a helicopter during a rainstorm.

I also attended the weekly meeting of the managing directors – the only non-managing director (MD) to do so apart from the (senior) note-taker. This was not only a privilege, but it was also highly instructive for me to see how big decisions were taken in a global company.

After this initial learning period I tried, with my team, to draw up a work programme for the MDs' approval. Our first attempt was not a success; we were told that some subjects had been covered before, others were irrelevant and yet others were the pet baby of some particular MD and should be avoided. We tried again. This time we drafted the subjects in such opaque terms that no-one could be quite certain what we were getting at. On that basis we were given the go-ahead.

My own main contribution arose from my perception, following my journey of discovery around BP, that the company bore a marked resemblance to a conglomerate. This was not only a controversial idea within the company, it was heresy. Conglomerates were deemed to be unserious. Furthermore, at the time of the diversification splurge, the deputy chairman had decreed that BP was not a conglomerate but a group. I therefore proposed to the MDs that my unit should do a study of conglomerates, find out how they operated, how their performance compared with that of the market and whether there were any lessons for BP. The reaction was sceptical on whether this would prove useful. But the chairman was interested, and I was sent forth with letters of introduction to talk to some conglomerates.

The most helpful of these letters was to Hanson Trust, one of the leading conglomerates of the day. They explained, with great frankness, how they went about their business. Put simply, they lived by making ever larger acquisitions of under-performing companies and turning them round. They steered clear of high-tech companies, which tended to be unduly complicated and high risk, and restricted their acquisitions to mid-tech. They then cleared out the top management level and promoted the second level, who were given tight financial targets which had to be met on pain of the sack. This style of management was light years away from that of BP, which offered a career structure more akin to that of the civil service.

In due course I made a presentation to the MDs. The crux of it was that, out of the eleven businesses in which the company was engaged, five of them were so different in character from its core oil and gas business that they should be managed quite differently – or spun off. My proposal was that they should be ring-fenced in a new entity, to be known, possibly, as 'BP Enterprises', with a different management structure and different incentives.

This was politely received by the great men and then consigned, as far as I could make out, to the bottom drawer of the desk! But the corollary is that, about two years after I had left BP and returned to the Foreign Office, I opened the paper to read that the businesses I had marked for the outer circle were being disposed of. Perhaps the amateur businessman had had some effect after all!

Shortly after this presentation, the Foreign Office called me back to the colours. At this point, my secondment to BP had given me such a rare experience of how a major British company operated that I probably knew as much about the workings of big business as anyone in Whitehall. The Office rose to the challenge and informed me that my next posting was to be a job where all this was totally irrelevant! I was to become, on promotion to the senior grade, Minister and Deputy Commandant in the British Military Government in Berlin – a purely political role, at the front line of the Cold War. Once again, we started packing.

Chapter 9

City in a Time Warp:
Berlin under the Allies

I arrived in Berlin, for the first time, on a freezing November night in 1984. I asked to be taken straight to see the Berlin Wall, at the Brandenburg Gate in the city centre. There, I climbed a viewing stand (named after Margaret Thatcher, for whose benefit it had been built) and peered through the fog over the Wall. On the other side was an East German guard tower, where I could just make out a border guard examining me through his binoculars. I stared back. Welcome to the Cold War was my unmistakable feeling. I was destined to be the last Minister in the British Military Government in Berlin

The offices of the (anachronistically named) British Military Government, Berlin (BMG) – my diplomatic mission – were co-located with the military Headquarters, Berlin (British Sector) in a Nazi-era building adjourning the Olympic Stadium which had been built for the 1936 Berlin Olympics. The arrangement enabled the military and diplomatic staffs of the Commandant and Minister (also Deputy

Photo: a rainy day at the Brandenburg Gate. The monument symbolised both the division and reunification of Germany.

Commandant), respectively, to operate as one team. In the past this had led to occasional frictions, but I found that it worked well, not least because, for most of my time, my opposite number, the Commandant, was Major General Patrick Brooking – a tall and genial officer who, as it happened, had been a contemporary at my prep school in Surrey.

Allied Berlin, I discovered, existed in a kind of strange time-warp. In a nutshell, it was still under occupation by the four wartime Allies – Britain, the US, France and the Soviet Union – who had taken over the devastated city after the defeat of Nazi Germany and at the end of the war. The military nature of the occupation – which had evolved over the years, as regards the Western Allies, into a relationship of partnership and cooperation with the Berliners, the West German government and the city authorities – explained the existence of a British Military Government headed by a Commandant. The system was replicated in the American and French sectors. The reason for not changing it to reflect the modern relationship was that it provided an unassailable legal basis for the Western Allies to remain, albeit in a greatly changed role, having originally arrived as wartime victors.

Already, at the end of 1984, what would become Mikhail Gorbachev's policy of economic reform had been enunciated, which together with his later policy of Glasnost (opening up the Soviet Union), would hold out the promise of change, not only in the Soviet Union itself, but also in its satellites in Central and Eastern Europe – even if, at that point, nothing much had actually altered. Margaret Thatcher, during Gorbachev's visit to the UK in 1985 before he became General Secretary of the Soviet Communist Party, would memorably say that Gorbachev was someone she felt she could do business with. The Cold War tectonic plates were shifting.

Whereas, as explained, West Berlin continued to be legally controlled by the three wartime Western Allies, East Berlin, beyond the Wall, had a more complicated status. This was the Soviet Sector of the city, but, at the same time, the capital – unacknowledged by the West – of East Germany, aka the German Democratic Republic (GDR).

How had all this come about? With the unconditional surrender of Germany on 8 May 1945, the four victorious powers assumed the supreme authority in Germany. They had conquered the country jointly and therefore all had the same rights. In the London Protocol of 1944 and other agreements, they had regulated in advance where and how they would exercise their authority. They agreed to form four separate zones of occupation. Berlin was to be within the Soviet Zone, but would, importantly, not be part of that zone. Instead, Berlin as a fifth (special) area was to be jointly occupied and administered by all Four Powers on the basis of equal rights. In spite of its being within the Soviet Zone, and surrounded by Soviet forces, the Soviet Union had no more rights in the city than the other three powers.

Although divided into four sectors, Greater Berlin was legally a single area of occupation. For the administration of this area the Allies had created a joint authority, the Allied Kommandatura (AK). At first the Four Power status and the Four Power administration went hand in hand.

But serious tensions arose when the Western powers – initially just the UK and US, but joined later by France – decided in June 1948 to introduce a new currency, the Deutschmark, into their zones of occupation in order to stimulate a revival of the devastated German economy. When the Western Allies started to introduce the D-mark into their sectors of Berlin as well, to counter Soviet moves to introduce their rival currency, the East-mark, into Greater Berlin, the Soviet Union, which was focused more on exacting reparations from its recent foe than on economic regeneration, was outraged. It was appalled at the prising open of its grip over the Western Allies' sectors of Berlin. As a consequence it withdrew its representative from the Kommandatura in June 1948. Thereafter the AK's jurisdiction was limited, in practice if not in theory, to the Western sectors.

The Soviet Union did not stop there. It blocked the Western Allies from access to the city by road and water. This blockade meant that no traffic was able to reach the city along the three land corridors through which it was supplied with food, medicines and fuel. A major East–West crisis followed.

In the Western part of the city the lights went out – literally. Hospitals were especially hard hit. Numerous factories had to shut down. There were enough food reserves to last thirty-six days, enough coal for forty-five days. A disaster seemed imminent. The American Military Governor, General Lucius D Clay, characterised the situation in the following words: 'It was one of the most brutal attempts in recent history to use mass starvation as a means of applying political pressure.'

Fortunately, although the land routes were blocked, there remained the possibility of air access. The reason was that, although the isolated position of Berlin made the access routes to the West by land indispensable lifelines for the Western Allies, the victorious powers had omitted to put down anything about them in writing in the Four Power agreements at the end of the war.

By contrast, the Four Powers had reached binding agreements in 1945 on the three air corridors leading to Hamburg, Hanover and Frankfurt-am-Main, providing for unimpeded communications. The Western response to the crisis, therefore, was to mount the famous Berlin Airlift. This was initially a British idea, promoted by the Foreign Secretary, Ernest Bevin. The Americans then shouldered the bulk of the operation with the first flight taking place on 24 June 1948, but the RAF was responsible for nearly a quarter of the supplies flown into the city, at RAF Gatow, the airfield in the British sector. They also flew Short Sunderland seaplanes, which, being resistant to corrosion, were particularly suited to carrying salt, onto the adjacent Havel river.

Nevertheless, it was unclear at the start whether it was technically feasible to satisfy the needs of a city of over 2 million inhabitants by such means. At best the planes would be unable to supply all needs. And how would the West Berliners react? Would they buy what they needed in the Eastern (Russian) Sector and thus demonstrate that they could not rely on Western aid?

At this critical moment it became apparent that, on the contrary, the West Berliners much preferred to bear great hardships than to come under Soviet influence. The charismatic mayor, Ernst Reuter – who famously called upon 'the people of the world to look upon West Berlin' in its troubles – answered Clay's question about the will of the people to hold out, 'General, there can be absolutely no question about where the Berliners stand. The Berliners will stand up for their freedom and gladly accept any aid offered them.' In fact, only a small minority of, at the most, 100,000 people did respond to offers of food from the East. The reaction of the vast majority was an unparalleled manifestation of their political willpower.

The Airlift lasted for nearly a year from June 1948 to May 1949, during which, once it was operating fully, even greater quantities of vital supplies reached the city's inhabitants – in addition to the Allied garrisons – than had arrived by land before the blockade was imposed. It was the success of the Airlift that convinced Stalin, the Soviet leader, that, since the blockade had failed to starve the city into submission, or induce the Allies to withdraw from it, there was no point in continuing it. The blockade was lifted, and on 12 May 1949 the first (British) convoy entered the city, to rapturous acclaim.

The success of the Airlift also changed the relationship between the Western Allies and the Berliners. The Allies' action during the blockade in providing not only for the needs of their garrisons but also for those of the civilian population transformed them, in the eyes of the Berliners, from an occupying force into partners in preserving their freedom. One of the abiding images of the blockade, for example, was of Lt Halvorsen of the US Air Force dropping bags of sweets out of his aircraft to the Berlin children below as he made his approach to Tempelhof airfield – earning him the nickname of the Candy Bomber.

An important event in our calendar was the annual commemoration of Allied losses in the Airlift in a moving ceremony, with the laying of wreaths, at the Airlift Memorial in the square in front of Tempelhof Airport. The memorial was in the form of a segment of a bridge, pointing to the west (the German term for the Airlift is Air Bridge). The corresponding, east-facing, segment of the bridge is at Frankfurt Airport.

The Allies' difficulties in Berlin were by no means over with the lifting of the blockade. Enraged by the steady haemorrhaging of people from the east to the west of the city (and on to West Germany), Stalin's successor, Nikita Khrushchev, issued an ultimatum to the Western Allies in November 1959. He demanded that they 'relinquish the remains of the occupation regime in Berlin, thus facilitating the normalisation of the situation in the capital of the GDR'. He gave them six months to enter into negotiations on leaving, after which it was clear that he intended to absorb the whole city into East Germany (the GDR).

The Allies stood firm, and the deadline passed with protracted negotiations, which took place in Geneva. Meanwhile the flow of refugees to the West became a flood. In July 1961 alone 30,000 refugees arrived in the West.

This was the background to the erection of the Wall in 1961. In the early morning hours of 13 August 1961, units of the GDR's People's Police tore up the pavement at street crossings to the West. They rammed in concrete posts, laid out barbed wire entanglements and dug trenches. At the same time the GDR authorities interrupted the subway and inner-city train lines running across the border. Not until a few days later did they start building the concrete and brick Wall itself. Construction gangs blocked the zonal border to West Berlin. The Wall, or in some places a secure fence, ran all around West Berlin. The purpose was not to keep the West Berliners from getting out, but to prevent the East Berliners from getting in.

In due course the barrier was strengthened by the addition of watchtowers with searchlights, raked sand with mines, tank barriers and dog patrols, as depicted in numerous atmospheric films. By the time of our arrival in the city some of the worst features had been removed, but the Wall still represented a formidable obstacle which had cost many lives, and stood as the symbol of the Cold War division of Europe.

25. A GDR watchtower, photographed as my first encounter with the reality of divided Berlin. (Photo: author)

*   *   *

This was the enclosed city in which I landed on that cold November night in 1984. It was a city, paradoxically, under the protection of its erstwhile Allied occupiers. Allied Berlin was the latest of the many layers which made up the story of this troubled capital, which had known so much history over the past two centuries, and which could be traced through its buildings, many reconstructed since the war. From the eighteenth-century elegance of Charlottenburg Palace, and Frederick the Great's summer retreat of Sans Souci in neighbouring Potsdam, via the pomp of the nineteenth-century imperial buildings that had survived the war – the most egregious being, in the West, the Kaiser Wilhelm Memorial Church, with its partly ruined spire standing like a filled tooth as a testament to the war's devastation – to such reminders of Nazi brutality as the torture cellars of Gestapo headquarters.

The political and security situation of Berlin had stabilised since the time of Khrushchev's threats through a landmark agreement negotiated in 1971. This was the Quadripartite Agreement (QA) between Britain, the USA and France, and the Soviet Union. The impulse for this on the Western side came from the desire of the West German Chancellor, Willy Brandt, to pursue a policy of improved relations (known as détente) between East and West, together with the Allies' interest in taking the heat out of the Berlin situation. The Soviet Union, for its part, aimed to gain Western recognition of its satellite, the GDR, and secure agreement to the holding of a European Security Conference as a framework for the promotion of its interests.

The negotiation was a hard-fought, and rather weird, affair. It was all about Berlin, but the city was not actually named in it. Instead there were references to 'the territory'. The outcome was that the Allies recognised the GDR. But, crucially, they did not recognise East Berlin as its capital (*Hauptstadt*) since, to do so, would have undermined the basic principle that the whole city remained under Four Power occupation. Nor did they accept the Soviet contention that it had handed over its responsibility for East Berlin to the GDR. In practice this meant that when the Allies wished to raise an issue concerning East Berlin they addressed themselves to the Soviet embassy in East Berlin, rather than to the GDR authorities. This convoluted procedure took some getting used to.

The essential point about the QA was that it brought stability to the previously febrile Berlin situation, which it was in the interest of neither side to disturb.

Such were the mysteries of Berlin's 'status', which, it should be said, were generally imperfectly understood, by the Germans on both sides, and even by many among the Allies themselves. One of the few who did, among West Berlin journalists, was Joachim Bölke, writing in Berlin's leading newspaper, *Der Tagesspiegel*. His articles helped to keep everyone up to the mark.

On the Allied side, the QA entrenched the position that West Berlin was not part of the Federal Republic and not governed by it. In practice, its system of government differed little from that in any other West German *Land*: it had its own Mayor, its own *Senat* (city government) and its own elected House of Representatives.

There were, however, essential differences: laws passed by the Bundestag in Bonn were only adopted in West Berlin once they had been screened, both in Bonn and Berlin, to ensure that they did not impact on, or detract from, the Allies' rights and responsibilities, in order not to compromise the city's security and the access to it. Another example was that the city remained a demilitarised area, free from the presence of the West German Bundeswehr (the Armed Forces of Germany), and in which West German conscription laws did not apply – which led, in practice, to it having a flourishing 'alternative' youth population, who were avoiding the draft. And, not least important, the West Berlin police came under the control, not of the Mayor, but of the AK.

My first attendance at the AK, as the newly arrived Minister in the British Sector, showed me Allied authority in action. The AK building was the imposing former headquarters of an insurance company. Each of the three Allied countries was represented by its Commandant (a two-star general) and his chief of staff. He was supported by the Deputy Commandant or Minister (a diplomat of equal rank). Administrative support was provided by the Allied Staff Berlin, a tripartite body formed from representatives of all three Allies, and interpreters. Each of the Allies took the chair in turn, following a fixed three-monthly rotation. The picture of the last Soviet Commandant, who had walked out of the AK in a protest in 1948, never to be replaced, looked down from the wall.

The formal proceedings of the AK normally dealt with routine business. On that, my first occasion, there was discussion of whether the

26. Soldiers of the four Allied Powers with their national flags, before the Soviet Union left the Allied Kommandatura in 1948. (Photo: author)

Allies should change the format of the Allied Forces Day parade – an annual event that highlighted their continued commitment to the city's security. Since it featured a number of tanks there was some inevitable damage to the road, not to mention traffic jams in that area of the city. Impassioned opposition to any change to the format was voiced by my colleague, the outgoing British Commandant, a charming but rather fierce Grenadier Guards officer, Major General Bernard Gordon Lennox, and it was decided to leave matters as they were.

An altogether more demanding test for the AK came with the bombing of a West Berlin discotheque, called La Belle, on 5 April 1986. It was a favourite resort of US service men and women in the city and there were a number of casualties. The AK met to decide what should be done. The golden rule was that the Allies should agree on joint action by consensus and none of them should act independently.

Unfortunately, in this case not all the three Allies were in possession of the same intelligence. It took a full week of deliberating, and consultation between capitals, before it was finally agreed that the perpetrators were members of the Libyan diplomatic mission in East Berlin. There was not a great deal that could be done with them. But we decreed that if they entered West Berlin they would be expelled into the GDR.

The incident had far-reaching consequences. On the basis of the Allies' determination of Libyan guilt for the La Belle disco atrocity, President Reagan ordered an airstrike on the Libyan capital, Tripoli. One of the alleged victims was Hana, a daughter of the Libyan dictator Muammar al Qaddafi. Libyan retaliation subsequently took the form of the appalling bombing in December 1988 of a Pan Am plane over the Scottish town of Lockerbie, with the loss of 259 lives.

* * *

Life in Allied Berlin normally followed an altogether calmer routine. The three Allied garrisons – with the US numbering about 11,000 troops, the UK 6,500 and France 4,500 – each mounted an impressive parade on its National Day. The UK held a Queen's Birthday Parade in June, at which a member of the Royal Family almost invariably took the salute. The three regiments of the garrison would be on parade, augmented by the resident tank squadron – against the backdrop of the Olympic Stadium, which had been the scene of Hitler's 1936 Berlin Olympics (and, after German reunification, would fulfil the same role for the FIFA World Cup Final of 2006).

Each of the Allies also had a less formal way of putting on a show for the Berliners. The Americans, one year, had a fun-fair themed on the Far West. The corresponding French event, as one would expect, gave prominence to food and wine. Our contribution, every other year, was an impressive British Berlin Tattoo in the Deutschland-Halle, Berlin's equivalent of Earl's Court. This was modelled on London's Royal Tournament and was a massive exercise in organisation and military showmanship. One year it took Scotland as its theme. I attended most performances over its two-week run. The result was that, at the end, I could barely sleep for the bagpipes playing in my ears.

It should not be thought that the garrison were chocolate soldiers who neglected their military duties. Its role, in the event of Warsaw

Pact troops coming over the Wall, would have been to act as a trip-wire until NATO forces could come to the rescue, like the US cavalry in Westerns. For this to be, even partly, credible the garrison needed to train. Sometimes, training exercises could lead to friction with the Berliners. The city within the Wall had, of course, limited space for recreation. A Berliner family wandering through the woods did not take kindly, for example, to being suddenly confronted by a Centurion tank. Nor did the Berliners, with their innate German love of trees, fully appreciate that those on the approach flight path into RAF Gatow had to be occasionally lopped for flight safety reasons.

My close association with the garrison – army and RAF – was a real pleasure, coming, as I did, from a military background. Similarly, attending the big show-piece parades of our French and American Allies was a chance to enjoy their different military traditions. The Americans would honour the flags of each of their state and territories, which were raised in turn. The names of the French tanks on parade evoked the victorious battles of the Great War and their commanders who made their names in Europe and Africa in the final stage of the Second World War.

A primary task for the Allies was to prevent any dislocation to the air services to the city. These were managed on a Four Power basis, including Soviet representatives, according to principles which were unchanged from the time they were instituted at the end of the war as part of the agreements on Berlin. They stipulated that the civil aircraft of the three Western Allies were only permitted to use the three corridors originating in their three erstwhile Occupation Zones – in what had since become West Germany. Each Ally had only one permitted carrier – respectively British Airways, Air France and Pan Am. The West German airline Lufthansa, on the other hand, was not allowed to fly into Berlin.

These restrictions all stemmed from the Soviet determination that nothing should change with regard to the Berlin situation, in case the whole ball of string began to unravel. They went further. Since the normal cruising height for a civil airliner in 1945 was 10,000 feet, this continued to be the required flying height for Allied civil flights into Berlin over the succeeding decades – in spite of anguished protests by British Airways bosses, and no doubt others, that the height restriction had become wholly uneconomic with modern aircraft.

The regulations were administered by air-force officers of the Four Powers in the Berlin Air Safety Centre (BASC), which was housed in the Allied Control Commission. This was the building in which Hitler's *Volksgerichtshof* ('People's Court') had pronounced summary judgement on the conspirators after the failed assassination attempt of Hitler in 1944, with Hitler himself enjoying the spectacle of the accused's humiliation through a peep-hole behind the notoriously aggressive judge Roland Freisler's chair. The Allies had governed conquered Germany from the building in the immediate aftermath of the war.

In my day the members of the Allied Kommandatura would also assemble there to receive the credentials of newly appointed ambassadors to West Germany, who were required to be accredited separately (to the Allies) in Berlin, due to its separate status. Before starting the accreditation ceremony, we would wait for a minute or two, without much expectation, in case our Soviet colleagues cared to join us for it – which had not actually happened for forty years.

The scene in the BASC was that each country's representative sat at his own desk. A docket containing the details of each flight preparing to use one of the air corridors to Berlin was passed round from desk to desk to obtain the approval of each country. The Soviets, stuck in their 1945 mindset, maintained that the post-war agreement only covered aircraft flying into Berlin from the 'Occupation Zones' (i.e. West Germany), and not those from further afield – such as London or Paris. So that on the dockets for the frequent flights from these capitals they would stamp 'Safety of flight not guaranteed'. It was just as well that this was not known to the passengers on these flights.

The Berlin air regime, freezing the air services of a major European city in a system created in 1945, was a constant source of irritation to the Allies, and of course to the West Germans. In President Reagan's speech at the Brandenburg Gate in 1987 (which I shall return to in the next chapter) the main concrete proposal he made to President Gorbachev was to hold discussions on removing the burdensome features of the air regime. There was no response from the Soviets at the time. It was only after the first opening of the Wall that they expressed some willingness to talk, but only in the context of much broader talks on slowing the pace of German reunification – which the Western Allies rejected.

Another emotionally encrusted area of Four Power business was the management of the Nazi War Criminals Prison at Spandau, which contained one solitary remaining prisoner, Rudolf Hess. Hess had been Hitler's Deputy and at the very centre of the Nazi regime. In

27. Rudolf Hess, the last remaining Nazi war prisoner in Spandau gaol, taking exercise. Though by now a frail old man, he had lost none of his certitudes about, and loyalties to, the Nazi experience. (Photo: author)

1941 he had flown an aircraft on a secret and unauthorised mission to Scotland, carrying proposals for peace between Britain and Germany, with which he intended to approach the Duke of Hamilton, whom he believed to be both a prominent opponent of the war and at the centre of British political power – wrong on both counts. The British decided that this was an eccentric freelance gesture not to be taken seriously, and he was interned for the remainder of the war, after which he was returned to Germany to stand trial at Nuremberg with the other leading Nazis. The court was not convinced by his claim of amnesia and he received a life sentence.

By the time I served in Berlin all the other Nazi inmates of Spandau had been released at the termination of their sentences, or had been released early due to ill-health. Hess's family were agitating for his release on similar grounds. The Western Allies were amenable due to his advanced age. But the Soviet Union was adamantly opposed in view of Hess's central role in the Nazi system, and out of respect for the 26 million Soviet dead in what they called their 'Great Patriotic War'. The Soviets may also have been mindful of the useful access to the Western Sectors afforded by their involvement at Spandau prison.

Although the Spandau prison was a Four Power responsibility, the UK had a particular role since it lay in the British Sector. For example, whenever Hess needed to be hospitalised he was taken to the British Military Hospital (BMH). It was on one such occasion that the myth arose that the prisoner was not actually Rudolf Hess. This came about because one of the crowd in the examination room (since all Four Powers had to be represented) happened to be a British doctor who observed that there was no scar tissue on the front of Hess's torso where a bullet had entered his body in the Great War. On this slender basis he constructed a case, writing articles, and even a book on the subject, attracting the support of some people who should have known better.

The case collapsed on the point that, as I understood it, although there was no wound mark on Hess's front, there was a mark on his back. Hess had been shot from the front. A bullet passing through the body leaves more scar tissue at the point of exit, in this case the back, than at the point of entry. Furthermore, Hess's family never subscribed to the unlikely conspiracy theory. The clinching point for me, however, was that, if the prisoner was not Hess, why had he not demanded to be let out?

On one or two occasions I accompanied the British Commandant on his routine visit to the prison during a British month in charge. There were strict rules for these occasions, agreed, as with every aspect of the prison protocol, on a Four Power basis. The Commandant asked Hess, as usual (using his prison number rather than his name), whether he had anything to say, and received his customary recital of (minor) grievances in reply. Under the watchful eye of the Soviet prison governor, I was not among those allowed to speak to the prisoner.

Looking at the slight and unimpressive old man in front of me, access to whom was so carefully controlled by four major powers in a huge nineteenth-century military prison, it was hard to believe that he had played a central role in the Nazis' rise to power as Hitler's deputy. The rambling testament he left behind after his suicide made it clear that his fanatical devotion to the Führer never wavered.

Hess's death, in 1988, had to be handled carefully. It appeared that he had finally drawn the conclusion that, although there was a possibility of a more favourably inclined regime in Moscow, represented by Mikhail Gorbachev, there was still no prospect of his being released. With all hope gone, he managed to commit suicide in spite of the close watch kept on him. He obtained a cord, attached one end to the window latch, looped the other end around his neck and dropped the short distance to the ground, killing himself.

The concern was that the nature of Hess's suicide would fuel conspiracy theories, as indeed it did. Fortunately, from the point of view of establishing the facts, he had left a note by way of a last testament. To forestall any accusation of forgery, we had this submitted to an internationally respected handwriting expert in the UK. He compared the note with examples of Hess's writing and concluded that it was compatible. Hess's body was flown to his native Bavaria and handed over to his family. His grave became a shrine for neo-Nazi sympathisers, which gave some support, in my view, to the Soviet case for resisting his early release.

※　　※　　※

Berlin was at the forefront of the Cold War. Not surprisingly, this led to its name being linked, particularly in the novels of Len Deighton and John le Carré, with spying activity. In fact, the Allies' intelligence record in the city was not especially good, given their failure to anticipate the building of the Wall in 1961, in spite of the extensive preparations in East Berlin that had led up to it.

The Allies had, however, enjoyed a notable intelligence success, some years previously, with the Berlin Tunnel. This was a 1953 joint CIA-MI6 project to construct a secret tunnel into East Germany from the American sector, from which a tap could be put on the cable carrying all Soviet military communications from their Berlin headquarters to Moscow. It proved to be very effective, and for about a year a huge amount of sensitive material came into the Allies' hands as a result.

The operation was only terminated following an accidental event. An East German engineer stumbled over a pothole in the road, beneath which the tunnel ran. When this was investigated, the East Germans, to their shocked surprise, came upon the tunnel and started to track back along towards West Berlin. At this point they were decisively blocked by US Military Police, who informed them that they were now entering the US Sector of Berlin and were allowed no further.

It was only later that the story behind the story came to light. This involved my old Arabic studies fellow-student in Lebanon, the spy George Blake. At the time of the tunnel's inception Blake had been serving in the MI6 station in Berlin. He had duly put his Soviet handlers in the picture over the whole plan. Amazingly, the Soviets decided not to interrupt the operation, and to allow some of their

28. A section of the genuine Berlin spy tunnel (rather than the mock-up used in John Schlesinger's film *The Innocent*, based on Ian McEwan's eponymous novel), now on display in the Allied Museum in Berlin. (Photo: author)

military secrets to be spirited away beneath their nose. The reason was to protect the cover of their ace double agent, George Blake. Such was the importance they attached to him.

The novelist Ian McEwan wrote a dramatic fictionalisation of the story of the tunnel in his book *The Innocent*, which was made into a film of the same name in Berlin, after the fall of the Wall, by the distinguished director John Schlesinger. Naturally a tunnel had to be constructed for the set, which we visited during filming. When filming was over the tunnel was transferred to the newly established Museum of the Allies in the former American sector to provide visual illustration of the tunnel story. The final twist is that a few years later, in 2012, a section of the original tunnel came to light, and, once it had been excavated and restored, it replaced the film-set version in the museum, where it is now one of the main attractions.

*   *   *

The glories of the Berlin cultural scene – even divided, as they were, between the two halves of the city – were the great joy of our time there. In the iconic Philharmonie – a state-of-the-art concert hall designed by Hans Scharoun – Herbert von Karajan, though becoming infirm, was still conducting the Berlin Philharmonic Orchestra with magisterial authority. Woe betide any latecomer: the maestro was liable to halt the performance and glare at the miserable culprit until they had taken their seat. His Sunday morning concerts, with Karajan wearing a black rollneck sweater, and drawing magical sounds from the orchestra with the slightest movements of his arthritic left hand, were particularly memorable.

At the German Opera (Deutsche Oper), in the West, highly innovative – or some would say wrong-headed – productions were the speciality of the director, Götz Friedrich. We were privileged to attend performances there by virtually all the great singers of the day. On my first night in Berlin my deputy, Roland Smith, took me to a performance of *Tannhäuser*, which was the start of a lasting devotion to Wagner.

When I noticed, some years later, that the square on the other side of the road from the Deutsche Oper, mysteriously, had no name, the thought occurred to me that it would be most appropriate to give it the name of William Shakespeare. Many streets in the British Sector bore the names of British literary giants (such as Dickensweg) but, for some reason, the Bard had been ignored. An opportunity arose when the Lord Mayor of London, who was due to visit Berlin, asked whether there was any particular present he could give the city to mark the occasion.

In a two-pronged operation, I called on the Lord Mayor at Mansion House and suggested to him that the best present would be a specially commissioned bust of Shakespeare, to which he agreed. When I told the Mayor of Berlin of the idea he was delighted and said he would arrange for the bust to stand in the square, which would be named after Shakespeare.

All went according to plan, and I was feeling rather pleased with myself, until the day after the ceremony of the Lord Mayor presenting the bust – in the square. Overnight it had been daubed with paint. It only then emerged that there was a reason why the square was nameless. In 1967 it had been the scene of the student riots against the state visit of the Shah of Iran (who was attending a performance at the Opera), in the course of which one student, Benno Ohnesorg, had been killed. This had been the spark which had lit the fuse of student protests in Germany. These had then spread across Europe and, in Paris, for example, had sounded the death-knell for General de Gaulle's presidency. Having had such momentous consequences, there was a strong view, on the left, in Berlin that if the square were to have a name, it should be that of Benno Ohnesorg.

The Berlin police cleaned up the bust. Next night the same thing happened, and so it went on for some time. But eventually the daubers tired of the game, and the Bard was left in peace, presiding, as he still does, over Shakespeareplatz. Benno Ohnesorg also has a monument, in the courtyard of the Opera, and a commemorative plaque.

All this cultural richness could not entirely make up for the fact that by the end of 1988, after being in Berlin for four years, I was finding the work somewhat monotonous. We lived a very comfortable life in a large villa on the edge of the Grunewald forest. We also had many friends. But as each year passed, following the unchanging rhythms of the Allied calendar, I felt in need of more professional challenges.

At the turn of the year, I was not to know that 1989 would more than meet that need.

Chapter 10

The Fall of the Berlin Wall: The Drive to Reunification

At the start of 1989, no-one in West Berlin, or elsewhere, had any inkling of the momentous events which would take place in the city before the year's end.

Two years previously President Reagan had made a significant speech at the Brandenburg Gate, in the course of which he had called on the Soviet leader: 'Mr Gorbachev, tear down this Wall'. The Mayor, Eberhard Diepgen, had appealed to the three Allied heads of state to visit Berlin in that year, which was the 750th anniversary of its foundation. The invitation had come at an opportune time for Reagan, providing a chance to divert attention away from the scandal of the Iran-Contra Affair – the covert sale of arms to Iran, in order to pay for arms to support the Contra rebels in Nicaragua.

Speaking from a stand directly in front of the Brandenburg Gate, the president also called on Gorbachev to 'open up this Gate', and to engage in talks with the Allies to update the obsolete Berlin Air Regime

29. Speaking in front of the Wall and the Brandenburg Gate, President Reagan calls on the Soviet leader to – in his famous words – 'Mr Gorbachev, tear down this Wall'. Some of the lettering of the bogus 'Welcome Reagan' graffiti can be seen on the Wall behind him. (Photo: © Alamy)

(which limited flights into West Berlin to three corridors from within West Germany). The speech was coolly received at the time on the German side. It was considered a flourish of rather embarrassing and provocative rhetoric, which was not helpful to the German policy of reducing friction with the GDR in order to make exchanges with it more productive, in the interest of its citizens.

For the same reason, the broader 'German Question', including the possibility of reunification of the two German states, was receiving little attention, apart from the occasional discussion in a restricted group at the Aspen Institute in Berlin, some of which I attended as an observer, along with the other Allied ministers. This was an American institution, and the meetings, which sometimes included such prominent figures as former Berlin Mayor Willy Brandt and former Chancellor Gerhard Schröder, were chaired by its distinguished American director, Shepard Stone. Discussions on German reunification were invariably interesting but inconclusive.

The Queen had also visited Berlin in 1987, in response to the Mayor's invitation, in order to underline British solidarity with the city. Her speech, delivered to a smaller audience than that of President Reagan, was no less prescient. 'The hope of all of us', she said, 'must be that the cruel division of this city will be overcome in the spirit of its long tradition of tolerance. May the same Berlin, which is now the symbol of the division of Europe, become on that day the symbol of its unity.'

*   *   *

Early in 1989, that day seemed far off. Our thoughts were less on the prospect of the Wall opening than on the day-to-day business of the city's security. On 5 February we were confronted by the sad reality of what turned out to be the last shooting of a young man attempting to escape from East Berlin. Chris Geoffrey, a 20-year-old barman, and his friend Christian Gaudian, were under the illusion that the regime's notorious 'Shoot to Kill' policy for dealing with escapes had been rescinded.

They succeeded in climbing over the first two fences of the border, but the second one triggered the alarm. The area was flooded with light and, as they attempted to surmount the third and final fence, two border guards fired at them. Geoffrey was hit by ten bullets and died instantly; he was the 238th and last person to be shot attempting to escape through the Wall. His friend Gaudian was hit in the leg and arrested. For once the East Germans were unable to hush up the murder, and there was an international outcry. A cross commemorating Geoffrey is one of those affixed to a wall of remembrance standing near the Reichstag building.

The following month another escape attempt, by Winfried Freudenberg, ended in tragedy. He flew a balloon over the Wall into the West Berlin district of Zehlendorf, but the balloon crashed on landing and he was killed.

A further escape attempt in the summer across the river Spree, where it flows past the Reichstag building, led to another international incident, involving the Allies, and me personally. Three young East Germans, two men and a woman, noticed that an East German patrol boat moored on the far bank seemed to be neglecting its watch. Taking their chance, they leaped into the river and swam across to the bank by the Reichstag, in the British Sector of Berlin. One of the men and the woman, although she was pregnant, managed to scramble up onto the bank.

But the other young man was still trying to heave himself onto the bank when the crew of the patrol boat woke up to what was happening, rapidly crossed the river and seized the luckless escapee, whose name was Martin Notev. Fortunately for him, however, the incident was witnessed by a passing British tourist, who took a photograph.

Armed with this evidence, the Allies made a strong protest to the Soviet government at this seizure of a German national from the Western (in this case British) sectors of Berlin. As explained in the previous chapter, East Berlin matters affecting the Allies were not raised directly with the GDR authorities in order not to compromise the status of Berlin. The Foreign Office Minister William Waldegrave, who was visiting Berlin, took a personal interest, which ensured that the matter was not dropped. He was warned by West Berlin leaders, whom we called on together, that any fuss made by the Allies would condemn Notev to a longer prison sentence. Nevertheless, Allied foreign ministers then took the matter up with Soviet Foreign Minister Edvard Shevardnadze himself – to the fury of the GDR.

While the matter was simmering, it occurred to me that future escape attempts using this route would stand more chance of success if ladders were placed at intervals along that particular stretch of the river, connected by a rope along the bank. The West Berlin authorities saw the force of this argument and put the ladders in place (but not initially the rope). The *Daily Mail* carried a photograph of the ladders, along with the story of the failed escape. All of this compounded the rage of the GDR, who pushed the Soviet embassy in East Berlin into making protests to us in the British Military Government.

At this point I went home for a couple of weeks of summer leave. When I returned, I was greeted with the news that, as a result of the escalating pressure from the GDR, via the Soviet embassy, for the removal of the ladders, the case had been reviewed by Foreign Office lawyers. They had come to the conclusion that, although the riverbank clearly formed part of the British Sector, the legal status of the water itself was more debatable. They therefore recommended that, to be on the safe side, the ladders should be cut off at the water level.

It seemed to me, on my return, that any such action would give the appearance of giving in to pressure from the GDR, and, given the attention the case had already received in the media, we would be left looking distinctly foolish. Making use of a Nelsonian blind eye, we therefore did nothing. Shortly afterwards, this bold policy of inaction was severely tested.

My Soviet opposite number, Igor Maximichev the deputy ambassador in the imposing embassy in East Berlin, came to my office to make a formal protest. There was no sign of the twinkle that was usually in his eye. This was deadly serious. He placed a written document, in Russian, on my desk, which, he said, outlined the strong objections of his government to the Spree ladders. They must be removed. If this did not happen his government could not be held responsible for the consequences.

Inwardly I quaked. Such language, in diplomatic terms, had the tenor of an ultimatum. Concealing my dismay, I looked Maximichev in the eye. I told him that I could not believe what I was hearing: that the representative of a great power should protest at measures which had been taken to provide for the safety of women and children who had fallen into the river Spree and had difficulty in climbing out, was deeply perplexing. Maximichev replied that he had never heard of women and children falling into the river, but he had heard of people attempting to cross the sector boundary illegally. I said this changed nothing.

We looked at each other steadily for what seemed ages. I thought I detected a softening in his gaze, and even a hint of the suppressed twinkle. I therefore concluded that the Soviet protest was pro forma,

30. Toasting the escapee Martin Notev on his release from East German prison, with Alan Charlton from BMG. Notev's failure to climb out of the Spree river, and subsequent apprehension by the GDR border guards, led to my having a serious confrontation with my Soviet number over the ladders we installed on the riverbank to help other escapees. (Photo: author)

in response to sustained GDR pressure, probably at a very senior level, and we could afford to ignore it.

Maximichev formally took his leave, leaving me to report the Soviet demarche and pray to high heaven that I had not misjudged the situation, and started a slide into the Third World War. Fortunately, the dramatic events in Berlin a few months later made the whole business academic. Visitors to Berlin today can spot the ladders as their pleasure-craft pass the Bode Museum at the tip of Museum Island, and the Reichstag building.

As a consequence of this high-level Allied pressure, Martin Notev was released from prison some weeks later and turned up at the Reception Centre in West Berlin. Together with Alan Charlton, the Deputy Political Advisor on my staff, I went down to welcome him, taking along a bottle of *sekt* to drink his health. A happy conclusion.

*   *   *

As the summer of 1989 progressed, the broader picture was that the storm clouds were gathering around the head of Eric Honecker, the GDR leader. In Poland, the military regime headed by General

Jaruzelski, seeing no other way of bringing the long-running strikes in the country to an end, had taken the fateful decision to open so-called Round Table talks with Lech Walesa, leader of the Solidarity trade union. These led to a power-sharing arrangement, which inevitably undermined the authority of the communist government.

Walesa, who was himself taking the risk of alienating his supporters by engaging in the talks, said 'I knew that the communist system was finished. The problem was what would be the best way to get rid of it.'

The major event of the summer was the brutal suppression of the student demonstrations in Beijing's Tiananmen Square on the orders of the aging Deng Ziaoping. The image of a single man standing defiantly in front of a column of advancing tanks went around the world. The massacre that took place provided a grim example of how protests could be dealt with by a regime that was not afraid of the international outcry which followed. That example must have been in the minds of the GDR regime and its opponents as events unfolded.

Hungary played a major part in the implosion of the GDR. At the instigation of Dr Otto von Habsburg, the claimant to the throne of Austria-Hungary (and a member of the European Parliament), a symbolic Pan-European picnic was held at Sopron on the Hungarian border with Austria on 19 August 1989 'to say farewell to the Iron Curtain'. The idea was that delegations from both countries would be present, and the border wire would be left unattended for a few hours to enable a number of East Germans (who had learned what was intended) to escape to freedom in Austria.

The number of refugees who made it was small – fewer than 2,000 – but the event made a huge impact in the GDR and growing numbers of refugees crossed into Hungary in the hope of a repeat. The Hungarians became increasingly concerned about what to do with them. They finally flew to Bonn for a secret meeting with the West Germans to discuss opening the border. As for the Soviets, in answer to the Hungarians' enquiry, Soviet Foreign Minister Shevardnadze informed them that 'this is an affair that concerns only Hungary, the GDR and West Germany'.

Given this Soviet green light, the Hungarian Foreign Minister Gyula Horn – who would later be feted in reunified Berlin for his action – announced on 10 September that all border controls would be lifted from midnight. The West Germans had sent scores of buses to ferry the refugees across Austria into Bavaria. The reaction of the GDR leadership was one of fury.

In the GDR itself there had been the first signs of opposition to the regime, following the election in May, when, for the first time, monitors had been allowed at polling stations. From their observations it was immediately clear that the count had been rigged in favour of the regime. For once, the stolen nature of the election was revealed when the monitors' conclusions were reported on West German TV, which was also received by households in the GDR. There were protests in a number of GDR towns – the most serious, which would eventually have a game-changing impact, being in Leipzig.

Leipzig was the second city in the GDR. The demonstrations there were centred on the famous Nikolaikirche. On Monday evenings groups of people, initially small in number, would gather in the church, and then parade into the square outside, holding lighted candles, to hold a silent vigil (as was recounted to the Queen when she visited Leipzig on her State Visit in 1992). After a break for August, and then the refugee exodus through Hungary, the numbers taking part swelled considerably.

The GDR leadership was blindsided in its response to the opening of Hungary's border with the West by the illness of Erich Honecker. He was suffering from cancer, the illness to which he would eventually succumb in 1994 while in enforced exile in Chile after the collapse of his country. This may have contributed to his botched handling of the next crisis of GDR refugees seeking passage to the West in September – this time via Czechoslovakia on the GDR's southern border.

The Czechs' response to Hungary opening its border to GDR citizens was to close its border with Hungary. This had the effect of leaving those East Germans on holiday in the country trapped, with their only route out being to return to the GDR, which was the last thing they wanted to do. Instead they made their way to the Czech capital, Prague, and besieged the West German embassy in the baroque Lobkovitz Palace below the castle – which now proudly displays photographs showing the large numbers of refugees it had to deal with.

By the third week of September the Czechs were in a quandary over what to do with the 4,000 or so refugees packed into the embassy and camped in its garden. They told Honecker, who was now back at his desk, that he had to find a solution, in conjunction with the West Germans. Honecker, who was handling the problem in person, reluctantly agreed that the 'traitors' should be allowed to go to West Germany. But, in order to humiliate them, he made it a condition that they would have to travel by rail – in sealed trains – through the GDR.

The arrangements for the exodus were made by the West German Foreign Minister, Hans-Dietrich Genscher, who had first to persuade the apprehensive refugees that his personal guarantee would be enough to secure their safety on the transit through the GDR. All went well, and on the train's passage through the GDR it was mobbed at every station by the enthusiastic citizenry, many of whom tried unsuccessfully to clamber onto it.

When, three days before the exodus took place on 2 October, Honecker had explained his plan to his Politburo, who had been kept in the dark, they were horrified. Honecker thought he had pulled off a diplomatic triumph, but his colleagues saw that it was deeply humiliating for the regime to actually make the arrangements for its own citizens to leave – their chagrin was further compounded when the refugees were cheered on by their fellow-citizens, and greeted ecstatically on their arrival in West Germany. It was the final blow to Honecker's waning authority.

*   *   *

Events now moved towards their climax. October was the critical month. On the seventh, a reluctant Gorbachev took centre-stage at the GDR's fortieth birthday party celebration in East Berlin. It was supposed to be Honecker's finest hour but it turned into a disaster for him. He had been opposed to Gorbachev's reform programme, declaring that just because your neighbour changed his wallpaper did not mean that you had to do the same. Gorbachev came to Berlin determined to show what he thought of Honecker, in his turn.

The torchlit parade of the party faithful was a dramatic humiliation for the GDR leadership, who had to keep up an impassive appearance as the marchers shouted 'Gorby save us'. It later emerged that, before leaving Berlin, Gorbachev ordered the Soviet authorities in the city not to oppose any move for Honecker's removal. The previously hardline Soviet ambassador, Kochemasov – whom I had had to listen to on numerous occasions advancing the Moscow line during his regular lunches with our ambassador from Bonn, Sir Christopher Mallaby (and before him Sir Julian Bullard) – had told the commander of the 380,000 Soviet troops in the country to restrict his troops to barracks and not to interfere in the GDR's internal political process.

The Soviet decision was critical for the outcome of the decisive event that took place two days later in Leipzig, on 9 October. The opposition had planned that the regular Monday night demonstration centred on the Nikolaikirche would this time be a mass display of defiance against the government. Their cries of 'WE are the people' amounted to a devastating attack on the leadership of a country claiming to be a People's Republic.

The communist authorities in Leipzig had to take the momentous decision whether to put down the demonstration with force – as had happened in Tienanmen Square – or let it go ahead peacefully. Thanks partly to the intervention of Kurt Masur, the highly respected conductor of the renowned Leipzig Gewandhaus Orchestra, who was pressing for a peaceful solution, and in the absence of any clear direction from the divided political leadership in Berlin, they decided to tell the police to stand aside and allow the demonstration to proceed.

Everyone, whether within the country or beyond, could now see which way events were turning. Finally, a week later, the members of the Politburo screwed up their courage and moved to depose Eric Honecker. By a unanimous vote – in which, by communist tradition, Honecker was eventually obliged to vote against himself – they forced him to resign. He left the building, never to return. His place was taken by his faithful deputy, Egon Krenz.

It was not long before the unfortunate Krenz was faced with the reality of the GDR's dire economic situation. The small group of officials who ran its finances, and kept the facts jealously to themselves, informed him that the country that had laid claim to having the twelfth largest economy in the world was in fact bankrupt. Krenz had to fly to Moscow and beg Gorbachev for a bailout. He was coolly received, and it was refused.

The final nail in the regime's coffin came at another massive anti-government demonstration, this time in East Berlin itself, on 4 November. Banners held aloft were openly critical of the regime, most of whom, including Egon Krenz, were booed off the stage. Only critical figures such as the writer Stefan Heym were applauded. For us in West Berlin, this was the first opportunity to see for ourselves what was going on, since, uniquely, the demonstration was broadcast live on West German TV.

* * *

And so to 9 November – one of the most fateful dates of the twentieth century. The GDR authorities had decided that, as a safety-valve measure, the restrictions on their citizens crossing the border to the West would be eased – eased, but, crucially, not abolished. Accordingly, the Politburo member who acted as spokesman, Günter Schabowski, held a news conference to announce the new measures, which contained few details but included the requirement to apply in advance for permission to leave. When asked by a Western journalist, Tom Brokaw of NBC, when these measures would come into effect, Schabowski, who was poorly prepared, became flustered. Not finding the answer in his notes he said that, as far as he knew, it was straightaway.

I happened to be at home in West Berlin watching developments on TV. This was unusual for me since the remorseless social round left few opportunities for evenings at home. I had used the pretext of my wife being away in London, accompanying the wife of Berlin's Mayor on an official visit, to decline an invitation to the glitzy birthday celebration of a newly established West Berlin Radio station, *Hundert Comma 6* – which the other top Allied officials were all attending.

Initially, it wasn't clear what was happening. But quite quickly there came reports of the dramatic developments at two of the Berlin crossing points in the Wall, Bornholmer Strasse and Checkpoint Charlie. When it became evident that East Berliners were starting to come through, and being ecstatically greeted by their compatriots in the West, I decided to resist the temptation to drive down to see what was happening (which would have meant my being out of telephone communication – in those days before mobile phones).

I thought that it was very important that the Berlin press next day should include a statement by the Allies, who bore the responsibility for the city's security, of their delight at the Wall being finally open. The absence of such a statement would not have been understood. I accordingly embarked on the cumbersome process of getting a statement drafted and then cleared with my Allied colleagues – late at night. A visit to the scene would have to wait until the next day. The telephone kept ringing, and the British Commandant, Major General

Robert Corbett, who enjoyed better communications than me, on the military net, called round to discuss developments.

Shortly after I finally got to bed, at about three in the morning, the Mayor of Berlin, now Walter Momper, rang (as he recounts in his memoirs) to say that he was on the far side of the Wall, and that he was being asked for instructions, or guidance, by three sets of police: the East German 'Vopos' (*Volkspolizei* – People's Police), the West German Police and the British Royal Military Police. What should he tell them? I suggested he tell them to keep order, each in their own way.

Next day I was able to join the joyous scenes at the crossing points. It was an amazing sight. A steady stream of East Germans was coming through the Wall, some waving banners proclaiming their newfound freedom. They were welcomed with hugs and kisses, and bottles of *sekt*. The band of one of the British regiments stationed in Berlin, the Royal Welch Fusiliers, played (in the rain), with their regimental goat mascot, Billy, in attendance. A British army NAAFI wagon dispensed tea and buns.

At the Checkpoint Charlie crossing point a long line of Trabants, the East German apology for a locally produced car, snaked its way

31. My wife's photograph of the East Berliners coming through to West Berlin on the day after the Wall opened. (Photo: author)

past the soon-to-be-obsolete Allied Military Police checkpoint, with well-wishers on either side waving excitedly at the occupants through the windows.

East German border guards were standing atop the Wall at the Brandenburg Gate, gazing down at the swelling crowd below on the Western side and looking decidedly uncomfortable. The situation was tense. At this point the Soviet leader, Gorbachev, who must by now have become aware that he was in the process of losing control of the GDR, the Soviet Union's most prized satellite, sent an urgent message to the heads of the three Allied governments, urging them to take action to prevent this potentially inflammatory situation getting out of control.

There was a hastily convened meeting of the Allied ambassadors, Commandants and ministers at the residence of the veteran American ambassador (General Vernon Walters, a prolific linguist, whose signature, and oft-told, anecdote was about how he had interpreted for General de Gaulle), to discuss what could be done. It was not straightforward, since the Wall at the Brandenburg Gate was set back from the boundary with the British Sector by a strip of land about ten yards wide (known as the '*Unterbaugebiet*'– 'Area under Construction'), which was legally part of the Soviet Sector, in practice the GDR. The reason for this was that, when the Wall had been erected in 1961, the GDR workforce had needed to operate on both sides of the construction.

Fortunately, we were able to come up with a solution from our experience in the British Sector the previous year. There was a triangle of land, known as the Lenné Triangle, which was a kink in the straight line dividing the Soviet from the British Sector. When the Wall was built, the GDR could not be bothered to take it around the triangle and continued it along the straight dividing line. Since the Triangle legally belonged in the Soviet zone – and such legalities underpinned the status of Berlin, with which one tampered at one's peril – the West Berlin police had kept out of it.

However, in 1988 a group of West Berlin hippies became aware that the Lenné Triangle was a legal no-man's land, and rapidly took advantage of the situation to set up camp there and have a good time. When lurid rumours spread about what was going on, the cry arose for something to be done. The Allies eventually decided to send in the West Berlin Police (WBP) to clear the area. But, given its legal status, this had first to be cleared with the Soviet authorities, and,

32. After the so-called woodpeckers – dedicated chisellers – had done serious
demolition work on the Wall it eventually became possible to see through to some
(now unthreatening) GDR border guards on the other side. (Photo: author)

through them, the GDR had to be warned about the impending operation. Once this had been done, the police action went off without a
hitch. In went the WBP, the hippies climbed over the Wall into the arms
of the East German border guards, who gave them breakfast. After
which they strolled back to West Berlin through Checkpoint Charlie.
A win-win solution.

Armed with this precedent, the meeting of the Allied authorities
concluded that, since the Soviets themselves had asked for action
to be taken, and the GDR was hardly in a position to object, we
were on safe ground in authorizing the West Berlin Police to enter
the 'Unterbaugebiet', take up position beneath the Wall and prevent
anyone in the crowd from attacking the East German guards who
were still manning it.

Once this had taken place, the Vopo guards were able to withdraw
from their deployment, no doubt with relief, and return to barracks.
In a flash their positions on the Wall were occupied by those eagerly
waiting to scramble up onto it, with the benefit of many helping hands.
The youth of the world began to converge on Berlin, including our

own two teenage children. They all wanted to stand, albeit rather precariously, on the Wall. They also began to dig chunks out of it; the so-called woodpeckers got to work. I drove out with my son Nicholas to an 'exclave' of Berlin (a village called Steinstücken joined to the city by a narrow corridor, flanked by a section of the Wall on either side – courtesy of the Quadripartite Agreement), where we could hack out a sizeable piece without being disturbed.

* * *

On the Saturday, two days after the first opening of the Wall, I spent time on the Kurfürstendamm, West Berlin's glittering shopping street, observing the *Ossies* (as GDR citizens were called – derived from the word *ost*, meaning 'east'), experiencing their first taste of the West. It was very instructive. They had been issued with 100 DM (about £30) of *Begrüssungsgeld* (welcome money). It did not go very far in face of their pent-up yearnings for the joys of the capitalist system. Mothers were scanning the fashion items (which were not cheap on that street), the fathers were interested in the porno magazines on the top shelf and the children were casting envious eyes at the toy department.

A great truth struck me. Whatever the politicians might say, the momentum of future events would be dictated by the *Ossies'* overwhelming desire to share in the good things of life already enjoyed by their Western compatriots and seen on TV. That meant acquiring the same currency that they used, the D-mark. And that, in turn, meant reunification of the two parts of Germany, and the two halves of Berlin.

I accordingly reported to the Bonn embassy and the Foreign Office on the following Monday that I thought we were experiencing the 'beginning of the endgame' for the Allied role in Berlin, and that we should start thinking urgently about how we should adapt to that reality.

I soon found, however, that I was getting rather ahead of the game. The first overseas leader to visit Berlin after what would be called the *Wende* (turning-point), was Douglas Hurd, newly appointed Foreign Secretary by Margaret Thatcher in succession to Sir Geoffrey Howe. The message he brought was that, as far as the Prime Minister was concerned, reunification was not on the agenda, and the subject should not be brought up. This was deflating, since what we thought the Allies had been doing in Berlin for the past four decades had been keeping open the door for Germany eventually to become reunited peacefully, and this was beginning to take place. I pointed out that the Berliners would not see things the same way as London.

However, at that stage, most German politicians were themselves adopting an equally cautious approach to the subject. Chancellor Helmut Kohl, nervous, like Margaret Thatcher, of undermining the reformist Gorbachev in the face of Soviet hardliners, talked initially of ten gradual stages needing to be gone through before 'confederal structures' between the two Germanies could be achieved. This was seen as well short of full unity. Once again it was the GDR city of Leipzig that provided the game-changer, when Kohl faced a huge and enthusiastic crowd there. Now their cry went up that 'We are ONE people'. He responded that his goal was 'the unity of our nation'.

I was able to glean an early impression of the Soviet view of developments the following week, when my wife and I crossed into East Berlin to fulfil a long-standing lunch engagement with my Soviet opposite number, Igor Maximichev (with whom I had had the face-off over the escapee Martin Notev), and his wife Anna. He heartily agreed with the Prime Minister that reunification should not be on the political agenda. As regards the prospects for the GDR, he said that the Soviet hope was that the leaders of the two Germanies could make a 'genuine Socialist alternative' work on the basis of democracy and human rights. He said, with some passion, that the latter were not capitalist concepts, but the basic rights of all mankind. I expressed doubt whether such a third way was achievable.

Maximichev was accurately reflecting his government's aversion to the idea of reunification, which would mean it losing control over the GDR. To prevent it happening, or at least to slow the process down, it came up with the forlorn idea of holding Four Power talks in Berlin to assess the situation. The chosen venue was the highly symbolic Allied Control Commission (ACC) building, from where the military authorities of the Four Powers had governed Germany immediately after the war.

The Western Allies could hardly turn down the Soviet proposal flat, but, in order to prevent the talks becoming a general and unfocused debate on reunification, they stipulated that the only subject on the agenda would be the implementation of the so-called Berlin Initiative, which had arisen out of President Reagan's famous speech at the Brandenburg Gate two years previously. The meeting duly commissioned expert follow-up talks on changes to the Berlin Air Regime, but no more.

The sting in the tail was the group photograph of the participants outside the ACC following the meeting. The spectacle of the ambassadors of the wartime Allies gathered together in an apparent attempt to keep their control over the Germans made an appalling impression in the German media next day. The meeting changed nothing, but, in retrospect, holding it had been misguided.

Officials of the West Berlin government were quick to establish working contact with their counterparts in East Berlin. They told us at our regular liaison meetings with them that they were finding a worrying lack of organisation there, bordering on chaos, which required their help. For example, officials on the other side were having difficulty over such a basic task as distributing food to the population. Matters improved when a new Prime Minister, Hans Modrow, took over in the GDR and formed an all-party government.

Prominent figures began to beat a path to Berlin to celebrate the historic *Wende*. One of the first was Mstislav Rostropovich, the great cellist. He took a private plane and went straight to the Wall at Checkpoint Charlie. Once there, he realised that he had no chair on which to sit, in order to play. The story was that he went to the nearest house, said who he was and asked if he might borrow one. Once she had resolved her understandable doubts, the astonished houseowner was happy to oblige. Rostoprovich played Bach, to a small but spellbound audience. Yehudi Menuhin was another early visitor, conducting Beethoven's Ninth symphony in the classical concert hall in East Berlin to great acclaim.

At the other end of the musical spectrum, a no less momentous event was 'The Wall' concert featuring Pink Floyd in July 1990. It took place in the no-man's land between the inner and outer Walls at Potsdamer Platz – the once and future centre of Berlin, like Piccadilly Circus in London. This presented fearsome bureaucratic problems in getting the necessary permissions from the authorities on both sides, plus the Allies – negotiated with skill and persistence by Leonard (later Lord) Cheshire VC, who saw it as an occasion to raise money for charities working for peace.

The concert, which was attended by an audience of over 350,000 people, was testimony to the long-pent-up enthusiasm for pop music in the GDR, which had been well understood in West Berlin. When any large pop concert had taken place in front of the Reichstag in the West, loud-speakers had been turned round to beam the music across the Wall to a sizeable crowd of young enthusiasts listening along Unter den Linden in the East, restrained behind barriers some way from the action, in order to prevent them from getting over-excited.

Shortly before Christmas in 1989, on 22 December, we were invited to attend the official opening of the Wall adjacent to the Brandenburg Gate, in the presence of Chancellor Helmut Kohl, as well as the East German leader Hans Modrow, the mayors of both halves of the city and many other dignitaries. The time was set for midday. We were then told that the ceremony had been cancelled due to reports of killings taking place in Romania, in the uprising there. Later, further word came that it was back on. The situation in Romania was only resolved with the execution of the Ceauşescu couple, who had tyrannised the country for so many years, on Christmas Day.

I was there with the family. As the sections of the Wall were lifted out by cranes, and the representatives on both sides came together to mingle happily, not even the steadily falling rain could dampen the joy of the occasion, the significance of which I found myself explaining to representatives of the UK media, with perhaps overuse of the term 'historic'.

The final event of the momentous year was the New Year's Eve celebration. Major General Robert Corbett (the British Commandant) and his wife Susie shared a minibus with us to transport our respective young to what promised to be a tumultuous event at the Brandenburg Gate. Together with our teenage children and their friends, we had a young house-guest for whom the evening would prove to be the launch of a distinguished journalistic career: Tom Bradby, later the presenter of ITN news. Then at Edinburgh University, he had been commissioned to get an interview with a student from the Humboldt University on Unter den Linden on the other side of the Wall.

When the last firework had exploded into the sky over the historic monument, and we found that the throng at the Brandenburg Gate was getting too much, my wife and I took the minibus and went home, leaving the young to find their own way back in due course. We woke in the morning to find that they had returned safely. We also heard that during the night there had been a collapse of the scaffolding at the Brandenburg Gate, with many injuries taking place.

When they surfaced, our children told us that Nicholas had thought of climbing the scaffolding, but had decided against it. Amanda's friend, Achara Tait, had become separated from the others and had been sitting on a wall when the collapse occurred. She had seen a young man wearing a leather jacket similar to the one Nicholas was wearing being carried off on a stretcher, badly injured. Only when the party were reunited did she discover her mistake, to her huge relief. Tom Bradby, after searching for much of the night, found his Humboldt University student and did his interview.

This was, I felt, a fittingly tumultuous end to a momentous year.

* * *

Like its predecessor, the year 1990 opened on a note of uncertainty. German reunification seemed a long way off. When Chancellor Kohl said to our ambassador, Christopher Mallaby, that 1995 seemed a possible date, it was considered a somewhat ambitious target.

There were many reasons for the cautious approach. The newly formed East German government was understandably reluctant to abandon the idea of a middle way between a reformed, but still socialist, state and the capitalism of West Germany – which would be the inevitable result of their country being folded into their hugely bigger neighbour.

As for the Four Powers, they were divided on their approach. Apart from President George HW Bush, who welcomed the prospect of reunification, each had its own qualms for its own particular reason. The Soviets faced losing their position in Central Europe, which had been underpinned by the Four-Power control of Berlin.

The British and the French were uneasy about the dominant role that a reunited and resurgent Germany, as the largest state, might be tempted to exercise in Europe. In the case of Margaret Thatcher, this was reinforced by her concern that Germany might revert to type and start throwing its weight about. This fear, it could be argued, was supported by Germany's twentieth-century history, but in her case, there seemed, for whatever reason, to be a strong element of emotion behind it.

Mrs Thatcher's concern was not shared by those of us serving in Germany at the time, particularly us in Berlin who were closest to developing events. Our strong feeling was that the momentum towards reunification was gathering pace, and the appearance of opposition to it in London was damaging Britain's standing in Germany as a long-standing supporter of the country eventually being reunified peacefully.

It was agreed that the Allies' concerns would be addressed in talks that would include not only the Four Powers, but also the two German states. They became known as the 2+4 talks. Their task was to resolve some of the loose ends from the Second World War, primarily the definition of Germany's eastern frontier with Poland, as well as providing for the withdrawal of Soviet forces from the former GDR and for a reunified Germany remaining in NATO.

It was only when the 2+4 talks had resolved these issues that the path was clear for reunification to take place. It also set the scene for the British and French governments to withdraw their reservations and endorse (in the case of Mrs Thatcher, with whatever misgivings she might privately feel) the reality of a reunified Germany. We in BMG had no such misgivings.

I had the opportunity of discussing the matter with (then) Lady Thatcher when she stayed with us in Prague, where I was ambassador, a few years later. On one of these occasions the conversation turned to Europe. Lady Thatcher was, of course, redoubtable, and could be pretty fierce. But I had had a frank discussion with her in the past (over a maritime frontier dispute between two Gulf States, so I felt able to summon up my courage and tell her that there was something I would like to say to her. She asked what it was and, sensing no doubt that it might not be entirely welcome, she fixed me with a basilisk look.

I said that I felt she had been poorly advised on Germany, and specifically Helmut Kohl's approach to European unity. His desire for a more closely integrated Europe was not, I argued, in order for Germany to be able to dominate it, but quite the reverse. His real concern was for Germany's demons to be constrained within European structures, so that the country would never again be able to follow an aggressive nationalist line on its own, which had led to two world wars. Lady Thatcher replied that no-one had said that to her (which was, I suspect, not the case) and that she was going to bed.

*   *   *

In June, just before the second round of these talks, the foreign ministers of the 2+4 countries came together in Berlin for a symbolic ceremony:

33. In a ceremony in the presence of six foreign ministers (the four wartime Allies and the two German states), Checkpoint Charlie is formally decommissioned and the military police hut is removed to the new Allied Museum in June 1990. (Photo: author)

the removal of the Allied military control hut at the Checkpoint Charlie crossing point in the centre of Berlin. They were Douglas Hurd for the UK, James Baker for the USA, Edvard Shevardnadze for the USSR, Roland Dumas for France, Hans-Dietrich Genscher for West Germany and Markus Meckel for East Germany. All the Allied authorities in Berlin were naturally present, as well as representatives of the Berliners.

It is worth noting the particular slant on the event some of the ministers gave in their speeches:

Shevardnadze: 'On this day marking the forty-ninth anniversary of the start of the Great Patriotic War, I express the confidence that all of us working together will be able to draw the final line under the past and move towards new horizons of understanding and cooperation.'

Baker: 'For twenty-nine years Checkpoint Charlie embodied the Cold War. Now, twenty-nine years after this barrier was built, we meet here today to dismantle it and to bury the conflict that created it.'

Hurd: 'So, from now on, Checkpoint Charlie will be part of history. We should not forget, our children should not forget, the reasons for which Checkpoint Charlie stood here for so many years, but no-one can be sorry that it is going. At long last we are bringing Charlie in from the Cold.'

The Deputy Mayor of West Berlin, Ingrid Starmer, spoke for the Berliners: 'Checkpoint Charlie was a pregnant symbol of the presence of the Western Allies in Berlin. It is for that reason that we view the dismantling of Checkpoint Charlie with a certain amount of regret, but above all with gratitude to our Protecting Powers. With Checkpoint Charlie we see the disappearance of a piece of practical solidarity during the time that the Wall isolated us.'

The speeches over, and with the band playing, the famous Checkpoint Charlie guard-hut, in which the Military Police of the three Western Allies had checked all Allied personnel in and out when they crossed from West to East Berlin, was lifted by crane onto a truck and borne away. It now forms one of the main attractions in the Allied Museum on Clay Allee in what was formerly the American Sector. It is well worth visiting – not least because it contains my photograph, as British Deputy Commandant at the time of its demise!

The 2+4 talks were concluded successfully. The main points were that the provisional definition of the German-Polish frontier along the Oder-Neisse Line, which had stood since the end of the war, was formally agreed; Soviet forces would withdraw, according to a time-table, from the GDR; and reunited Germany would remain in NATO – but NATO forces would not be stationed in East Germany.

With this agreement, the reservations of the Four Powers were largely laid to rest – although there would be subsequent recriminations over what exactly was agreed over NATO. The way lay open to German reunification. An intra-German agreement on monetary and economic union was also put in place. Reunification Day was set for 3 November.

As the reunification date approached, the Allies prepared to carry out their final duty – signing off, at the conclusion of their forty-five-year role as Occupying and then Protecting Powers. It was not an entirely straightforward process. Apart from the British Commandant, Major General Robert Corbett (who had succeeded Major General Brooking), his fellow Commandants initially found it hard to accept that the conclusion of the Allied role inevitably entailed their departure; as the physical embodiment of Allied authority, they could scarcely remain once that authority had come to an end. The US Commandant was particularly obdurate.

The Allies' last official act was the signing of a letter to the Mayor and Assembly of Berlin, at the concluding session of the Allied Kommandatura. The letter was a British draft. Before the signature ceremony each of the AK committees – for political and legal affairs, protocol and public security – delivered its final report.

Unfortunately, the signature ceremony itself was in dispute. The US Commandant was insistent that only the Commandants should sign the historic document. I had been arguing for some time, with the support of my fellow Allied ministers, that this was inconsistent with the spirit and practice of the AK, which had over the years operated on the basis of military/diplomatic teamwork: the Deputy Commandants (ministers) should also therefore append their signatures. This was finally agreed, but only after the French Commandant had been won round 'in the interest of solidarity', and the US Commandant had found himself isolated.

Masking our emotions, we then trooped outside, leaving the building for the last time, for the formal lowering of the Allied flags. From there we drove to the Rathaus Schöneberg to call on the President of the House of Representatives (*Abgeordnetenhaus*) and the Mayor, Walter Momper (in the presence of Willy Brandt who had been the iconic mayor in the 1950s and 1960s before going on to become West Germany's Nobel Peace Prize-winning chancellor from 1969 to 1974). Presenting the AK letter in the House, Robert Corbett made a speech, in German, with skill and charm. His reading of the letter was frequently punctuated with applause. Many of those present later confessed to lumps in the throat and a few tears. After the Commandants and their wives had signed the Golden Book of Berlin, the House and the audience gave them a standing ovation.

It only remained for us to watch the Reunification Ceremony at midnight, which was greeted by a huge crowd in front of the Reichstag building. We were invited to a reception and dinner in the Rooftop Restaurant of the Intercontinental Hotel, overlooking the great square in front of the Reichstag building, generously offered by Daimler-Benz and its chairman Edzard Reuter (son of Ernst Reuter, the famous Mayor of Berlin at the time of the Airlift). Once again Robert Corbett made an elegant, and impromptu, speech of thanks to our host, and of appreciation for the consistent support which the Berlin business community had given the Allies. It was fitting that my wife and I took along with us for the occasion Sir Frank Roberts, a very distinguished, and well-remembered, former ambassador in Bonn (and Moscow), who was staying with us.

Just before midnight, the German band in front of the Reichstag, to my surprise and delight, struck up with 'Land of Hope and Glory'. It seemed a nice compliment.

Chapter 11

Through the Wall and into the East: Promoting Britain and Observing a New Germany

The reunification of Berlin failed to make the city one and whole, except in a purely formal sense. People were now able to travel freely throughout it, but the Westerners – *Wessies* – showed little inclination to avail themselves of the pleasure, except to visit the historic centre around the broad avenue of Unter den Linden and attend a concert or the opera. For their part, the *Ossies* did not have the money to enjoy the bright lights of the Ku'damm in the centre of West Berlin. It did not take long before it was said that the physical Wall may have gone, but the wall in people's minds remained.

Politically the most important event was a speech that Chancellor Helmut Kohl delivered from the balcony of the Crown Prince's Palace

---

Photo: The Reichstag building 'wrapped' by the performance artists Christo and Jeanne-Claude (before it housed the Bundestag after reunification). This proved a controversial treatment of the newly restored German Parliament building.

on Unter den Linden to a large and expectant crowd. I managed to find a spot at a window below the balcony and heard it live. He made the momentous promise that within a few years the economy in the new *Länder* would be a *'blühende Landschaft'* ('a blossoming landscape').

It turned out to be far from the case, and Kohl was much criticised for creating false expectations. His justification, which was not unreasonable, was to give people hope that their lives would improve. Otherwise, they would pack a suitcase and move westwards in search of work, as many were already doing. The Bonn government transferred massive sums to the East, largely for the purpose of improving the moribund infrastructure. But this did little to raise the standard of living, or employment prospects, of the majority of people in the short term, partly because the West German unions, fearful of losing jobs to cheaper labour in the East, hastened to encourage their Ossie counterparts to press for a progressive rise in pay scales to bring them into line with those in the West. The result was yet further unemployment. Germany remained two countries for many years to come. The *Wessies* resented the enormous cost of uplifting the new *Länder*, and the *Ossies* felt that they were being colonised by, and condescended to, by their richer neighbours.

One issue which had not been resolved at Reunification was whether Berlin would resume its role as the capital of Germany. This was being strongly contested by Bonn, the capital of West Germany, where there was widespread dismay at the prospect of the move to Berlin – led, it was said, by the dentists of Bonn, who were horrified at the thought of losing their patients!

The case for Berlin was powerfully argued by the Federal President Richard von Weizsäcker, who was himself a former Mayor of Berlin. In an address given in the neo-Gothic Friedrichswerder church in East Berlin (at which I was present), he raised the level of the debate, arguing that the city's historic credentials, and its artistic tradition and tolerance of foreigners, outweighed the dark chapter of the earlier part of the twentieth century. The speech made an impact, but the question was not finally settled until Chancellor Kohl spoke up for Berlin in the critical debate on the subject in the Bundestag in June 1991.

Until then Bonn continued to carry out the functions of the capital city. In Berlin, the situation for the Allies was that, apart from the departure of the Commandants, little changed. The garrisons remained in place until the final departure of all the Soviet forces from East

Germany in 1993, commanded by the brigade commander in each former Sector. The British commander was Brigadier David Bromhead, who now liaised with a West German Bundeswehr General, who became the senior commander in the city.

But for me, everything changed, starting with the nature of my job. As regards the British diplomatic presence, the position was initially somewhat confused. The British embassy in East Berlin ceased to exist, as such, with the disappearance of the GDR. The British Military Government (BMG) in West Berlin also ceased to exist, with the ending of Allied rights and responsibilities on Reunification. In fact, it had formally ceased to exist, under that name, several months before.

The story behind that is that I had been recommending, since my arrival to head BMG, five years previously, that its title was both obsolete (since it was no longer a military government in any meaningful sense) and misleading. The uninitiated might, for example, not immediately realise that a telegram of advice reaching the FCO from Berlin, over the signature of a military commandant, in fact emanated from a political mission, headed by a minister (an FCO official) of equal rank to the commandant. At times, such as during the highly charged period through which we had just lived, this lack of clarity could have affected the weight given to the advice, which could have mattered.

My proposal had not been accepted when I had first made it, due to the fear of unintended consequences that might flow from any change in the delicately balanced Berlin situation. But after the fall of the Wall, the change was finally agreed. The British Military Government became the British Mission, Berlin. The sky did not fall in – any more than it had fallen in when the Americans had made an identical change in the title of their Military Government as long ago as 1948, over forty years earlier.

Now, after Reunification, the post went through another name change, to British embassy, Berlin Office (BEBO – an unlovely acronym). My new task was not only to head it, but also to integrate it with the former embassy in East Berlin – the ambassador to the former GDR, my old friend Patrick Eyers (from Dubai days), having left to return to the Middle East, as ambassador to Jordan. I also moved out of my office in London Block at the Olympic Stadium and into his embassy in a charmless communist-style building on Unter den Linden.

It was not an easy time. The termination of the Allied role, and the special status it had afforded to the Allies, left me with a feeling of deflation. The merger of the two diplomatic posts led to a number of the local staff becoming redundant. UK-based friends and colleagues in BMG also left for pastures new. My 'God speed' remarks at their farewell drinks began to sound rather well worn.

Furthermore, the change of status coincided with a world event which turned the erstwhile Allies from the city's 'Protecting Powers' into something approaching 'Public Enemy No. 1'. Many of the Berlin public reacted strongly to the First Gulf War, culminating in the Allied Coalition's eviction of Iraqi forces from Kuwait, following Saddam Hussein's invasion of that country. There were noisy demonstrations in the streets. For the first and last time in my career I was temporarily accorded a close protection team of highly trained officers from the Berlin Police for my safety.

This somewhat bizarre situation eventually came to an end when the straight-talking President of the Berlin House of Representatives, Hanna-Renate Laurien, pointed out that the three countries that were the target of the demonstrations, Britain, France and the USA, were exactly the same countries that had been protecting the city for the past forty-five years. After that, matters slowly returned to normal.

In any case, my low spirits did not last. My new responsibilities included not only promoting the British presence in unified Berlin, but also getting out into the former GDR (now known as the *Neue Bundesländer* – the New Federal *Länder*) and doing the same there. This was an enticing prospect.

* * *

With a newfound sense of freedom at being finally allowed to travel through the Wall, which was increasingly disappearing, and beyond the city limits, my wife and I began to explore the region around Berlin, made famous in German literature by the nineteenth-century writer Theodor Fontane's *Ramblings in Brandenburg* (the *Land* in which Berlin is situated), a landscape of lakes and woods.

I was afforded an excellent start in making contact with opinion-formers in the new *Länder* by the fortunate coincidence that there was a long-arranged British Council exhibition of the great British Romantic water-colourist painters of the eighteenth century, including Constable and JMW Turner, on tour in the former GDR. It was a real treat, and made a big impact, not least because the paintings rarely travelled abroad due to their fragility. I was invited to open the exhibition both in Schwerin, a picturesque town on the Baltic coast, and in East Berlin.

Further afield, I worked my way along the east–west highway that bisects the state of Thuringia, passing through a succession of famous towns, starting at Jena (the scene of a key battle in the Napoleonic Wars). These are, in succession, Weimar, Erfurt (the state capital), Gotha and Eisenach, where Luther translated the New Testament into German while in hiding from the Holy Roman Emperor in the Wartburg fortress, and where the first stirrings of German democratic protest took place in 1848, known throughout Europe as the Year of Revolutions.

Weimar, apart from being the capital of the ill-fated German Republic after the First World War, and being associated with both Germany's leading literary figures, Goethe and Schiller, prided itself on its link with another literary giant, Shakespeare. It featured a bust of him in the city park, and its Shakespeare Society was in the habit of celebrating the Bard's birthday by adorning it with a wreath. This charming event had fallen by the wayside during the Nazi and communist periods and a rival German Shakespeare Society, in the Rhineland, had taken over the honours. But with the ending of the GDR, normal service was resumed, and I had the pleasure of attending the revived ceremony, laying a wreath and joining the lunch that followed – in the hotel from the balcony on which Hitler, when visiting, had been in the habit of addressing the Nazi Party faithful.

I was particularly taken with Gotha. When I first visited, I called first, as was my habit, on the Mayor. He was a young man, who told me, with disarming candour, that when municipal elections had taken place a few weeks previously, he and his friends had decided that, for a lark, they would all stand for the City Council. To their surprise they had all been elected, but were now at a bit of a loss what to do next. He asked if I could help. I offered to arrange for him to go on a short course in England to study how a mayor in the UK went about his/her functions. He was delighted by this.

My next stop in Gotha was at the massive Renaissance-Baroque Schloss Friedenstein, dominating the town. I found the curator welcoming and impressive. He explained the castle's links with the British Royal Family: Prince Albert (of Saxe-Coburg and Gotha), the Prince Consort, had spent much of his youth there. This gave me an idea.

When the Duke of Kent visited the new *Länder* a few months later, in his role of Special Representative for International Trade and Investment, to highlight the opportunities for UK-German trade, we arranged for him to host a dinner in the castle (with the support of the Department of Trade and Industry). This was a memorable occasion, attended by the prominent personalities of Thuringia and serenaded by a string trio. It was the first time that a member of the Royal Family had visited the castle since before the Great War. To mark the event, the curator had arranged an exhibition recording some of the highlights of Prince Albert's stay there.

The interest of the new *Länder* generally for British business was less in finding new markets – given the low purchasing power of the east German currency before monetary unification on 30 June 1990, and the East's general economic weakness – than in identifying investment opportunities. An exception was BP, the company where I had spent eighteen months immediately before my Berlin posting, which jumped in with both feet and built an ultra-modern service station, in record time, on the road leading off the motorway into Dresden. When I attended the opening, the host of the occasion, a colleague from my BP secondment, informed me with pride that the facility had already registered the largest monthly through-put of fuel of any BP service station in Europe, since fuel suitable for Western vehicles was hard to find in the heart of the former GDR.

In order to stimulate investment, the Federal Government had set up an agency in Berlin, known as the *Treuhandanstalt* (Trust Agency), a unique organisation which took over the assets of the GDR prior to reunification, and was charged with the massive task of restructuring, and finding investors for, about 8,500 state-owned companies, with 4 million employees. We kept in close touch with it, in order to be in a position to advise and support potential UK investors. The Federal Government were keeping a scorecard of how much each country was investing, which seemed to me slightly pointless. However, the UK was high up the list.

* * *

The main attraction in the new *Länder*, as far as I was concerned, was Dresden, known as 'Florence on the Elbe'. Pictures of the baroque city before the war, passed around the class by my German teacher at school, PK Bourne, had fired my interest in Germany. I was now able, at last, to see the city for myself.

In many ways it was a sad sight. The buildings were still blackened by the firestorm created by the air-raid in 1945. The magnificent Protestant Frauenkirche (Church of Our Lady), built with the subscriptions of the citizens in the eighteenth century, to rival the Roman Catholic cathedral which their newly converted ruler, King Augustus the Strong, had erected to strengthen his claim to be elected to the throne of Catholic Poland, still lay in ruins – a calculated act by the communist regime to keep alive the people's memory of the horror of the Anglo-American raid.

But not all was doom and gloom. The Zwinger, the great baroque palace complex built by Augustus, was being restored. It had been largely destroyed in the Allied air-raids, but fortunately the art collection had been evacuated beforehand. After the war some rebuilding had taken place with the help of the Soviet military authorities. Some galleries were now open, displaying Augustus' spectacular picture collection and incomparable pieces of early Meissen porcelain.

It was in Meissen, near Dresden, in the eighteenth century, that the breakthrough took place in discovering the formula for creating fine hard porcelain as produced in China. Augustus had lured an alchemist into his service who had escaped from the Prussian Court, Johann Friedrich Böttger, and then virtually imprisoned him until some years later, and at great detriment to his health, he had found the formula. Works of other great porcelain artists, such as Johann Joachim Kändler, who took up the baton from Böttger as modeller for the Meissen factory, were also on view in the Zwinger.

During the war the incomparable treasures of Augustus's collections were removed for safe keeping to Königstein, the highest fortress in Europe, on a plateau dominating a valley of the Elbe river not far from Dresden. In this way they, happily, escaped the Allied air-raid.

Another revelation in Dresden was the Green Vault (*Grünes Gewölbe*), the largest treasure collection in Europe – one of its greatest splendours being a model, created in Augsburg, of the people and animals of the Court of the Mughal Emperor Aurangzeb, all in precious and semi-precious stones.

To begin with, finding somewhere to stay for the night in Dresden was not easy. The best option was to stay on a cruise-boat, moored on the river Elbe beneath the elegant eighteenth-century Brühl Terrace, which was known in its heyday as 'the balcony of Europe'.

*   *   *

Back in Berlin, my longevity in the post meant that I had become the senior diplomatic representative in the city and therefore the Dean of the Diplomatic and Consular Corps. This was not a particularly onerous task, but it was up to me to act as the channel of communication between the Rathaus (City Hall) and the Corps, and vice versa. The Rathaus in question was once again the Rotes (Red) Rathaus in the city centre, rather than the West Berlin government's temporary residence in Rathaus Schöneberg in the western sectors – in which it had taken refuge when the city split in two.

One duty which did fall to me was to reply, on behalf of the Corps, to the Mayor's address at his annual New Year Reception. The Mayor of Berlin at this point was once again Eberhardt Diepgen, who had won back office from the SPD at the latest election. We had for years not only been in frequent contact in the course of Allied business, but also close neighbours. As I remarked in my final speech in Berlin, when I came to sign the city's Golden Book, neither of us could ever have imagined at that time that we would one day be exchanging official addresses in the Rotes Rathaus, from which the non-communist city politicians had been ignominiously ejected so many years ago.

There was no shortage of visitors from Britain. Among members of the Royal Family, Princess Anne came for a meeting of the Olympic Equestrian Committee, on which she represented the UK. Prince Edward came to visit the Irish Guards, one of the regiments in the garrison, which gave me the opportunity of hosting a lunch in his honour with slightly younger, and less staid, guests than usual (including our son Nicholas).

The architect Norman Foster came to receive a prestigious prize for architecture. He was later to make a significant mark on the city when he designed the glass cupola over the remodelled Reichstag building. This was a controversial commission, but the generally accepted view of the outcome is that it is a triumph: the public ascend the dome in circles, in the sight of the legislators in the chamber beneath, who are thus reminded of their democratic responsibilities.

Other visitors connected with the Reichstag were the artists Christo and Jeanne-Claude. They had built a worldwide reputation under the brand name 'Christo' with their original artworks, which consisted in wrapping well-known landmarks in special plastic sheeting for a short period, in order to make people look at them with fresh eyes. An early example was the Pont-Neuf, the oldest bridge across the Seine in Paris.

They had long held the ambition of wrapping the Reichstag building in Berlin. The proposal was inevitably controversial, with some people strongly opposed at what they considered a belittling of Germany's parliament, while others believed that it would give it an exciting new prominence. A close friend of ours, the German-American architectural historian Michael Cullen, was coordinating Christo's lobbying campaign (he was also leading the opposition to Norman Foster's proposal for the new Reichstag cupola). Through him, we met Christo and Jeanne Claude and were intrigued by their vision.

Christo eventually got the green light, thanks to winning the support of Chancellor Kohl, and the project took place in 1995. By then we had moved on, to the embassy in Prague. But our daughter Amanda had gone to live in Berlin, to experience the city for herself. We drove up to see her and view the Wrapped Reichstag (where she was acting as one of Christo's team of monitors) at the same time. It was a truly spectacular sight: a huge, gleaming white shape like a massive iceberg, conferring a new significance, and beauty, to the well-known seat of German democracy, with its chequered history.

*   *   *

In Berlin, the ghosts of the past lie not far from the surface, none more so than that of its appalling record of anti-Semitism. During the Allied era, the forceful leader of the renascent Jewish community, Heinz Galinski, had made a practice of inviting (although 'commanding' might be a better word) Berlin's political leaders, as well as the Allies, to attend an annual commemoration of the Holocaust on 9 November, the anniversary of Kristallnacht in 1938. Recalling that night of shattering glass, when the Nazis unleashed a concerted pogrom against the Jews, Galinski would admonish his somewhat cowed audience with the words 'We do not forget – and we do not forgive', which made a powerful impression.

On the first anniversary of Kristallnacht after the Wende, I was invited to join the Mayor and other prominent people in a silent torchlit procession along Unter den Linden and through the centre of the reunified city to the main synagogue in Oranienstrasse. It was the most moving occasion of my time in Germany. Once free to travel outside Berlin after reunification, my wife and I also visited the two Nazi concentration camps situated north of the city, Sachsenhausen and Ravensbrück. Both visits provided chilling experiences.

I was involved in a commemorative event of a different sort in April 1992, shortly before my departure from Berlin. There was an approach to the Air Attaché in the embassy in Bonn from the authorities in the Baltic port of Rostock. Their request was for a suitable RAF representative to attend a wreath-laying ceremony to commemorate the RAF air-raid on the city, half a century earlier, in 1942. Ideally, they said they would like someone who had been involved in the raid. It was intimated that it would also be nice if he would apologise for the loss of life the raid had caused.

The message back from the embassy was that, not only had the MOD failed to find anyone suitable, but that the Air Attaché himself was unfortunately unable to attend on the day in question. They asked whether I could stand in for him, which I agreed to do, although I found the prospect somewhat daunting.

On arrival in Rostock, I found a large crowd gathered in the cemetery. The event was being organised by the pastor of the cathedral, who had been 10 years old at the time of the raid. The speeches before mine described the events over three nights in April 1942 when RAF Bomber Command had launched successive raids on the city. The main objective had been to knock out the Heinkel factory outside the city that produced aircraft for the Luftwaffe. On the first night the bombs missed the factory entirely and fell on the city. On following nights the factory was hit, but so, once again, was the city, resulting in a firestorm in which thousands of people died.

I began to feel the responsibility of my participation. I could not apologise for the raid, a legitimate act of war – a war we had not started. Besides, in the world of diplomacy and international relations, apologies imply the acceptance of guilt, leaving apologisers open to claims for reparations and other consequences which can hugely complicate the conduct of international affairs. What I did do, with feeling, was to express regret for the tragic events of that time and the loss of life. I went on to say that the lesson for all of us was that such a war should never happen again. This went down well, and I laid the wreath with due solemnity.

The ceremony over, the gathering moved into the large brick-built cathedral (typical of its kind around the Baltic). It was freezing cold. The high point of the service was the address by the pastor. He told the congregation that, although he had been only 10 at the time of the raids, he could remember them well, in all their full horror. He went on to speak along these lines (with a certain exaggeration, not to say inaccuracy, to make his point): 'My friends, we should all bear this in mind: when the Nazis came to power we voted for them by 90%; and when the Communists took power we voted for them also by 90%; we can only hope that no-one else will come along for whom we shall vote by 90%. This must never happen again!'

You could have heard a pin drop in that vast and icy cathedral. The main participants in the event then repaired to the cellar restaurant in the Rathaus. The mood lightened, and we enjoyed a convivial dinner, with many toasts and expressions of esteem. At the end, I congratulated the pastor on all he had done, and said, and returned to Berlin.

*   *   *

The question of an apology also loomed large in the event that was the climax of my seven long years in Berlin, a state visit by the Queen and the Duke of Edinburgh in 1992. The Queen had paid a number of state visits to Germany in the course of her reign, but this would be the first to a reunified Germany and reunified Berlin. Together with my staff, I was in charge of the arrangements for the Berlin and eastern *Länder* part of the visit (after the customary arrival formalities had taken place in Bonn), which was clearly likely to excite the most media interest.

The most difficult question to be addressed in the planning stage was whether a visit to Dresden should be included. One school of thought was that, in view of the 1945 air-raid, in the last months of the war, this could provoke strong feelings and should be avoided. The contrary view, which eventually prevailed, was that not to go there would have appeared to be avoiding the issue. But this decision then raised another question, whether the Queen should apologise for the raid, which was being advocated, in particular, by a canon of Coventry Cathedral; his proposal was that the Queen should place a bouquet of remembrance at the ruins of the Frauenkirche, as a symbolic gesture. Neither of these ideas was accepted.

But, in the light of this, the Dresden visit had to be particularly carefully choreographed. It was agreed that it would contain only one event, a symbolic service of reconciliation in the restored Kreuzkirche (the Church of the Cross), at which a joint German-British choir would sing. The Federal German President, Richard von Weizsäcker, would read a lesson in English and Prince Philip would read one in German. There would be no stopping at the Frauenkirche ruin on the way to the church.

Unfortunately, in the build-up to the visit there was an event that raised the temperature surrounding the Dresden bombing. By a coincidence, the statue of Air Chief Marshal Sir Arthur Harris (known as Bomber Harris), the head of Bomber Command and the man who issued the order for the Dresden bombing (which had been authorised by Winston Churchill in the margin of the Yalta Conference), was unveiled in front of St Clement Dane's church in the Strand. The unveiling was performed by the universally loved Queen Mother, but on this occasion, and perhaps for the only time in her long life, her speech was greeted with some boos. If the raid was controversial in Britain, as the occasion demonstrated, it was of course many times more so in Germany.

On the day of the Dresden visit, the advance party, including me, all flew down from Berlin, with the exception of the Queen herself and President von Weizsäcker, who followed in a later plane, and were driven straight to the Kreuzkirche. I realised, immediately on landing with the advance party that, when the two principals followed shortly afterwards in their car, there would be no-one with the necessary political background accompanying them, to report if there were an incident of some kind. I therefore stayed back from the main party, and found a seat in the car carrying the Queen's Equerry, immediately following the royal car.

The drive from the airport to the Kreuzkirche, following the principals' car, was eerie. Dresden, by some geographical quirk, had not been able to receive West German TV, unlike other GDR cities. The crowd did not know how to react to the occasion. The cheering and flag waving, which would normally be evident for such a visitor, were absent. The presence of a number of curious, but silent, off-duty Soviet troops among the crowd lining the road added to the unreality.

Things started to go wrong when the convoy came level with the ruins of the Frauenkirche. Ignoring the agreed arrangements,

34. Dresden's Frauenkirche (Church of Our Lady) was left in ruins by the communist authorities after the Allied air-raid of April 1945, to remind the population of Western 'iniquity'. (Photo: author)

President von Weizsäcker told the car to stop while he explained the ruins to the Queen. Fortunately they did not alight, and, after a short pause, the car moved on. However, worse was to happen when the convoy stopped in front of the Kreuzkirche. To my horror, an egg was thrown at the royal car, just as the occupants alighted, narrowly missing them. The police moved in. The President looked incandescent with rage. The Queen looked utterly composed. They went into the church, followed by the Equerry and myself. The service, which went ahead as planned, was beautiful. After the service the royal party drove, as planned, to the railway station without more ado. The egg incident was played down in the German media; there was general approval over the Queen having made the visit to Dresden.

A postscript was that when plans were made for the great Frauenkirche to be rebuilt, a Dresden Trust was set up in the UK, headed by the Duke of Kent, to contribute towards the cost. It received donations of more than a million euros. The Golden Cross and orb, surmounting the cupola, was donated by the city of Coventry, with the involvement of the son of one of the pilots who took part in the raid. This was the real, and most meaningful, act of reconciliation. The restored Frauenkirche is now, once again, one of the glories of Germany and of Europe.

The next stop on the programme was Leipzig, which we reached by the German bullet train. It had not yet been certified for travel at full speed, so it sheathed its power and kept to a normal speed for the journey. In Leipzig the atmosphere was very different from that in Dresden. Again, there was a church to be visited, this time the St Nicholas church, which had played such an important part in the peaceful protests leading up to the critical demonstration of 9 October 1989 that had exposed the GDR regime's lack of resolve to suppress mass dissent by force. Pastor Christian Führer gave the royal party an account of that dramatic event, after which the Queen and Prince Philip went out into the square, as had been the practice of the candle-bearing regular Monday demonstrators, for a walk-about. There was great enthusiasm from the crowd.

Accompanying the Duke of Edinburgh down one side of the square for the walk-about (the ambassador was accompanying the Queen down the other side), I became aware how trying Prince Philip must occasionally have found his role. The crowd on our side, who had little

35. The church, one of the greatest Protestant churches north of the Alps, was rebuilt after German reunification with public donations, including the gift of a new Orb and Cross from contributions raised in the UK by a charitable fund headed by the Duke of Kent, whose father had been an RAF officer during the Second World War. (Photo: author)

**36. The Queen and Prince Philip with Mayor Diepgen in front
of the Brandenburg Gate. (Photo: © Alamy)**

idea of who he was, frequently asked him to get out of the way so that they could have a better view of the Queen.

In Berlin itself, the highlight of the visit was the picture taken of the Queen walking through the Brandenburg Gate, a symbolic consecration, by one of the three Allied heads of state, of the peaceful reunification of the city.

Another highlight, this time away from the public gaze, was the Queen's return dinner for President von Weizsäcker's state dinner in her honour on arrival, which had taken place in Bonn. This was held in Charlottenburg Palace. It was on a different scale of magnificence from the many formal dinners I had attended there during the Allied period, when the Mayor entertained important visitors. Since the Queen herself was the hostess, the most splendid gold-plate dinner service was flown out from Buckingham Palace, with cutlery and crystal to match. The State Trumpeters summoned the guests to dinner. It was unforgettable.

Also unforgettable was that, at the end of the visit, Her Majesty dubbed me a Knight Commander of the Royal Victorian Order, in a private ceremony in the ambassador's residence. The Order, along with the Garter, the Thistle and the Order of Merit, is in the personal gift of the sovereign, which makes it very special.

One final engagement which the Queen undertook before her departure was to unveil the foundation stone for the new British embassy, at which I attended her. The site for the building on Wilhelmstrasse was the same as that of the pre-war embassy, which had been damaged during the war and demolished some time thereafter. We had been quick off the mark, in comparison with the other Allies, in getting permission to rebuild on the prime site near the Brandenburg Gate.

Finally, on 10 December 1992, the time came for me to end my long tour in Berlin. The practice had been that each departing senior member of the Allies (ambassador, commandant or minister) had signed the Golden Book of Berlin and been decorated with the Berlin Order of Merit. Now it was my turn, the last in the line. It was an emotional occasion, both for me and my wife. In my speech I spoke of the many memories we would take away with us, thanked Mayor Diepgen for the honour Berlin was doing us and promised in future to act as an ambassador for the city in the wide world – which I have tried to be.

Among the press coverage the following day, the comment which touched me most was the simple headline '*Ein Gentleman sagt good bye.*'

Chapter 12

Policy-Making at the Centre: Director, Middle East and North Africa in the Foreign Office

My next move, in January 1992, was back to the Middle East, not, this time, physically, but as Director for the Middle East and North Africa in the Foreign Office. At the time, the position rejoiced in the traditional, and more sonorous, title of Assistant Under-Secretary of State, which I preferred. But the change of title to Director took place during my time in office.

Either way, it was an exciting and demanding job – one of the best in the Foreign Office. Since it involved supervising two departments – Near East and North Africa Department (NENAD) and Middle East Department (MED) – I was responsible for advising ministers on an area ranging from Iran in the east to Morocco in the west.

My office, in the Old India Office part of the Foreign Office complex, was spectacular. It was on the ground floor, looking directly over St James's Park. It benefited from having not one entrance door, but two, so that two Indian princes could be received at the same time without a problem arising over precedence. It was disappointing that the problem did not arise during my tenure.

The political picture in the region had changed greatly since we had returned home from Kuwait thirteen years earlier, when Iran was in the grip of the Islamic Revolution. Iraq and Iran had fought a bloody eight-year war. Saddam Hussein had then invaded and occupied Kuwait, in order to seize its oil, only to be evicted from the country by a US-led Allied coalition in the First Gulf War.

My period as Director fell between the two Gulf Wars, the second of which took place ten years later, over the issue of Iraq's supposed non-compliance with UN Resolutions divesting it of its weapons of mass destruction (WMD).

The UK had played an active part in the First Gulf War and in the subsequent Security Council debates. These had resulted in demands on Iraq to cease from all aggressive acts, to co-operate in the delimitation of its border with Kuwait, to declare the full whereabouts of its stocks of chemical and biological weapons and to allow inspections of its stocks by UN inspectors. It was laid down that there would be consequences if Iraq failed to comply with any of these provisions.

Iraq also had to accept the setting up of no-fly zones over areas in both the north and the south of the country. These were a response by the Allies to Saddam Hussein's continuously provocative and aggressive behaviour in the aftermath of the ceasefire that ended the war, after his forces had been chased out of Kuwait. He had taken repressive measures against the ancient Shi'i communities living in the marshes to the south of Basra (known as the Marsh Arabs, whose way of life had been described in lyrical terms by writers such as Wilfrid Thesiger). In the north of the country he had attacked the Kurdish population from the air, forcing large numbers to flee into the surrounding mountains.

It was Prime Minister John Major who had reacted with outrage to the treatment of the Kurds and initiated demands for a no-fly zone. The result was regular overflights in the two zones by the RAF, together with the USAF and the French Airforce. If the Iraqis locked their radar onto the Allied aircraft, meaning a preparation to attack, as they not infrequently did, they became liable to reprisals by the Allies, based on the principle of self-defence (under the terms of the relevant UN resolutions).

The system generally worked well. But towards the end of my time in the job, Turkey was beginning to have qualms over allowing the

Allies to make use of their base at Incirlik, in the south-east of the country. Together with my US and French colleagues, I held talks with the Turks in Ankara. These steadied the ship, at least for a time.

I should, at this point, make clear my position on the invasion of Iraq – the Second Gulf War – which took place in 2003, six years after my retirement. I was against it. I explained my reasons in a debate at Chatham House (the Royal Institute of International Affairs) about six months before the invasion. The case for an invasion was put forward, cogently, by the writer William Shawcross. Although I was sitting between two former ambassadors to Iraq, I was the one who felt moved to take issue with his arguments.

I said that when I had been Director for the Middle East in the Foreign Office in the 1990s (as described in this chapter), the regional threat presented by Saddam Hussein, and the highly repressive nature of his regime, had been well understood. Our policy had been to deter him from aggression against his neighbours, and to contain him through the disarmament measures undertaken by the UN.

Iraq, I argued, was a country ruled by a strongman. If the West were to invade, it could shatter the political structure of the country, with wholly unpredictable consequences. At the end of the day another strongman would be likely to emerge. That person would have to be dealt with by the same mixture of deterrence and containment. It would be better to continue with the present strategy of containment and deterrence and forgo a risky invasion. I still believe my argument was valid, or at least the first part, about the unintended consequences of an invasion.

*   *   *

The Director job involved a lot of travel. There were visits to Paris, Washington and Moscow, for wide-ranging discussions with my counterparts in those capitals on how they saw the region.

I also visited all the posts, except two, in my parish, in order to hear from them directly about their hopes and fears. These included managerial as well as policy issues, since, together with a changed title, regional Directors in the Foreign Office had taken on responsibility for the efficient deployment of resources in their area. This was a positive development.

My travels took me, on one particular journey, to Sudan, Egypt and Lebanon. In Khartoum I found little changed since my posting there twenty-five years earlier; it seemed that the same drainage trench was open and untouched in the street where the ambassador's residence stood, still waiting for new pipes to be laid. I did, however, have the opportunity to call on Sayed Sadiq al Mahdi, who had been Prime Minister for part of my posting and was now an elder statesman, having gone through many vicissitudes in the intervening period. He was, understandably, mournful about the current state of the country, under the repressive regime of Omar al Bashir.

I also had a meeting with Hassan al Turabi, one of the most significant, and intriguing, figures in Sudan. I remembered him from my earlier time as a radical, Paris-educated lawyer (and relation of Sadiq al Mahdi's) who had agitated for a Muslim Brotherhood-style government. He was highly articulate – one of the three great talkers I would encounter on this particular journey. He had started as a supporter of the military regime of Omar al Bashir, but had fallen out with him, and spent time in prison.

Turabi's analysis was that Sudan had experimented with military rule (General Abboud), then with democracy (Sadiq and Mahjoub), followed by a form of socialism (Nimeiri). None of them had worked. An Islamist regime (Bashir) was best suited to the country, but unfortunately this had also degenerated into rule by a strongman. Turabi and the National Islamic Front, the hard-line political party he headed for thirty years, was the intellectual force behind Bashir's regime, imposing a top-down ideological system on the country with scant regard for human rights, particularly in the South. As with the Muslim Brotherhood, Turabi's answer to every question was that 'Islam is the answer'.

However, at our meeting Turabi cut a sadly disillusioned and even rather tragic figure, whose death in 2016 would mark him down in history, like Robespierre, as a revolutionary who had been eaten by his own revolution.

Moving up to Cairo, I found our ambassador, Sir James Adams, whom I had succeeded in Paris, ensconced in the impressive, but unfortunately leaking, embassy beside the Nile (buckets were placed in strategic positions). My main interlocutor there was Osama al Baz, diplomatic advisor to President Mubarak. Another highly articulate observer of the diplomatic scene, he gave me a thoughtful account of how it was seen from Cairo. The chill wind of the Arab Spring was a decade away.

Next stop, Beirut. The security picture there was, as so often, fragile, and our ambassador, Maeve (later Dame Maeve) Fort, was being looked after by a UK-based close security team. On the drive into town from the airport Maeve pointed out the locations where British hostages had been seized by militias at the start of their long ordeals. The atmosphere in the ambassadorial Rolls was subdued. I felt thankful for Maeve's support team in the following car.

In Beirut I called on the third of my outstanding Middle East interlocutors, Fuad Butros, a veteran Lebanese diplomat. Our interesting and informative talk was lubricated, as I found not unusual in the case of Lebanese diplomats, with a glass of champagne. Taking my leave in a relaxed frame of mind, I was momentarily disconcerted to find journalists and TV cameras waiting outside the door, which would be expected for a visiting minister, but not normally for an official. Fortunately, Maeve just had time to whisper in my ear 'Don't forget Security Council Resolution X' – I forget exactly which, since there have been so many in relation to Lebanon – before I faced the cameras. The first question was indeed on Britain's position on Resolution X, to which I was able to confirm the UK's firm commitment.

A similar problem arose when I called on the Palestinian leader, Yasser Arafat, at his Tunis headquarters, after the breakthrough in the Israel-Palestinian talks in Oslo had led to his visiting London and being accepted as someone the UK was prepared to do business with. After our conversation, which consisted of him delivering his familiar monologue on the injustices heaped on the Palestinians, we came out together to find the media, in substantial numbers, awaiting our appearance. Whereupon Arafat repeated his monologue, with the additional twist of declaring that his British visitor was in full agreement with all he had said. I got out of the trap by asserting the UK's well-known position that it was in full agreement with the need for a two-state solution to the problem. This was one occasion when I, as an official, had to deploy the skills of a politician.

My visits to the region naturally included Israel, as well as Jerusalem and the West Bank. In Jerusalem I was given an official lunch in the famous King David Hotel, which provided an opportunity for some plain speaking across the table. I found the Israelis to be much preoccupied with security matters. But rather than the threat from their Arab neighbours, which had become stabilized, the new and serious threat they perceived was from Iran. At the time this was a relatively new strand in their thinking.

My talks with the Israelis were balanced with talks with Palestinian leaders in Orient House, their headquarters at the time, in Jerusalem. In the West Bank town of Ramallah I called at the home of Hanan Ashrawi, whom I found the most impressive of them. An Anglican (as she mentioned), with perfect English and the recipient of numerous international awards, she made a persuasive spokeswoman for their cause at peace talks and on TV. I found the Palestinians to be increasingly depressed at the oppressive nature of the Israeli occupation. A striking example was the stories I was told in the highly impressive St John's Eye Hospital in Jerusalem about the difficulties placed in the way of Palestinian patients trying to reach the hospital at the numerous Israeli checkpoints in the West Bank. A relatively short journey could take hours, I was told.

All the Palestinian politicians I encountered (below the level of Yasser Arafat) were of high quality and a match for their Israeli counterparts. In addition to Hanan Ashrawi they included Nabil Sha'th, Faisal Husseini (of the prominent Jerusalem family) and the late Saeb Erekat, their long-time spokesman.

In Tel Aviv the Defence Attaché in our embassy took me on a fascinating drive around the north of the country, including a call on the mayor of Qiryat Shemona, the most northerly town, nestling below the Golan Heights, which Israel had captured from Syria in the 1967 Six Day War. The mayor recounted how intolerable life had been in the town before that war, when it had been regularly subjected to Syrian shelling from the Heights. The inhabitants had been forced to spend long periods in air-raid shelters.

I also learned how, by an inspired act of psychological warfare during the fighting, the Israelis had induced the Syrian forces to abandon their positions on the Heights and retreat in confusion by telling them that Israeli forces were already behind their lines in Damascus, having their way with their womenfolk there! By this means, the resistance to the potentially costly assault had been weakened.

The Foreign Secretary Douglas Hurd, who took a close interest in the Middle East, decided that Syria's participation in the Allied coalition that had evicted Iraqi forces from Kuwait in the First Gulf War made it timely for him to visit the country in an effort to improve our bilateral relationship. It was also at a point where Israel had made some progress in its talks with the Syrians and the prospect of a peace deal – between these most intractable of enemies – seemed not entirely fanciful. I accompanied Hurd as his advisor.

We called on President Hafez al-Assad in his hill-top palace over-looking Damascus. Assad had in effect ruled Syria since 1970 as Prime Minister first, then President, and became a fixed item on the Middle East strongman scene, to be followed in the same role after his death in 2000 by his son Bashar. Hurd led off by observing that the Syrian-Israeli talks seemed to have made gratifying progress, and that the only remaining territorial issue was a strip of Syrian land on the east bank of Lake Tiberias (which the Israelis were determined to hang on to for security reasons). Did the President think that this obstacle was surmountable?

Assad was a sick man and looked decidedly frail. But the question caused him to throw off his lethargy and launch into an hour-long tirade on the iniquities of Israel. The burden of his discourse was that every single inch of Syrian land was sacred, and could under no circumstances be bargained away. We got the message.

The visit was otherwise memorable for the tourism the Syrians laid on for us the following day, in the course of which, accompanied by the Syrian Foreign Minister, we visited the two spectacular sites of the desert city of Palmyra and the great Crusader castle of Krak des Chevaliers, many miles apart. We accomplished this feat by a combination of helicopter and aircraft flights, which seemed like cheating!

In Palmyra, the city of the fourth-century Queen Zenobia (who had modelled herself on another queen, Cleopatra), where Lady Hester Stanhope, in the nineteenth century, had been welcomed in triumphal style under Hadrian's Arch, we were shown round by the learned and delightful Director, Khaled al-Asaad, whose grisly fate it was to be brutally beheaded in the Roman theatre by the so-called Islamic State (or Da'esh), when they captured the city from the Syrian forces, twenty years later. Both the sites we visited would become egregious examples of the incalculable harm that the Syrian civil war would do to the country's great cultural heritage.

*   *   *

Iran was a major preoccupation during my time in the job. During my Kuwait posting, thirteen years earlier, it had been in the throes of the Islamic Revolution. Since then it had suffered a grinding eight-year war with Iraq. One way in which that had impacted on the Office was the so-called Arms-to-Iraq affair. This involved the sale to Iraq of manufacturing equipment with a dual use, in that, in addition to its civil application, it could be used to manufacture highly sophisticated armaments. The question was how far the government had supported the sale, misleading parliament in the process. When the trial of the manufacturers for illegal arms exporting collapsed, after a minister, Alan Clark, had admitted to not having given truthful evidence, it developed into a major scandal. A senior judge, Lord Justice Richard Scott, was appointed to head an inquiry into the whole affair.

The inquiry was under way when I became Director, Middle East. I was not directly involved because I had been in Berlin, far from the action, when it happened. But Foreign Office colleagues were being summoned as witnesses. Some were finding giving evidence a bruising experience, due to the forensic intensity of the questioning. I found myself having to give comfort to the walking wounded.

UK relations with Iran were in a poor state. Full diplomatic relations had been broken off over the Iranian *fatwa* on the author Salman Rushdie in 1989. Rushdie had provoked the rage of Ayatollah Khomeini and others in the Islamic world with his book *The Satanic Verses*, which Khomeini perceived as being blasphemous in its treatment of the Prophet Mohammed. In the *fatwa*, an instruction to the faithful, the Ayatollah had called explicitly for the author to be killed, along with anybody else who had a part in the book's publication.

The *fatwa* had a number of violent consequences. Some of the bookshops in London and a number of other countries were hit by firebombs. The book was banned in India and many Muslim countries. It was also burned on the streets of Bradford. Iranian officials offered a bounty of $6 million to anyone who killed Rushdie, who had been put under police protection.

I had taken over from my predecessor, Sir David Gore-Booth, the role of Salman Rushdie's contact point in the FCO. Rushdie would call on me, accompanied by Dr Frances D'Souza, the executive director of the human rights organisation Article 19, who acted as his main spokesperson (she was later to become Lord Speaker of the House of Lords). The purpose of the meetings was to discuss whether any progress could be made on the diplomatic front to get the *fatwa* lifted. The UK's efforts in this regard were supported by the EEC, who had withdrawn their ambassadors, for a short period, in a coordinated gesture of solidarity.

Events took a turn for the better when the Iranians indicated to our embassy in Tehran that they would like to resolve the problem

– short of lifting the *fatwa*, which as a religious edict promulgated by Ayatollah Khomeini, who was no longer alive, was irrevocable. But they would first like to see a positive gesture from our side. That desire was reciprocated in London, particularly by the business community, who were exasperated at seeing profitable opportunities being seized by their competitors, benefiting from the freeze in UK–Iran relations.

One way of meeting the Iranians' desire for a gesture from us was for a senior official to go to Tehran to discuss the issue. Our ministers were somewhat nervous at the political risks involved, but eventually decided that I should fly to Tehran and test the water.

In Tehran I stayed with Jeffrey (later Sir Jeffrey) James, the Chargé d'Affaires, in the leafy embassy compound in the north of the city. The historic official residence in the downtown compound, in which the Chancery offices were also situated, had been vacant since the departure of the ambassador. During the Tehran Conference in the Second World War, meetings of the Big Three (Churchill, Stalin and Roosevelt) had taken place in the dining-room.

My initial interlocutor was the director-general for Western Europe in the foreign ministry. He led off with a prepared statement that the Iranians would not send any 'commandos' to assassinate Rushdie.

I responded that this statement was welcome, but not enough. The *fatwa* should be set aside. We needed to be satisfied that there was no longer any threat to Rushdie from Iranian leaders, government agencies or associated organisations, and that they would not incite others to carry it out.

I added that we understood the offence caused by the book, and had great respect for Islam. Our defence of Rushdie's right to live in peace, free from death threats, did not mean that we endorsed his views. Our European Community partners shared our concerns, as did other countries.

At a follow-up meeting with Deputy Foreign Minister Mahmoud Vaezi, I argued that the central point was that UK ministers needed to be able to convince Parliament that they genuinely believed there was no further threat to Rushdie's life. We parted on amicable terms, with Vaezi underlining the Iranians' desire for a constructive bilateral relationship.

I flew home – after blowing away the cobwebs with a hard game of tennis with Jeffrey – confident that some progress had been made, but with the feeling that what had stood in the way of our reaching agreement on a resolution of the problem had been the lack of an endorsement by the religious leaders in the holy city of Qum. I gave Salman Rushdie the (qualified) good news.

Ten days later, Douglas Hurd went over the same ground with the Iranian Foreign Minister Ali-Akbar Velayati, an articulate and professional diplomat, at a meeting in the margin of the UN General Assembly, at which I was present. The two ministers, who were keen not to let the *fatwa* get in the way of other business, agreed that discussions should be carried forward by Vaezi and me. In practice I was unable to play any further part in the story, as I left the FCO shortly afterwards to take up my post as ambassador in Prague.

It took a further five years before Salman Rushdie was able to live as a free man. After Foreign Secretary Robin Cook (Hurd's successor) had met his Iranian counterpart at UN headquarters in New York, again in the margins of the General Assembly, the two men stood together in front of the world's media, and the Iranian minister read the following statement:

> The Government of the Islamic Republic of Iran has no intention, nor is it going to take any action whatsoever, to threaten the life of the author of *The Satanic Verses*, or anybody associated with his work, nor will it encourage or assist anybody to do so.

The text was little different from the one I had discussed with Vaezi five years earlier. But, this time, its presentation in the most public fashion provided the necessary guarantee that it would be adhered to, which had been absent previously. The matter was over, although Salman Rushdie would continue to receive threats for years to come.

*   *   *

The Arab-Israeli dispute was the central issue in the Middle East. In my previous postings in the region – both in Sudan, during and after the Six Day War, and even more in Jordan, a front-line state – I had seen how it absorbed the attention of Arab leaders, as it did equally the leaders of Israel.

Returning to the subject, from the vantage point of FCO Director for the Middle East, I found that the agenda had been set by the conference held the previous year in Madrid. Co-sponsored by the US and the Soviet Union (making its last appearance on the international stage before its demise), the Madrid Conference brought together Israel, Jordan, Egypt, Lebanon and Syria for 'direct' talks. The Palestinian delegation, in order to meet Israeli objections to direct contact, had formed part of the Jordanian delegation. The conference had led to bilateral talks in Washington that seemed to be making little progress.

The EU had a joint policy, which was coordinated in a Middle East Working Group. Whenever I attended this group I found that Britain and France played the leading role, which was understandable, given their long experience in the region, and that the other member states tended to follow their lead.

In my experience, incidentally, the UK played a significant part in whatever discussions I attended in Brussels, not only on the Middle East, but on such varied subjects as Afghanistan, the environment, terrorism and the Law of the Sea. It is sad to think that we have no further voice there.

The EU kept in touch with the Madrid follow-up talks by meeting all the delegations separately at the UN General Assembly in New York to be briefed on progress, and to report back subsequently to the EU as a whole. The EU team was composed of the so-called Troika of states: the member state currently holding the six-month presidency, together with the next state in line and the former state in that role. When I became involved, the UK had just handed over the EU Presidency to Denmark, but we were still a member of the Troika.

By this time, the EU team's calls on the delegations in New York had become somewhat ritualistic. One could write the report before the meetings took place. Having completed the round of the delegations, my overriding impression was that the Madrid process had reached stalemate. That stalemate was about to be broken in dramatic fashion.

On August Bank Holiday 1993 I was telephoned by Christopher Long, a fellow Arabist and, at the time, our ambassador in Cairo, who was home on leave. He said that he had been contacted by a senior member of the PLO named Nabil Sha'th. The PLO, under its leader, Yasser Arafat, having been ejected from Jordan and then suffering the same fate in Lebanon, had made its base in Tunis. From there it kept in close contact with the government of Egypt, as a leading Arab country. Sha'th was the unofficial foreign minister of the PLO; in the course of his visits to Cairo he had come to know Long.

Long said that Sha'th had told him that he had an important message he wished to convey to the British government. He would like to have a meeting over the coming weekend, including with a senior member of the Foreign Office. We arranged to meet Sha'th for breakfast on the Bank Holiday Monday at the Kensington Hotel.

It was an extraordinary meeting. Sha'th's message was that he was a member of a PLO delegation that had been holding direct talks with an Israeli delegation in Oslo, secretly brokered by the Norwegians. These had resulted in substantial progress being made towards a peace deal between the two sides. He was passing through London on his way to report to Yasser Arafat (whom he spoke to on the phone during breakfast).

This was momentous news. The Israelis had hitherto refused to engage in direct talks with the PLO, which they had branded a terrorist organisation. At Madrid they had insisted the PLO should form part of the Jordanian delegation. Their change of heart had only come about when the veteran Foreign Minister, Shimon Peres (a dove in Israeli terms), had managed to persuade the Prime Minister, Yitzhak Rabin – a hawk, whose main preoccupation was the country's security – that it was time to try to break the post-Madrid logjam. Not even the Americans knew that the talks were taking place, by their own choice (as I later learned from Mona Juul, their main Norwegian promoter) – though whether this was really because they did not want to know, or because they knew but did not want to be seen to know, was unclear.

Sha'th was very open in giving us the details of the agreement reached, which I frantically scribbled down. The stage had been set by the two sides exchanging Letters of Mutual Recognition. Israel had recognised the PLO as the legitimate representative body of the Palestinian people. The PLO, for its part, had recognised, for the first time, Israel's right to exist in peace. I considered this the most significant part of the whole package, since recognition, once accorded, could scarcely be withdrawn. (Time has shown that I was over-optimistic on this point, since the PLO 'suspended' its recognition in 2018.)

This vital preliminary step out of the way, the agreement – what came to be known as the Oslo Process – was divided into two stages. A first stage, or Interim Agreement, provided for Israel to gradually withdraw its forces from the Gaza Strip and parts of the West Bank, which would be handed over to Palestinian self-government. Yasser Arafat and the PLO leadership would return to their homeland from Tunis and form a Palestinian Authority to govern the areas from which Israel would withdraw, although Israel would retain a security oversight.

The PLO would accept that its 'armed struggle' would be replaced by negotiation and diplomacy.

The second, or Final Stage, provided for negotiations to take place after five years on the deeply contentious issues of the return of Palestinian refugees, Israeli settlements in the Occupied Territories, the borders between the two states and, last but not least, the status of Jerusalem, which both sides claimed as their capital.

After the meeting I made haste back to the Foreign Office, clutching my notes, to compose a report to ministers and a telegram to posts overseas. In Whitehall the news was greeted with some scepticism. What was the likelihood that this agreement was not just another false start on the long and tortuous road to an Arab-Israeli peace deal? I was in favour of giving it a chance.

One issue requiring immediate attention was adjusting the UK's attitude towards the PLO, now that it had seemingly adopted the path of peace in place of armed struggle. Even after the Madrid Conference in which the US had dropped its classification of the PLO as a terrorist organisation, UK ministers had continued to be reluctant to receive any PLO representative, until Faisal Husseini, a respected member of one of the leading Palestinian families in Jerusalem, called on Douglas Hogg, a minister of state in the Foreign Office, the previous year. The Palestinian cause was ably presented in London by Afif Safieh, who was accredited within the Arab League mission. Safieh had great verbal dexterity and was adept in argument. But the time had now come to raise the level of our contact, which meant inviting Yasser Arafat himself to London. I was apprehensive how this would go, but I need not have been. Scruples were swallowed. Arafat came to London that December on an official visit and was delighted with his reception, including the symbolic photograph of him shaking hands with John Major outside the door of 10 Downing Street. The Foreign Secretary, Douglas Hurd, also hosted a convivial lunch in his honour in his official residence.

Another step we took, to celebrate and promote the new hopeful atmosphere, was to hold a one-day Round Table with the title 'Towards Peace in the Middle East', in the prestigious Locarno Rooms in the Foreign Office, bringing together prominent members of the Jewish and Palestinian communities in London for the purpose of getting to know each other. It concentrated on two issues: how the two communities could contribute to the peace process, and the prospects for economic development and British trade with the region. We also laid

37. After the so-called Oslo breakthrough in Israel-Palestinian talks the Palestinian leader Yasser Arafat was invited to London and received at 10 Downing Street by Prime Minister John Major. Arafat's mood was positive and optimistic, though 'breakthrough' became viewed as a misnomer. (Photo: author)

on a good lunch to help things along. It was a great success. There was much appreciation of the FCO's role in organising this important and worthwhile occasion.

Middle East Heads of Mission Conferences were held periodically to bring together our representatives in the region to discuss the issues of the day. After the Oslo breakthrough we decided to hold one, for the first time, in Israel and Jerusalem. At our meeting in Tel Aviv we invited an Israeli official, who had played a big part in the Oslo talks, to give us an Israeli perspective. This was Yossi Beilin, one of the brilliant young team brought into Israeli diplomacy by the Foreign Minister Shimon Peres. We then moved up to Jerusalem to hear the Palestinian side of the story, from their chief negotiator, Saeb Erekat. They were, in my view, equally persuasive – which is the essence of the whole tragedy.

After Rabin and Arafat had signed the Oslo Declaration to plot the course towards Palestinian self-government, and formally end the Palestinian campaign of violence known as the First Intifada, Israel began to withdraw its troops from most of Gaza and Jericho, the

West Bank town in the Jordan Valley (where the British archaeologist Kathleen Kenyon had discovered one of the first constructions of human habitation). This enabled Arafat to move his base to Jericho from Tunis. Thereafter Rabin, Arafat and Peres jointly shared the Nobel Peace Prize.

So far, so good. But progress in the talks was slow, and Palestinian groups that rejected the Oslo agreement (known as 'rejectionists') continued their attacks on the Israelis. There was also continuing opposition to the agreement among Israelis themselves, particularly those on the right wing. The tragic outcome was that two months after Rabin and Arafat had signed the Interim Agreement for a further transfer of power and territory to the Palestinian National Authority, Rabin was shot dead by an Israeli right-wing extremist.

This proved to be a fatal blow to the Oslo Process, although it suffered a lingering death. Five years later, in 2000, talks between Yasser Arafat and the new Israeli Prime Minister, Ehud Barak, broke down over the timing and extent of further Israeli troops withdrawals. Israeli reluctance to hasten their withdrawal was due to the Palestinians' failure to convince them that they could be trusted to play their part by establishing sufficiently tight security control over the areas where they exercised authority.

The *coup de grâce* was administered later that year by the Likud Party leader, Ariel Sharon, visiting the Temple Mount in Jerusalem (Haram al Sharif to the Muslims), with a large group of supporters, in a manner which Muslims considered to be a desecration of their holy places. Buoyed by his resulting popularity with the right wing in Israel, Sharon defeated Ehud Barak in elections the following year. Once he became Prime Minister, he declined to resume peace talks with the Palestinians. The consequence was the Palestinian uprising known as the Second Intifada.

It was a matter of deep personal regret to me that the secret Oslo talks, so brilliantly orchestrated by the Norwegian diplomats and husband-and-wife team Mona Juul and Terje Rød-Larsen, did not ultimately lead to that 'just and lasting peace' between Israel and the Palestinian people, which has proved so elusive.

The talks themselves were the subject of an excellent play, *Oslo*, by JT Rogers, which was later staged, to acclaim, in New York and London.

*   *   *

My regrettably short time in the Director job ended, once again, with a royal visit, in this case a Gulf Tour by the Prince of Wales. Prince Charles had delivered a powerful speech in Oxford in October 1993 on Islam and the West. The thinking behind it was to correct the negative image of Islam that was being created by 'Islamic fundamentalism', as it was called at the time.

In his speech Prince Charles had argued that Islamic law, rather than being a medieval construct, was based on principles of equity and compassion, at least when it was administered with integrity and not deformed for political reasons.

As regards the vexed question of the position of women, the Islamic world should not be judged by extreme cases. Women in Turkey, Egypt and Syria, for example, had been given the vote as early as women in Europe, and women prime ministers had emerged in both Pakistan and Bangladesh.

He had given examples of the cultural and scientific richness of the Moorish empire in Spain, which had lasted for eight hundred years – exemplified by the magnificent library in Córdoba – and which had bequeathed numerous advances in science, mathematics and medicine, and more besides, to the West. He had concluded with a plea for mutual understanding, on the basis that Islam and the West had much to learn from each other.

Invited to do so, I had made some modest contributions to the drafting of the speech. One point I remember making was that 'Islamic fundamentalism' should not be considered a monolithic doctrine, based on some central agenda; it was more of a protest movement rooted in the specific grievances within each particular country, expressed in different ways. Prince Charles thanked me for this.

A few months later he embarked on a tour of the Gulf as a follow-up to his speech, which had been warmly appreciated in the region. I was invited to accompany him as one of his advisors, together with General Sir Peter de la Billière, who had played a prominent part in the Gulf War, and Lord Denman, a banker (and President of the Royal Society for Asian Affairs) who was highly respected in the region. Also on board was Jonathan Dimbleby, together with a film crew, who were filming for the TV interview Dimbleby conducted with Prince Charles.

Much of the tour took place from the Royal Yacht *Britannia*, starting in Kuwait. For me it was a privileged experience. Prince Charles made few demands on us trio of advisors, other than asking us to join him for the occasional discussion, and accompanying him on his calls on the Rulers along the way. They were uniformly delighted by the Oxford speech and went far beyond the norm in the warmth of their reception of the Prince of Wales. The normally taciturn Amir of Kuwait, for example, made a gracious dinner speech, and King Fahd of Saudi Arabia received Prince Charles in Jedda with great ceremony, and at a civilised hour. The goodwill generated was tangible.

The formalities of the day over, we would all gather to relax over a glass of whisky in the wardroom of HMY *Britannia*. Prince Charles showed himself to be a gifted mimic in recalling some of the day's events.

I left the party when the official part of the tour was over and followed my own programme of visits to a few posts I had not yet included in my tours of my parish. One of these was to Bahrain, where, probably because of my association with Prince Charles, the Amir, a figure of well-known amiability, was even standing on the steps of his palace to greet me!

Another bonus from the tour was that it enabled me to make a return visit to Jordan, of which I had happy memories dating from our time there in the 1970s. On this occasion I was received in audience by King Hussein himself. One of the reasons for this audience may have been that the king was taking any opportunity to repair his relationship with the UK, which had been temporarily damaged by his support for Saddam Hussein of Iraq (no relation) in the First Gulf War.

I had been a strong admirer of King Hussein since our tour in Amman, and was delighted not only to be received by him, but also to be a beneficiary of his legendary habit (acquired at Sandhurst) of addressing lesser mortals as 'Sir'. My admiration was based on observing his skill and courage, firstly in keeping his country stable in the face of conflicting pressures from the traditional tribal element in its population, and the more urbanised Palestinians who formed an increasingly large proportion of it; and secondly in maintaining a relatively balanced position in the Arab-Israeli dispute which was the all-consuming obsession in the region.

The stability of Jordan under King Hussein struck me as a partial answer, apart from the limited powers enjoyed by the elected assemblies in Lebanon and Kuwait and some other countries, to those who argued that Israel deserved to enjoy more support from the West than the Arab countries, because it was the only functioning democracy in the region. This argument only had any force as long as one stuck to the narrow definition of parliamentary democracy, which Israel itself had imported from the West. But Jordan – to take one example among the Arab countries – managed to be a stable and harmonious country, with an acceptable, if not ideal, level of human rights, although power was essentially held in the hands of the king. The security forces kept a tight rein, but the king remained demonstrably popular. It was a system that suited the history and culture of the region.

*   *   *

Back in the UK, there was an interesting sequel to the Royal Tour. Prince Charles held a seminar at his country house, Highgrove, to consider ways of building on the tour's success. A number of distinguished academics and religious leaders were invited, and I was also included. When my turn came to make a contribution, I offered the thought that the main priority should be to avoid entering the twenty-first century (still seven years away) refighting the Crusades of the twelfth and thirteenth centuries.

With the bombing of the World Trade Center and the subsequent invasion of Iraq a decade later, this proved to be a salient observation. When President George W Bush then talked of a 'crusade' against terrorism, this was taken by a new generation of Arabs as indisputable confirmation of the West's intentions.

Sadly, my days in the Middle East Director's hot seat were numbered. I was told that, since I had little more than three years in the Service until my fixed retirement date at the age of 60, and this was the minimum period to make one eligible for an ambassadorial appointment, I had better make a move. Three posts were about to fall vacant: Madrid, Cairo and Prague. It was clear that I was not a credible candidate for Madrid since I had no Spanish, but I was credible for either of the other two posts. The (Spanish-speaking) incumbent in either Cairo or Prague would go to Madrid, and I could then slot into the vacant embassy.

Thus it was that, when David Brighty was appointed to Madrid, I went to Buckingham Palace, with Henrietta, to kiss the Queen's hand as her new ambassador at Prague in the Czech Republic. The wheel of fate had come full circle since, twenty-eight years previously, Foreign Secretary Michael Stewart had laid down the conditions for my remaining in the Foreign Office on marriage – including never being able to serve in my wife's country of origin. This was where we were now going.

Chapter 13

Ambassador in Prague: The Post-Communist Czech Republic in a State of Transition

A month after the Fall of the Berlin Wall, in November 1989, the process started in Czechoslovakia which would become known as the Velvet Revolution. It culminated, shortly before the end of the year, with the overthrow of the hard-line communist government, and demands by the vast crowd gathered in Wenceslas Square, in the centre of Prague, for the installation of the dissident playwright Václav Havel in Prague Castle as the new president. This was the ignominious end of the communist regime that had ruled the country since it came to power in a *coup d'état* in 1948.

The state of Czechoslovakia was created at the end of the First World War out of the collapse of the defeated Austro-Hungarian empire. It was a federation composed of Bohemia and Moravia, which together make up the Czech lands, and Slovakia to the east, adjoining

---

Photo: Our Prague Residence and garden, taken from the grounds of Prague Castle, and looking down to Prague Old Town below, did much to enrich our Czech experience.

Hungary. Its first president, Tomáš Masaryk, had found influential advocates for the formation of the new state in the British political activist Robert Seton Watson and the *Times* correspondent in Vienna, Henry Wickham Steed.

Neville Chamberlain, when attempting in 1938 to rationalise his appeasement policy vis-à-vis Hitler's determination to annex the Sudetenland, a part of Czechoslovakia, into Germany, notoriously described Czechoslovakia as 'a small, far away country of which we know little', ignoring its important historical links with Britain. For example, Anne of Bohemia, the daughter of Charles IV, the most important medieval Bohemian monarch and Holy Roman Emperor, married the English King Richard II in 1382.

Another link lies in the story about the origin of the Prince of Wales's device of the three feathers at the Battle of Crécy in 1310, during England's Hundred Years War with France. Charles IV's father, the blind King John of Luxembourg and Bohemia, fighting on the French side, told his knights to guide his horse in a charge on the Black Prince (of Wales). He was cut down before he reached his target. But the Black Prince was so impressed with his bravery that he adopted the king's three feathers and the motto 'Ich dien' (I serve).

Coming more up to date, England was closely involved with the Czech nation at the beginning of the Thirty Years War, the continent-wide religious struggle for power that dominated Europe in the early seventeenth century. A dynastic link had been created by the marriage of Elizabeth Stuart, daughter of King James I of England, and VI of Scotland, to Frederick, Elector of the Palatinate in the Rhineland.

Having been made King of Bohemia in 1619, Frederick – the Winter King, as he became known thereafter – and Queen Elizabeth (the Winter Queen), had to flee Prague after the Bohemian nobility were defeated at the Battle of the White Mountain in 1620. Their sons Rupert of the Rhine (born in Prague during their brief reign) and Maurice returned to England to play a prominent part in the English Civil War.

Anticipating the death of the childless Queen Anne (all of whose children predeceased her, including many still births or miscarriages), when the English nobility were casting around for a member of the royal house with no connection to Catholicism to whom to offer the throne, their choice fell on Elizabeth's daughter Sophia. Unfortunately, she died shortly before Queen Anne, so it was her son, the Elector of

Hanover, who assumed the British throne in 1701 as King George I. From him the Crown has passed by direct descent to Queen Elizabeth II.

We were reminded of the dynastic link between the English and Bohemian royal houses on a daily basis in our residence, the Thun Palace, situated directly below Prague Castle. In the Reception Room hung twin portraits by the Dutch painter Gerrit van Honthorst of the Winter King and the Winter Queen of Bohemia. And the Dining Room was graced with a magnificent portrait of their son, Prince Rupert, as a dashing young cavalier, by Sir Anthony Van Dyck.

Britain's relations with the newly formed Czechoslovakia between the two world wars reflected its policy at that time of appeasing Hitler, culminating in the infamous Munich Agreement in 1938. The effect of this was to give Nazi Germany a free hand in occupying the Sudetenland, along the German-Czech border, followed some months later by its occupation of the whole country. Hitler travelled from Berlin to review his troops in the Giants' Courtyard of Prague Castle.

In this dismal picture of the more recent connections between the two countries, there were mitigating shards of light. A number of Jewish Czech children were rescued from the approaching Nazis by a philanthropic British businessman, Nicholas Winton, who arranged for their transport by train to Britain as part of what came to be known as the Kindertransport. Each little figure wore a label bearing the name of the British family who had agreed to take them in – after heart-breaking partings from their parents at the Prague station. It was only more than fifty years later that Winton's role was recognised (with a knighthood), and he was reunited with some of 'his' children, in a highly emotional programme of Esther Rantzen's *This is Your Life*.

During the war, Britain became a refuge for the Czechoslovak leadership fleeing from Nazi oppression. Edvard Beneš led the exiled democratic government of Czechoslovakia in London, and Jan Masaryk, the former president Tomáš Masaryk's son, made inspiring broadcasts on the BBC to the Czechoslovak people during and after September 1939.

Making common cause with the Allies during the Second World War, many Czechs and Slovaks served with distinction in the Royal Air Force and with the British Army. Czechoslovak soldiers fought beside Allied forces in Western Europe and North Africa. Czechoslovak airmen fought with the RAF's famous Duxford Wing during the Battle of Britain, destroying at least ninety-two aircraft. They also served with distinction during the invasion of Normandy in 1944. On returning home after the war, many were to suffer years of imprisonment, persecution and even death at the hands of the communist regime. Having fought together with the Western Allies, these ex-combatants, were distrusted by the paranoid new regime, who saw them as potential fifth columnists.

After the birth of Czechoslovakia in 1919, Britain had had to find a suitable building for its legation (later embassy) to the new state. It managed to lease the Thun Palace from Count Thun, and bought it outright six years later, together with its furniture and all its contents, to house both the legation's offices and the Residence.

The building had a colourful history. It was originally one of the properties of Albrecht of Wallenstein, the successful commander of the Habsburg army in the Thirty Years War. When the emperor became suspicious of Wallenstein's continued loyalty, he arranged for him to be assassinated. One of the assassins was Walter Leslie, a Scottish soldier of fortune, who received the palace as a reward for his work. In due course Leslie sold the palace to Count Guidobad Thun, the Prince Archbishop of Salzburg. It remained in the hands of the Thun family for the next 260 years until eventually being acquired by Britain in 1919.

The most noteworthy event during that period was that Mozart stayed there, under the patronage of the Thun family, when visiting Prague. On one of these visits he realised that he had not written the Prelude to his opera *Don Giovanni*, which was about to receive its first performance in the Estates Theatre in the town below. He sat down at the piano and put this to right.

The Residence is one of the glories of the British diplomatic estate. It is co-located with the embassy offices and reached through an imposing gatehouse which gives onto a large courtyard. Beneath the royal coat-of-arms, a dedicated door leads to a stately lift, serving the Residence on the third floor.

On leaving the lift, visitors find themselves in an imposing hall. To the right are the large reception rooms; to the left are French windows leading (unexpectedly, since one is on the third floor) to a large garden backed by a high stone wall. Above this are the gardens of Prague Castle. From the reception rooms one looks down in the other direction onto the river Vltava (or Moldau) and the old town of Prague, with its lights twinkling at night. The views in both directions are magical.

* * *

I flew to Prague in July 1994, a few weeks ahead of Henrietta in order to spend some time in a Czech family, in the university town of Olomouc, in an effort to improve my somewhat rudimentary knowledge of the language. My teacher, a lecturer in the English and American department, told me he had learned his English mainly from listening to the Beatles' songs. My command of the language made only modest progress (coming to my first Slavonic language in my fifties, I found it difficult to achieve the level of proficiency of my other languages, French, German and Arabic), but through conversations with my teacher, and travelling around the countryside with him in the car the embassy had provided me with, I began to get some feel for the country.

As Henrietta joined me in Prague a few weeks later it really felt that the wheel of fate had come full circle. When the Foreign Secretary had agreed to my both marrying her and remaining in the Service, nearly thirty years before, one of his main conditions had been that we could never serve in her native country. And here we were.

Henrietta had been born in the Moravian town of Zlín, north of the regional capital, Brno. Zlín was a company town, the home of the world-famous shoe company Bata, of which her father had been a senior executive. The founder of the company, Tomáš Bata, was one of the more remarkable entrepreneurs of the twentieth century, credited with achieving for the shoe industry what Henry Ford had introduced in the car industry – the manufacture of good-quality, good-value shoes which were made and sold on an international scale. His untimely death in a plane crash in 1932 left the company in the hands of his 17-year-old son, also Tomáš, who went on to extensively expand the brand and its worldwide shoe manufacturing.

Aware of the growing threat of a communist take-over in the country at the end of the war, Henrietta's father had been advised to take up an opportunity to fill a managerial post with Bata overseas. When he left with his wife and Henrietta, their only child, he little thought that, due to the communist take-over that eventually occurred in 1948, they would not return. In due course, after working for a time in Egypt, he accepted a challenge to establish a Bata factory, in Cyprus, then still a British colony. The family loved Cyprus, not least because a number of Czech RAF personnel were serving there. The parents made it their home and are buried there.

As for Henrietta, when the attacks by EOKA terrorists on British personnel, including school buses, made it too dangerous to remain on the island, she was sent to a boarding school in England, Hollington Park School in St Leonards-on-Sea, East Sussex. She emerged a few years later as a typical English schoolgirl, having lost her Czech, which her parents, having in due course abandoned hope of returning to their native land, no longer used when speaking to her. When she arrived to join me in Prague, she set about (re)learning Czech, by attending classes at Charles University – which she found both enjoyable and productive.

Henrietta was welcomed to Prague with a full-page profile in the English-language *Prague Post*, under the headline 'Jindra (Henrietta) Honešová is Lady Burton now'. Written by the editor and founder of the paper, the veteran American-Czech journalist Alan Levy, it recounted how 'a British diplomat sacrificed his career for the Czech-born woman he loved – and became ambassador to her homeland'.

The country in which I was starting my mission was in a state of transition, five years after the end of communism which had suppressed its natural verve for the previous forty-one years, leaving its mark on every aspect of life, including the drab appearance of towns and cities and the degrading of the environment. Driving in from the German border to the north, for example, as I first did on a cold and foggy night, I was greeted by a forest of dead trees, killed by pollution, and scantily clad prostitutes lining the road in the hope of attracting the attention of truck-drivers. A dispiriting impression.

But the Czech Republic had started with many advantages. Under the avuncular leadership of Tomáš Masaryk it had been a functioning parliamentary democracy between the wars, the only one in Europe east of the Rhine. Its economy had a strong industrial base due to a tradition of engineering excellence. One example was the Bren light machine-gun used by the British Army in the Second World War (and still in use when I did my military service in the fifties) – and a strong automotive tradition (Skoda cars) without mentioning its famous beer. Its world-class cultural heritage in music, literature, architecture, the cinema and other arts and sciences meant that it was a natural fit with the Western liberal democracies.

An ambassador's mission begins officially with a ceremony in which he or she presents 'credentials' to the head of state of the country to which they are accredited. These take the form of two letters: one informing the president of the withdrawal of the previous ambassador, and the other introducing, in suitably formal language, the new ambassador. The letters – officially known as Letters of Credence – are signed by the Queen herself, reflecting the fact that an ambassador is her personal representative – correctly described as 'Her Majesty's Ambassador'.

A highlight of my career in the Diplomatic Service was the presentation of my Letters of Credence to President Václav Havel in Prague Castle. I drove to the castle with the senior members of my staff, alighting from my official car at the entrance to the Giants' Courtyard (so called because of the figures of two giant warriors over the gates). Then came the emotional experience of standing to attention before a guard of honour, while the band played 'God Save the Queen'. I then inspected the guard, whose colourful – some would say Ruritanian – uniforms had been introduced by the first post-communist chancellor to the president, the immensely grand Prince Karel Schwarzenberg.

I was the first British ambassador to be accredited to the Czech Republic, rather than to the former state of Czechoslovakia. From the time of its creation, the two component parts of that state had never been easy bedfellows. In the Second World War, Nazi Germany had treated them differently: the Czech part was a Protectorate under the direct control – until he was assassinated by commandos sent from Britain – of the vicious murderer Reinhardt Heydrich, whereas Slovakia retained a measure of independence under its quisling leader Father Tiso (who was hanged after the war for treason).

After the fall of communism, the two leading figures (under President Havel), in Prague and Bratislava respectively, were of a very contrasting stamp. The Prague government was headed by Václav Klaus, a self-assured professor of economics and a great admirer of Margaret Thatcher, whereas his opposite number in Bratislava was a tough crypto-communist named Vladimír Mečiar. Mečiar resented what he saw as the patronising attitude of the Czechs towards Slovakia.

Matters came to a head in a confrontation in 1992 between the two men in Brno, in which Mečiar demanded that Slovakia be allowed to secede from the federation. Somewhat to his surprise, Klaus agreed, and the split was formalised on 31 December 1992, without delay and, crucially, without parliamentary approval, in the Villa Tugendhat in that city – an iconic modernist building designed by Mies van der Rohe. The separate Czech and Slovak Republics came into existence the following day.

So, the Velvet Revolution, which saw the end of the communist regime, was followed by the Velvet Divorce which, fairly amicably, divided the country into two, about eighteen months before my taking up my post. To alleviate any problems for those living immediately on either side, the border remained fairly porous, with some crossing points left lightly manned. Since the populations of the two new countries divided neatly as two-thirds Czech and one-third Slovak, it made sense for Czechoslovak assets, such as central bank reserves and the armed forces, to be divided broadly on a similar ratio. This resulted in remarkably little friction.

*   *   *

On my arrival in Prague – whose baroque beauty was a constant delight – in the hot summer of 1994, I found the political discourse in the Czech Republic framed by the competing visions of the two Václavs (pronounced *vatslav*), Havel and Klaus. Havel was by now a highly regarded international figure, an icon of post-communist democratic values in Central Europe. He had been the driving force in the establishment of the Visegrad Group of countries in the region, named after the small town on the Danube in Hungary where the leaders of the four component countries – Poland, Hungary, Slovakia (after the divorce) and the Czech Republic – came together in 1991. Their shared objective was to join NATO and the European Union and to pool their experience in making the transition from communist-style command economies.

Havel's ambition for his country was that it should re-join, as he saw it, the community of democratic nations of which it had been a member in the inter-war years, but from which it had been effectively severed from the time of the Munich Agreement in 1938 up to the Velvet Revolution fifty-one years later. The Nazi occupation during the war had been followed, after a brief and uneasy period of restored democracy under President Edvard Beneš, by the *coup d'état* that brought the Soviet-backed Communist Party to power in 1948 – and led, incidentally, to the creation of NATO by an increasingly alarmed West.

Internally, Havel aspired to be a moral influence on his countrymen as they faced the challenge of changing the ingrained habits of the communist years, particularly the need to take responsibility for one's actions. He was concerned to combat both the moral and actual corruption in the country. He delivered a weekly 'fireside chat' on the radio to share his thinking, which did not always make him popular. Unfortunately, the hardships he had endured during his periods of imprisonment under the communists, together with his heavy smoking, had taken a toll on his health, which had become precarious.

As for Václav Klaus – an astute politician – he had outflanked the more unworldly Havel after the Velvet Revolution and set up a centre-right Eurosceptic party, the ODS (the abbreviation translating into Civic Democratic Party), with which he had won the first democratic election, leading to him becoming Prime Minister. He was not greatly interested in foreign affairs, which he tended to leave to Havel.

But Klaus took great credit for the successful transformation of the economy, which he claimed was due to the application of economic principles he had developed as an academic economist, specifically the requirement for two 'cushions'. He argued that, firstly, the liberalisation of the country's foreign trade had been cushioned by devaluation of the currency. And secondly, painful restructuring of the economy to Western standards had also needed to be cushioned by holding down real wages. The three essential elements in the transformation of Czech society were, in Klaus's view, liberalisation, deregulation and privatisation. He recognised, however, that the systemic transformation of a command economy into a market economy was not merely an exercise in applied economics or political science; it was also a process involving millions of human beings with their own dreams, preferences and priorities – which were not so easy to alter.

James M Buchanan, a Nobel laureate in economics, wrote that 'Almost uniquely, Václav Klaus combines a classical liberal vision of socio-political order and an understanding of the realities of modern democratic politics'. This made him one of the most sought-after Central European politicians in some circles in the West, notably by Thatcherites in Britain. Others were more inclined to be put off when Klaus emerged as a forthright Eurosceptic and climate-change denier.

Klaus believed that the Czech Republic had been fortunate in having had to haul itself up by its own bootstraps. He told me that he contrasted this achievement with the progress of East Germany, which, contrary to appearances, had suffered by being able to rely – after the implosion of the GDR – on boundless support from West Germany, so that it had avoided the painful transformation that it really needed.

I found both Havel and Klaus to be impressive, in different ways. The problem for the Czech Republic was that they could not stand each other. The diplomatic corps were shocked when, at his New Year Reception for all the gathered foreign envoys, Klaus gave a detailed exposé of the budget which had been passed by the Parliament that day, without mentioning that Havel had just come through a life-threatening heart operation that afternoon. One felt that Klaus resented the high regard in which Havel was held by world leaders, such as President Clinton.

The group of EU ambassadors, of which I was of course a member, would regularly invite each of the two Václavs, President and Prime Minister, separately, to a lunch discussion. These occasions were always worthwhile and each of them answered our questions freely. There was a sharp contrast between them in tone. What struck us about Klaus was that he displayed a marked lack of enthusiasm for the EU, bordering on disdain. It was also particularly striking that, counter-intuitively, he showed little interest in attracting EU investment. Indeed, he had taken the same approach to UK investment during my initial call on him, much to my surprise.

I was fortunate that my mission in Prague came at a formative time in the country's transition process. Britain was well placed to exercise an influential role, due, not least, in my opinion, to the high regard in which our ambassador at the time of the Velvet Revolution, Laurence O'Keeffe, had been held. Prior to being posted to Prague, before the Revolution, O'Keeffe had been a forceful critic of the human rights performance of the communist countries in the Helsinki Conference – which they had not enjoyed. He was rewarded by being sent to one of the worst offenders, Czechoslovakia. He had compensated for the frosty welcome he had received there by getting to know the leading dissidents, including Václav Havel, who were shortly to find themselves in power.

When I arrived in mid-1994, the former dissidents now running the country had not yet settled into the normal bureaucratic way of doing business. One practitioner of a less formal approach was Alexander Vondra, the young deputy foreign minister, who was close to Havel. A small discussion group consisting of Vondra, my American, French and German colleagues and me, was in the habit of meeting for a strictly informal dinner in one of the excellent local restaurants once a month to exchange ideas. The golden rule was that these were *bez kravaty* (no tie) occasions. We took it in turns to act as host.

Over (incomparable) Czech beer and good Czech food, Vondra could draw our attention to any ways in which he thought the West was not taking Czech concerns sufficiently into account. And we could suggest actions that the Czechs could take which would be well received in Western capitals. It was a creative, and effective, way of doing business.

Václav Havel's ambition for his country to join both NATO and the European Union was based on a perceived need for greater security. The memory of the Warsaw Pact invasion of 1968 was still raw. Not all his countrymen were of the same mind; some felt that their enforced membership of Comecon and the Warsaw Pact, under the previous regime, had hardly provided a good experience of belonging to such collective organisations.

There was also some reticence in London about extending NATO's security guarantee to the potentially unstable region of Central and Eastern Europe. This was gradually overcome through the shared experience of military exchanges, a successful visit by Defence Secretary Malcolm Rifkind and the secondment of a senior British officer as advisor to the Czech Chief of Staff.

On the Czech side there was, on the other hand, genuine concern, particularly in the mind of Foreign Minister Josef Zieleniec, at the possibility at some future point of repeated Russian expansion to the West. He pointed out that Russia had no natural Western border. The solution was NATO membership, although for Czechs who still thought in the terms of the former communist regime, jumping straight from the Warsaw Pact into NATO was a step too far.

The decisive development, from the Czech point of view, was the appointment of the formidable Madeleine Albright as US Secretary of State. She was of Czech origin and she made it her business to ease the Czechs' path into the alliance. With her backing, the country celebrated becoming a NATO member (before my departure) in a solemn ceremony in the Charles University, attended by Havel and Albright. Joining the EU came later, in 2003.

It could be argued, in retrospect, that the adhesion of the Central European countries, including the Czech Republic, to NATO was too precipitate and fuelled resentment in Russia, which was destabilising in the long run for European security. There may be an element of truth in this – but only when added on top of what Russia saw as President Reagan's provocative 'Star Wars' initiative (for the stationing of advanced anti-ballistic missiles in Poland and elsewhere), and the deployment of NATO units into the area of the former Warsaw Pact.

Furthermore, for what it is worth, I picked up no suggestion of this feeling in my many informal discussions with my Russian colleague, who always spoke very openly. He seemed relaxed on the point.

*   *   *

The British contribution to reconnecting the Czech lands with the West was not confined to the embassy. The British Council, for example, moved fast to offer its services to eight of the main cities outside Prague. Its energetic Director, Bill Jefferson, called on each of the town's mayors. They were all interested in gaining access to Western culture and the English language (the main foreign language taught in schools under the previous regime having been Russian). The solution Jefferson offered them was to have a British Council Centre to forge educational, cultural and other links with Britain – provided that they accommodated it in a prominent position in the town square. If they could provide the premises, he would bring the centre. They all enthusiastically agreed, creating the basis for fruitful cooperation.

The setting up of these Regional Resource Centres as centres of information about Britain, not only providing English Language Teaching (ELT) and hosting British arts events and exhibitions, but also developing business contacts, was a pioneering effort, which was later copied by other countries.

The BBC had enjoyed a high reputation in the country since the broadcasts from London by Jan Masaryk (the son of the first president) in the dark days of the Second World War. The presenters in the Czech Service were well known, not only by their voices, but also by their names. They were now able to visit, make new contacts and expand the content of their broadcasts.

The Prince of Wales had made an early visit after the Velvet Revolution and established a good dialogue with President Havel. Together they had set up two institutions of which they were Joint Patrons. One was the Prague Heritage Fund, which worked to restore and safeguard Prague's unique cultural heritage, including the statues on Charles Bridge – visited by every visitor to the city – and the elegant baroque Lebedur Gardens stretching down from the castle, and adjoining the embassy's own garden.

The other was the establishment of the English College in Prague, at Havel's request, to take the place of the earlier much-loved English Grammar School, which had been closed down by the Nazis. This was a private charitable institution supported by a fundraising committee in London. It produced excellent results and became extremely popular with Czech families and the international community. Formally opened by Foreign Office minister Baroness Lynda Chalker in 1995, the Queen herself visited the college during her state visit in 1996.

The scientific equipment for the English College, and books for its library, were provided by the UK's Know How Fund (KHF), set up after the fall of communism to help newly democratic and market institutions in Central and Eastern Europe by the transfer of British know-how. In its first few years, the fund – which was separate from, and more effective than, the EU's rather slow-moving development programme – concentrated on headline projects, often related to the Czech mass privatisation programme and the creation of Czech capital markets.

Government ministers and key officials visited Britain to see market systems in action and to gain advice about their creation, operation and supervision. Two British investment bankers were seconded to the largest Czech bank, where they were instrumental in setting up its investment banking division. In my final call on the Finance Minister before my departure I proposed to him the attachment to his ministry of an advisor on combating fraud and insider trading. He was politely receptive, but took some convincing that this was necessary.

Later the KHF branched out into small programmes with more grassroots participation: a senior British civil servant worked inside the Prime Minister's Office to advise on retraining policy and the creation of a national network of Job Centres; the fund paid for the creation of a model privatisation plan of a large state farm; and local government benefited from the technical twinning of British and Czech towns, for example Liberec and Bradford, and the open cast mining town of Děčín in the north with the northern county of Northumberland.

The promotion of business links was done mainly by the embassy's commercial section. But, apart from my regular meetings with the leaders of the British business community, we hit on an effective way to support their efforts. The community was small but growing and, since there was no Chamber of Commerce when we arrived, it was not always easy for it to make new contacts among Czech business and government circles.

Our solution was to host an evening At Home in the Residence, which always took place on the first Tuesday evening of the month. Any British business person could turn up, having notified us in advance, and was encouraged to bring along their Czech contacts – for whom an invitation to the Thun Palace was usually an attractive proposition – as well as any visitors from the UK who would benefit from the networking opportunity.

The idea – which was more my wife's than mine – rapidly caught on. The unchanging regularity of the reception made it a predictable event to put in diaries and plan ahead for. During my time in Prague, business links between the two countries grew exponentially and, shortly before my departure, a Czech-British Chamber of Commerce was launched, which took the operation to a higher level and was a great success.

The Residence's reception rooms, in all their splendour, made the ideal setting for many different kinds of event, ranging from charity concerts, business receptions and cultural occasions, to the promotional tasting of British tea.

One of these events was very moving. It was a reading by Dr Jana Moserová, the Czech representative to UNESCO, of a letter she had written to her brother Tom in Australia about the events surrounding the death of the student Jan Palach, who had set fire to himself in Wenceslas Square in January 1969 as a protest against the Warsaw Pact invasion of the previous year. She had been one of the team treating him in hospital during the three days before he died.

Entitled 'A Letter to Wollongong', it was a harrowing description of the pressure put on her twenty years later by the security apparatus to make her divulge the names of those who had written letters to the dying Palach. Unable to remember any names, she had eventually succumbed, under threats to her family, to signing a document to collaborate – over which she felt deep remorse.

Dr Moserová's poignant reading brought out not only the cruel methods of the communist regime, and the appalling choices many people were made to face, but also the tragedy of families driven apart for many years and unable to see each other. This resonated powerfully with my wife.

*   *   *

My own contribution to promoting British culture, apart from working closely with the British Council, was to install an iconic sculpture by Henry Moore, no less, in the garden of the Residence. This was not easy to achieve. The gardens of Prague Castle, directly above, sloped down-hill to a boundary railing surmounting a twenty-foot retaining wall, below which lay the British embassy – identifiable by the Union Jack flying above it – fronted by an immaculate lawned garden stretching away to the left for about fifty yards. Any visitor gazing down from the castle grounds might easily wonder that only the British could be responsible for such an impressive lawn.

Early in my time in Prague I stood at that railing, looking down into the garden. The thought came to me that what it lacked was a work of art, something to carry the eye towards the far end of the garden and provide a point of focus. It should be recognisably British. The ideal, I felt, would be a sculpture by Henry Moore, one of Britain's leading twentieth-century sculptors.

When I put this suggestion in a letter to the Foreign Office, I got a polite brush-off to the effect that I was being overly ambitious. They mentioned the name of another sculptor whose work was available in the Government Art Collection.

I was reflecting on this offer when I had a stroke of luck. The head of the Arts Council, Lord (Grey) Gowrie, came to lunch. As we stood on the steps outside the large French windows leading from the hall to the garden, I mentioned my presumptuous dream. To my delight Gowrie thought the idea had merit and promised to support it by writing to the Henry Moore Foundation, the keepers of the master's work.

In due course the Foundation wrote offering the loan of one of Moore's famous works, *Seated Woman*, dated 1951. The condition was that I would have to find a way of paying for the cost of freighting the large sculpture from the UK, and insuring it. After much cajoling, I managed to get these costs covered, half by the British Council, and the other half (thanks, possibly, to my monthly At Home for the British business community) by a generous British firm with investments in the Czech Republic.

However, my problems did not end there. The Thun Palace is built into the slope of a steep hill. It is entered via a rather forbidding gate-house which gives onto a cobbled courtyard with the massive height of the embassy on the left-hand side, with the garden behind it. There was no vehicular access to the garden. The only way to manoeuvre *Seated Woman* into the garden, therefore, was to hire a large crane to lift it off the lorry bringing it from England and lower it/her into the garden. More grateful thanks to the sponsors!

All went well, and the sculpture became, in time, a much-admired adornment of the embassy garden. It particularly attracted comment at the annual Garden Party which took place every June (as in other British diplomatic missions worldwide) to celebrate the Queen's Birthday. The garden would be looking at its best. I was required to perform a traditional ritual before it began in order to ensure fine weather.

There was a small ornamental pond and fountain in the garden, in the centre of which stood a statue of a little boy doing a piddle. In order to mollify the weather gods and secure a fine day, the ambassador's task was to take off his shoes and socks, roll up his trousers, get into the (mercifully shallow) fountain and offer a glass of whisky to the little boy by placing it on his head. Woe to him, or her, if they failed in this duty – which did not happen in my time!

The Garden Party itself was always a jolly occasion, with the embassy team ensuring that we put on a good show. The guests were a mixture of diplomatic colleagues, prominent Czechs and members of the British community. The two Václavs, Havel and Klaus, would normally attend, but happily, from a protocol point of view, at different times (perhaps their offices got together over this!). We had a British military band who played the National Anthem at the conclusion.

A third Václav, our head gardener, could be seen, after the main dignitaries had departed, making frequent visits to the stall dispensing Baileys Irish Cream, for which he had a particular fondness.

Seated Woman's moment of glory came during the state visit of the Queen, who was scheduled to unveil the statue at the conclusion of the lunch my wife and I hosted at the embassy in honour of her and Prince Philip on the last day of the visit. As we walked across the lawn for her to perform the little ceremony, I unwisely mentioned that the statue was on loan from the Henry Moore Foundation. She gave me a questioning sideways look, which suggested that she was not unduly impressed to be unveiling a statue that was merely on loan.

What I did not mention to the Queen was that the Foundation had written asking for the statue to be sent back to them, since it was needed for the events surrounding the centenary of Henry Moore's birth. So, a matter of days before our own departure from Prague, the lorry and crane were back in the embassy courtyard and *Seated Woman* departed for home at the end of her Bohemian adventure.

*   *   *

Living and working in Prague, particularly in the Thun Palace, was both a privilege and a delight. From the windows in our large bedroom we could look both up to the castle (the largest in Europe) and down to the Old City, with the river Vltava snaking through it.

The Czechs are known for their quirky sense of humour. A recent example was an art work called *London Booster*, which consisted of a double-decker bus with hydraulic arms, doing push-ups every day for half an hour, which accompanied the Czech team to the 2012 Olympics in London. Another example from literature, which also demonstrates the Czech art of dumb insolence in the face of authority, is Hašek's novel *The Good Soldier Schweik*.

And then of course there is the beer. On my first visit to the city, for a weekend staying with ambassador Laurence O'Keeffe in November 1990, a year after the Velvet Revolution, I had walked down to the river, early on a cold and misty Sunday morning. Crossing a deserted Charles Bridge, I had ambled through the winding cobbled streets – which were later to become almost impassable with tourists – past the Old Town Hall, with its famous Astrological Clock, and into the Old Town Square.

I had it to myself. As I stood in the middle, by the monument to the fifteenth-century martyr Jan Hus – himself an example of unflinching Czech opposition to oppressive authority, in his case the dominance of the Church, for which he was burnt at the stake in 1415 – with the great Baroque church of St Nicholas to its left, a horse pulling a cart carrying a large barrel of beer slowly emerged through the mist, clip-clopping over the cobbles into the square. The beer man pulled me a tin mug-full, which cost no more than a few pence. It tasted superb.

My wife's family had already introduced me to the simple pleasures of good beer, a nourishing pork, dumplings and cabbage meal, and the delights of picking wild mushrooms. There is also a fondness for singing and dancing (particularly in Moravia).

In literature, Prague is a city of mystery and magic, and the depth of winter is the best time to explore it. It was then free of the hordes of tourists who, in summer, trooped in a continuous procession past the Thun Palace and up the steep hill to the castle. To feel its atmosphere, I would occasionally climb the steps along that route on a winter night, walk through the deserted castle courtyards and round St Vitus cathedral, to the Golden Lane of small ancient houses that lies behind it. In one of these had lived the writer Franz Kafka, who best captured the essence of the place.

When we arrived in Prague it still had the dead feel of a communist city, and it was hard to find a decent restaurant. Within a fairly short time this changed. The city became transformed from a black-and-white photograph into a colour photograph, as its fine baroque buildings were restored and repainted. The scaffolding that had encased some buildings for years, seemingly in order to keep them from falling down, began to be used for its proper purpose in renovation work.

One example of the successful restoration of historic buildings being carried out was a baroque corner building in the square below the embassy, earmarked as an annex to the Czech parliament. Betty Boothroyd (later Baroness Boothroyd), the Speaker of the House of Commons, was shown round when she visited Prague, as the work was nearing completion. She greatly admired not only the authentic nature of the building's restoration, including its frescoes, but also the speed and low cost with which it had been carried out. She remarked on how favourably it compared with the construction of Portcullis House, the costly parliamentary offices beside the Palace of Westminster.

As for the restaurants, one of our favourites, which served excellent Czech food, was housed in a medieval building linked to the Sovereign Order of Malta (which was working hard, with the backing of the Pope, for the return of its extensive property holdings, expropriated by the communists). Round the walls of the restaurant, which was reached down some steep stairs to the cellar, hung the coats-of-arms of some of the knights. It was allegedly haunted by the ghost of one of them who had met a gruesome end there. The custom was that the lady of the house would descend during the course of one's meal and recount the story in dramatic detail. We once subjected a royal house-guest, the Duke of Kent, to the experience. To our relief, he seemed to enjoy it.

The Czech Republic was a fascinating country to explore, with its many picturesque towns and castles. The much-visited royal castles in the vicinity of Prague were Karlštejn, associated with the Emperor Charles IV (who also gave his name to the Charles Bridge in Prague and the ancient university), and Konopiště, which belonged to the Archduke Franz Ferdinand, whose assassination in Sarajevo in 1914 precipitated the First World War. The Archduke was an obsessive hunter, and the walls of Konopiště were bedecked with trophy heads, to a rather grisly extent, although his family pictures revealed a softer side to his nature.

Wider afield, particularly vivid memories of our travels around the country include a spectacular midsummer Masque at Český Krumlov, a Renaissance castle of the Schwarzenberg family, dominating a bend in the Vltava river, halfway between Prague and the Austrian border. The castle, a UNESCO World Heritage Site, contains one of the few baroque theatres still in working order. The Masque, which told the story of the castle's history through its three centuries of ownership by successive noble families, with lighting and dance and specially composed music, was staged on an outside terrace and viewed by the audience from the opposite side of the river. It made for a truly memorable evening.

Another occasion was a weekend organised by the World Monument Fund to draw attention to the restoration work it was undertaking at Valtice, a palace on the former estate of the princely Liechtenstein family on the Austrian border in southern Moravia. The huge estate, which almost rivals Versailles, includes another palace, Lednice, which was rebuilt in the neo-Gothic style in the nineteenth century, reminiscent of Horace Walpole's Strawberry Hill House in London. At the end of the war the Liechtensteins were accused of having collaborated with the Nazis, the estate was requisitioned and they had to make a rapid departure. But, allegedly, they had enough time to load up eight waiting railway wagons with the princely treasures, to be transported to the family seat in Vaduz. Litigation has continued over the decades.

A great pleasure of our time in the Czech Republic was getting to know Henrietta's Czech family. Her relations on her mother's side lived in Zlín, the Bata company town in Moravia in which she was born. Conversations with them gave me an invaluable insight into the way ordinary Czechs felt about the transition through which the country was passing. Many of these took place in the bucolic surroundings of the family *chata* (equivalent to the Russian *dacha*) in the nearby village of Bystřice. The village had been in the front line during the

Mongol invasion into Europe in the thirteenth century. Frescoes in the pilgrimage church of Hostyn, on a hill above the village, told the story of how the villagers, who had taken refuge there from the invaders in 1241, had been saved by the intervention of the Blessed Virgin Mary, who had called up a great storm and lightning which had thrown the Mongols back in disarray.

The family also introduced us to wild mushroom picking. This involved going to their favourite spot in the woods, which they kept a closely guarded secret, and learning how to distinguish edible mushrooms from the others. It was as well to pay attention, since a mistake could be fatal!

A cousin on Henrietta's father's side was a French teacher, living with her family in Mělník, the town at the junction of the Vltava river with the Elbe – which then flows north into Saxony, through the picturesque 'Saxon Switzerland' beloved of the German romantics. The town contained one of the many castles of the Lobkovicz family. At another of their castles, at Nelahozeves, William Lobkovicz and his wife Sandra, returning from America after the Velvet Revolution, had reassembled the family's incomparable art collection, which included two magnificent Canaletto paintings of London and original Beethoven scores. The collections have now been transferred to yet another of the family's palaces in the castle area in Prague. Nelahozeves is also where the great Czech composer, Antonín Dvořák, was born – in his father's inn.

*   *   *

The year 1997 was my last year in the diplomatic Service before retirement, and also the year in which we were visited in Prague by three prime ministers – the current, his predecessor and his successor: John Major, Margaret Thatcher and Tony Blair.

John Major, whom I had worked with on Middle East matters in my previous appointment, came to Prague in April 1997 for an overnight stopover on his way to Kiev. In the great debate of the time between enlargement and pursuing deeper integration within the European Union, he had shown himself to be a staunch advocate of enlargement, in the twin beliefs that it could not rightly exclude the newly democratising states in Central and Eastern Europe, and also that enlargement was the best way of heading off the federalist tendencies of some of the existing members, such as France. His preferred vision was of a community of nation states (in an echo of General de Gaulle long before, as well as Margaret Thatcher), in pursuit of which he saw the Central Europeans as natural allies, not least the eurosceptic Czech Prime Minister, Václav Klaus, who was instinctively opposed to outside interference in the running of his country's affairs. There was a good rapport between them.

The visit, which was billed as support for another centre-right leader who was facing a general election, consisted of a meeting with Klaus in his office, a dinner in a restaurant, hosted by Klaus, and a night at the embassy. The talks covered, in a general way, developments in NATO and the European Union. These were followed by a joint press conference in the garden of the prime minister's office. To my horror, the first question, from an aggressive reporter, was along the lines of, 'Mr Klaus, what possible benefit can it be to you to receive a visit of support from the most unsuccessful British prime minister ever?'

38. In conversation with Prime Minister Václav Klaus at my last Queen's birthday reception in the Residence garden. Klaus was a shrewd and ambitious politician, the polar opposite of the idealistic President Havel. (Photo: author)

Klaus was struck dumb, but Major, a smoother and more subtle politician, took over and replied that the questioner had seemingly not heard him say that the two of them had had very constructive discussions about NATO and so on. The press conference was rapidly brought to a close and Major and I left in my car. I turned to him and said, jokingly, that I was astounded at his forbearance in not climbing over the rope barrier and clocking the reporter on the nose. John Major, who was in his last months in office, replied that he was getting rather used to that kind of attack. It was clear, however, that he had gone into shock, because he then asked me what he had said in his response.

I found all this rather sad. I had, and have, a high regard for Sir John Major as a steady, if unexciting, leader, with a number of achievements to his name. In the European sphere, he had managed to secure vital opt-outs for Britain from joining the euro single currency, as well as the Schengen Agreement on passport-free travel within Europe. In the Middle East, following the First Gulf War, he had saved the Kurds in Northern Iraq from the vicious reprisals of Saddam Hussein. But his government had run out of steam and his own morale seemed to be at a low ebb.

A few months earlier, the Leader of the Opposition, Tony Blair, had spent a week-long holiday in Prague over the New Year, with his wife, Cherie. He had made his own accommodation arrangements with a friend, but he contacted the embassy to help with communicating with his office in London. As a consequence, we saw quite a lot of the couple over the week. I took him to call on Prime Minister Klaus, whose economic thinking he found disconcertingly inflexible.

Talking to Blair about the EU, I was surprised at his relaxed approach to the possibility of Britain joining the euro, which was the hot topic at the time. For him, sovereignty was not an issue, and he saw no great difficulty in Britain losing the ability to manage its exchange rate policy – which, I pointed out, had proved to be a useful tool to reduce unemployment in the past – provided it managed its overall economic policy right.

On one evening, we took the Blairs out for a relaxed dinner in our favourite Lebanese restaurant. It was the first time that they had tried Lebanese food. Tony and Cherie also came to our monthly At Home the following evening and charmed everyone with their ease of manner. We ended the evening at our local jazz club in the square below – jazz, much beloved by Václav Havel, having, incidentally, played a significant role in undermining the pomposity of the communist regime in their final phase.

We were impressed by the Blairs' naturalness, once they were at ease in our company. Tony Blair showed genuine interest in everyone he met. He was keen, for example, to learn as much as he could, at lunch in the residence, from the vast experience of Sir Frank Roberts – the veteran former ambassador in Moscow and Bonn – before Sir Frank had to rush to the airport to catch a plane. But he seemed no less interested in probing the thinking of a teenager, our daughter Amanda, who was also at the lunch. I also found him a good listener, showing a polite, but seemingly genuine, interest, in my own views on how to insert the UK between France and Germany in the critical EU dynamic, as well as my thinking on the Middle East (which I had come from dealing with in the Foreign Office). His energy and charisma were unmistakable.

Lady Thatcher's three-day stay in Prague (in May 1996) was to attend, and play a starring role in, a think-tank-sponsored conference titled 'The New Atlantic Initiative', at which there was a strong delegation from London. I accompanied her to unveil a statue of Winston Churchill in a Prague square on the side. She stayed in the Residence (without her husband, Denis), and after the evening events organised by the conference, we would sit and enjoy a quiet nightcap, sometimes talking into the early hours.

As a house-guest Lady Thatcher was warm and charming. Before she left, Henrietta took her on a successful shopping expedition to buy Czech crystal glasses. She wrote on her return to say that her husband had approved of them. She insisted on her departure that we look her up when we returned to London. We did not take her up on this, but in her final years I would occasionally see her when she visited the Hurlingham Club in West London, where I was chairman at the time, for a quiet tea on a Thursday afternoon.

* * *

The state visit of the Queen and the Duke of Edinburgh to the Czech Republic took place at the end of March 1996. It was the second half of a week in which the royal couple had first visited Poland. As the first official visit by a British monarch to the Czech lands as they were emerging from communism, like all three previous state visits in which I had been involved – France in 1972 (a new relationship after de Gaulle's departure), Kuwait in 1979 (first visit to Arabia) and Berlin in 1992 (first visit to the reunified Germany) – it was historically significant.

The months of advance preparation were spent, not only in agreeing the programme with the Czechs, and making the detailed arrangements, but also in trying to get this message across. I was able to draw on my experience of the Berlin visit, five years earlier, in doing this. As on that occasion, the embassy produced an excellent coloured brochure as an introduction to the visit. Entitled 'Britain and the Czech Republic' (in Czech), its cover carried a watercolour by Chris Vinz, a young British artist living in Prague, showing the embassy in its central position beneath the castle. There was an introduction by Prince Charles, and sections on the wide range of links between the two countries – historical, political, cultural, economic, business and sporting.

We also arranged, as in Berlin, for an exhibition of replicas of the British Crown Jewels in the crypt of the town hall of Brno (the country's second city) during the month leading up to the visit. Having opened the exhibition, together with the mayoress, I asked Charles Hay (the embassy Second Secretary), to check, before we left Brno to drive back to Prague, whether anyone was visiting it. He reported that there was already a queue round the block. Thereafter it attracted more than 25,000 visitors, helping to prime the city's inhabitants for the Queen's visit.

The highlight of the formal part of the visit was the State Banquet hosted by President Havel. Exceptionally, he had arranged that it should take place in the magnificent Spanish Hall of Prague Castle, holding 250 people, rather than in a smaller hall holding seventy, where these events were normally held. At the glittering occasion the Queen addressed the big question mark hovering over the visit, namely whether she would apologise for Britain's role in the 1938 Munich Agreement.

There had been exchanges between the embassy, the Foreign Office and Downing Street, and there was general agreement that an apology was not appropriate. In diplomatic and political terms, apologies are extremely rare and have to be viewed in their wider historical contexts. A further complication was that, on his return from Munich waving the piece of paper, proclaiming, as he said, 'Peace in our time', Prime Minister Neville Chamberlain had been invited by the King, George

39. The Queen with President Václav Havel before the magnificent state dinner in the Spanish Hall at Prague Castle in March 1996. The event symbolised Prague's unambiguous shift towards a Western orientation. (Photo: author)

VI, onto the balcony of Buckingham Palace, to receive the cheers of a huge and enthusiastic crowd. Furthermore, Churchill had declared the agreement null and void shortly after the start of the war, and Prime Minister Margaret Thatcher, in her turn, had expressed the government's regrets for it. But the Queen could not ignore the issue in her keynote speech at the dinner, reviewing the course of UK-Czech relations. She covered the point in the following sentence, having noted

Britain's active support for the creation of the first Czechoslovak Republic, under President Masaryk:

> The events which brought it to an end are the only shadow over our relationship, and I understand, and sympathise with, the feelings in this country over the Munich Agreement.

This formulation was considered by those present, and in the Czech media, to have drawn a line under a deeply contentious subject, and to have struck just the right note.

The other highlight of the visit was the Queen's visit to Brno. It was a triumph. President Havel was particularly keen that she should make Brno, the principal city of Moravia, as her out-of-town destination, rather than one of the many scenic medieval towns in which the country abounded. His reason was that her visit would enhance the status of the Czech Constitutional Court which was situated there. Furthermore, he indicated that if she went to Brno he would accompany her – which was unprecedented.

We were hugely fortunate that the visit took place on a cloudless spring day. We flew down from Prague (minus Prince Philip who was following a separate programme). As the cars, to which we had transferred, turned into the city's Town Hall Square we were astonished – since the Czechs are not normally given to displays of enthusiasm – to be met by a sea of cheering people. Every balcony and window was occupied. Even the doctors, wearing their green operating robes, were cheering from the balcony of the hospital. One wondered who was taking care of the patients!

The Queen's visit to the Constitutional Court, after an elaborate civic lunch, was the moment for the fulfilment of Havel's objective, of a royal benediction for the Court's role in cementing democracy in the country. The Vice-President of the Court, Justice Ivana Janu, spoke eloquently of Britain as the very model of a free country, adding that Tomáš Masaryk had found there three important elements that contribute to its development as a free country: a sense of respect for human rights, a sense of continuity and a sense of compromise.

After this the Queen undertook a walkabout, back in the town square, with Havel's personal interpreter, a large lady, doing the translating. Then it was back on the plane for the flight to Prague, with me sitting opposite her. She remarked that during the walkabout she had wondered what she had said that was so important, when her normal light conversational approaches were rendered into Czech in the sonorous tones of the lady interpreter.

The final event of the tour, before the royal couple took their leave of President Havel in the castle, was a more intimate affair. My wife and I entertained the royal party, together with a select few outside guests and members of our embassy staff, to luncheon in the Residence. Prime Minister Klaus and his wife Livia were the main Czech guests. All went well, and the Queen was amused at our cook Maria, when she was presented at the end of the meal, saying that she had been at the Residence so long that she had become part of the furniture.

Prince Philip did however cause a bit of a flutter at his table, which my wife was hosting, when the window in the castle above was pointed out to him, from which the famous defenestration of Prague took place in 1618, which led in due course to the Thirty Years War. Defenestration was the wrong word, he asserted, since it meant throwing out the window, rather than throwing someone out of it. (According to the dictionary it has both meanings.) This provoked Mrs Klaus, who responded that the Czechs knew exactly what defenestrations were all about, since there had been several in their history. After lunch I accompanied the Queen into the garden to unveil the Henry Moore statue. Then, after the embassy staff had been presented, there came a gap of a few minutes in the programme which we had not fully anticipated. The embassy staff needed those minutes to descend the stairs into the embassy courtyard, in order to wave off the royal party as they departed through the gate.

Extemporising, we filled the time by conducting the Queen and Prince Philip back into the main reception rooms. In contrast to their being thronged with guests enjoying pre-lunch drinks, as they had been earlier, we now had them to ourselves, giving the royal couple the opportunity to enjoy the spectacular views over Old Prague.

I drew the Queen's attention to the two large portraits by the Dutch painter Gerard van Honthorst of the Winter King and the Winter Queen, remarking that it was, of course, through their daughter Sophia of Hanover that her own claim to the throne arose. The Queen replied that she used to be rather good at such matters – but she had since forgotten some of the details!

And so, with waves (of relief) to the departing royal plane from the tarmac of Prague airport, it was all over.

Before our own departure, nineteen months later, there occurred another major, and this time unscheduled, event. In late August we spent a week visiting Kraków in southern Poland. On our drive back home we made a diversion to visit the death camp at Auschwitz-Birkenau, which was an emotionally draining experience. As a result, we arrived back in Prague late in the evening and tired, and dropped into bed.

I woke early and turned on the TV to catch up on the news, having been out of touch for a few days. It was hard to take in what I saw – the flashing lights surrounding a car crash in the tunnel by the place de l'Alma (near where we had lived in Paris), and the shattering news that Princess Diana was injured. I barely had time to wake Henrietta and tell her what had happened before the follow-up news came through that the Princess had died.

It was a Sunday, and none of the embassy staff was in the office, so I decided to lower the embassy flag to half-mast, although no instructions from London had been circulated at that stage. This turned out to be challenging, as I found myself crawling through a dusty attic to reach the flagpole.

By mid-morning a few people were starting to arrive with flowers and messages that they placed outside the embassy gates. The accumulation of flowers reached massive proportions in the succeeding days and almost blocked the entrance to the embassy for traffic. The flowers were accompanied by candles which, when lit in the evening, gave the small cul-de-sac in which the embassy stood the air of a shrine, accentuated by the fact that at night people knelt in the street in prayer.

On the following Monday we opened a Book of Condolence. Over the next two days it was signed by the presidents of the two chambers of Parliament, political leaders, prominent businessmen and hundreds of ordinary people who, at some points, were having to queue for up to two hours in the late summer heat.

Among the many expressions of condolence that I received from prominent Czechs was a proposal by Pastor Tomáš Halik, a leading former dissident and theologian (who was later to receive the prestigious Templeman Prize in London), to hold a memorial service to commemorate both Princess Diana and Mother Teresa, who had died in the same week. I naturally welcomed the idea and took the opportunity to ask that the Anglican padre in Prague should be robed and included in the service, to which Halik agreed.

Father Halik told me afterwards that this was the first time ever that a joint Roman Catholic/Church of England service had been held in Prague. I thought it poignant that Princess Diana's tragic death should have produced a moment of ecumenical reconciliation.

Finally, six weeks later, we ourselves drove through the embassy gate, after an emotional farewell from our staff and a formal call by the Czech Foreign Minister, to begin our retirement. It was good-bye to being addressed as Your Excellency, good-bye to the official car with driver and the Union Jack flying, and hello to a normal life, and the pleasure, for example, of walking to the corner shop each morning to buy the newspaper to read at breakfast.

To break the journey back to England, we spent the weekend at the Kempinski hotel in Heidelberg, where we had long-standing German friends. Visiting the city's museum, housed in the former palace of the Electors, it was almost eery to be faced, in the final room, with almost identical portraits of the Winter King and the Winter Queen (also painted by Honthorst) as those we had just left behind in our Prague residence. The explanation was that King Frederick had been the Elector Palatine, and Heidelberg had been his capital.

Coming down to breakfast the next day – my sixtieth birthday, which was then the mandatory retirement age in the Diplomatic Service – the Hotel Director approached our table carrying a cake and a bottle of champagne, greeting me with a bow and saying, 'Mr Ambassador, Happy Birthday!' It was an elegant and unexpected way for the curtain to fall, and a new life to begin.

Reflections

Looking back on my thirty-seven-year career in HM Diplomatic Service (from 1960 to 1997) I can see that it was affected by three broad historical currents, running beneath the surface of daily events. These were firstly the Cold War, secondly the movement towards the peaceful integration of the countries of Europe, and thirdly Britain's search for the right place for itself, both as a global player and a European country.

The Cold War, with the West pitted against its erstwhile wartime ally, the Soviet Union, impacted on me from the time when I first peered at the Iron Curtain in the German city of Lübeck when touring around Europe as an Oxford undergraduate in the 1950s. It impinged on me from the start of my time in the Middle East, with the arrest of my fellow student, George Blake, as a double agent, and was a continuing background theme throughout my involvement in the region. It then had a very direct impact on my career when I married my wife, and life-long partner, in spite of initial opposition from the Foreign Office due to her Czechoslovak origin.

A battleground of the Cold War in which I became involved in the 1980s was the Soviet invasion of Afghanistan. This was a case of Soviet over-reach. The mounting Soviet casualties in an unpopular war on the home front created one of the first cracks in the legitimacy of the Soviet leadership and paved the way for the rise of the reforming Mikhail Gorbachev.

When I commenced my term as Minister and Deputy Commandant in Berlin in 1984 the Cold War became, for me, a daily physical reality. Berlin was on the front line of the Cold War, as one was reminded not only by the Wall but also every time one flew into and out of the city along the air corridor, at the maximum permitted height of 10,000 feet, or drove through the GDR under Military Police escort from Checkpoint

Bravo in Berlin to Checkpoint Alpha at Helmstedt, at the point where the, very visible, Iron Curtain divided the two German states.

It was only when the Wall fell in 1989 that the confrontation with the Soviet Union, on military and other levels, finally drew to a close. The hard-line German Democratic Republic, and then the Soviet Union itself, shortly afterwards ceased to exist. Later, as I inspected the Soviet and GDR military paraphernalia on sale at makeshift stalls by the Brandenburg Gate, I reflected on what the American academic Francis Fukuyama called 'the end of history' would actually mean. I hoped that it would include Britain, now relieved of its role as Protecting Power in Berlin, also taking a long, hard look at its position in the world, scaling back its strategic obligations to better match its resources, and giving more attention to the weaknesses in its own society. It was not to be. It was, I suppose, asking a lot to expect Britain to voluntarily scale back its world role – and leave the field to the French! Instead, together with the United States, we invaded Iraq in 2003.

Secondly, the coming together of Europe was something I first, dimly, discerned when, again when on vacation from Oxford, I was in Düsseldorf in 1958 for the sake of my German, and joined a day's river cruise on the Rhine. The other passengers were mostly groups of young people from both Germany and France. They were mixing happily together. I could not imagine this being the case with British kids. It was clear that, only twelve years or so after the war, the old enmities had been set aside, at least among the younger generation. The political consequences of Franco-German reconciliation as the foundation of a European community were far-reaching.

The EEC that Britain joined (not least due to the diplomatic achievements of the UK's Paris embassy under Lord Soames, as recounted in Chapter 5) consisted of the original six members, of which the most significant were France and Germany. By the time of my retirement in 1997 it had grown, through a series of enlargements, to fifteen and, with the release of the countries in Central and Eastern Europe from the Soviet grip, that number later rose to twenty-eight – before the UK's departure. The ability to attract ex-communist countries into its democratic and free market system through enlargement (actively promoted by John Major) has been one of the great achievements of the European Union.

In that time, the EC/EU's most significant developments were the Single Market, which was largely a British initiative under Margaret

Thatcher; the move towards a single currency, culminating in the euro; and the EU's transformation into a border-free area by the Schengen Agreement. Throughout these changes, the direction of travel remained towards what the French like to call 'the construction of Europe'. This was based on the blueprint drawn up by the Founding Fathers (such as Jean Monnet) in the 1958 Treaty of Rome, which aimed at the integration of Europe through a series of small steps in order to prevent any more intra-European wars.

Another unchanging feature of the process was the shared leadership role of France and Germany, the engine driving the machine. Although that engine has occasionally stalled, in recent years there has been less tension between the two main players than between the founding member states and some of the more recent members in Central Europe, who feel that their interests are not being sufficiently taken into account. These countries also tend to be less welcoming of immigrants and asylum-seekers.

Turning to the third strand, how did Britain fit into the picture? Before considering this question in the European context, I need firstly to recall the pithy observation of former US Secretary of State Dean Acheson in 1962 that 'Great Britain has lost an empire and has not yet found a role'. His much-quoted comment was made not only in the context of Independence for India and Pakistan (1947), but also after the disastrous Suez Crisis of 1956, when Britain had to pull back from its occupation of the Canal Zone in Egypt (following President Nasser's nationalisation of the Canal) under extraordinary and unexpected US pressure, leading to a run on the pound. This had done huge damage to Britain's standing in the Middle East.

By the time of my arrival in the region, in 1960, the US had already supplanted Britain as the main external player. US marines had landed in Lebanon two years previously, to shore up the Christian Maronite President, Camille Chamoun, who was facing overthrow, under the new Eisenhower doctrine. This was the first US incursion onto Arab soil. There were to be many others subsequently. The US had also supplanted British influence in Iran, where American political influence reigned supreme between 1953, when the CIA-led coup ousted Prime Minister Mohammad Mossadaq, and the 1979 Islamic Revolution.

The next blow to British influence was its military withdrawal from the Gulf in 1972 brought on by economic weakness (the pound sterling had been devalued in 1967). This was a low point. Thereafter,

Britain did not cease to count in the Middle East, but its influence had to be furthered in other ways: through its role as a Permanent Member of the UN Security Council; the nurturing of traditional friends and high-level contacts; the popularity of the BBC, particularly the Arabic Service, the British Council, the British communities throughout the region; and, last but not least, skilful diplomacy.

Taking a narrow focus – and ignoring developments elsewhere such as those in Africa, or the agreement with China on handing back Hong Kong (which coincided almost to the day with my retirement from the Service), or the Falklands War – Britain was indeed (perhaps unconsciously) searching for a new role in the Middle East. Those other momentous events were, as far as I was concerned, going on elsewhere. As regards the Commonwealth, which some people used to think of as a substitute for lost empire, although it is an institution which its champions view as of great benefit to its members, encompassing about a third of the human race, it cannot be considered an instrument for the projection of British power.

If one looks for an instrument for the projection, not of power, but of influence, the Queen, and other members of the Royal Family, were and are, in my experience, one of the most significant contributors to maintaining Britain's high standing in the world. As I have recounted in these pages, I was fortunate in being able to play a part in four of her overseas visits, each one of which had a positive impact in the country visited.

It is not sufficiently recognized at home that these tours are not merely about protocol and pageantry. They can make a powerful statement about what Britain stands for. Memories and impressions linger on, long after the royal visitor has departed.

As regards Britain's role in Europe, I saw, when following the course of our negotiations to join the EEC (from the embassy in Paris), that we had to pay a heavy price for having rejected the possibility of joining the process at the beginning, playing little part in the discussions leading to the Treaty of Rome. The founder members had, naturally, constructed an economic system that suited their own requirements, including the Common Agricultural Policy (CAP) which subsidised agricultural exports and taxed imports.

As a major food importer, Britain was a big loser from this arrangement. It also had to allow access to the fishermen of the other member countries into its richly stocked fishing areas, in accordance with the

EEC principle of solidarity. And, as one of the largest EEC countries, it had to pay one of the largest contributions to the budget.

It is therefore not surprising that, at the point of entry, the EEC was not a comfortable fit for this country. But, over time, many of these problems were made less irksome. For a start, Margaret Thatcher, addressed the unfavourable budgetary burden by memorably demanding 'our money back'. Foreign Office mandarins winced at her negotiating style. But she succeeded in getting a sizeable rebate on our contribution, which became the envy of other countries. The CAP, with, for example, its butter mountains and wine lakes of surplus produce, became indefensible in the long run, and was modified.

Margaret Thatcher's other great contribution towards making EC membership more comfortable for Britain was her championing of the single market. She was persuaded by the UK commissioner Lord Cockfield that extending the common market into the area of services (such as financial services), based, crucially, on common standards, would do away with some of the non-tariff barriers standing in the way of Britain, as a largely service economy, gaining full benefit from its membership.

Later John Major, when the integrationist Maastricht Treaty was under negotiation, managed to secure opt-outs for the UK in two important areas. We would not have to remove our border controls in line with the Schengen Agreement, and we would not join the single currency, which led to the creation of the euro.

As the EU, as it had become, extended its reach, some of the new policies, for example those designed to fight organised crime, suited this country, whereas others did not. We continued to have to fight against the protectionist tendencies of some of our partners and the Commission's inclination to regulate and control matters that were better left in the hands of the individual member states.

Nevertheless, in my view, when the Brexit referendum took place in 2016, Britain was well placed in Europe. Standing apart from the euro and the Schengen Agreement, we were not drawn into the most troublesome areas of European integration. In short, the country was, on balance, benefiting greatly from its membership. If there was a concern for the future, it was that, as a non-euro member, we were not part of the EU's central project and could have found it increasingly difficult, in time, to make our voice heard in the face of the main preoccupations of most of the other member states. We shall never know.

The attraction of the Diplomatic Service is that it offers a rich variety of career paths. No two officers' careers are the same. At the same time, the varied nature of the work makes it difficult to sum up a career in retrospect, and to give it some coherence. This is particularly true in the case of my own career – touching on the Middle East, Europe, the Cold War, South Asia and more besides – as described in these pages. The connecting thread is the need to do a professional job, to the best of one's abilities; diplomacy is a profession demanding its own particular skills, every bit as much as the professions of medicine, the law, the stage or any other. The Service, which is not large, is like a family. This is why I felt it to be a privilege to be a member, and fought against my enforced retirement at the time of my marriage. It is for others to mark my record within it.

However, there was one respect in which my career can be seen as a well-shaped narrative. My final posting, as ambassador in Prague, in Henrietta's home country, was more than a fitting last chapter. It was an opportunity to make a difference. The Czech Republic, in which we arrived in 1994, was a damaged country. Its experience over the previous half-century of war, occupation and living under a grinding

40. With my wife Henrietta in the garden of our Prague residence. (Photo: author)

communist regime (with the Warsaw Pact invasion of 1968 thrown in) had left deep marks. The command economy was ill-adapted to the challenges of the free market, the rivers were poisoned and the forests dying, and the people suffering from what the president, Václav Havel, called moral pollution.

This meant there was plenty for the embassy, the British Council, and me personally, to do: bringing targeted aid to bear through the excellent Know How Fund, helping to build the foundations of a restored democratic system, and forging links with Britain in the political, economic, military, cultural and other spheres – as well as the key diplomatic task of helping to steer the country towards its desired destination of membership of NATO and the European Union.

I could not have asked for a more rewarding assignment. It enabled me to end my career doing demanding and constructive work in a country to which I had become personally attached (through my wife and her family), in one of the most glorious capitals in Europe. As I sat with Henrietta in the garden of our residence, the Thun Palace, I reflected, 'Thank you, Pa, for having set me on the path to diplomacy!'.

Index